Roy Huggins

ALSO BY PAUL GREEN
AND FROM McFARLAND

*Jeffrey Hunter: The Film, Television,
Radio and Stage Performances* (2014)

Jennifer Jones: The Life and Films (2011)

*Encyclopedia of Weird Westerns: Supernatural and
Science Fiction Elements in Novels, Pulps, Comics,
Films, Television and Games* (2009)

Pete Duel: A Biography
(2007; paperback large print edition 2009)

A History of Television's The Virginian, 1962–1971
(2006; paperback 2010)

Roy Huggins

Creator of *Maverick*,
77 Sunset Strip, *The Fugitive*
and *The Rockford Files*

PAUL GREEN

Foreword by JO SWERLING, JR.

McFarland & Company, Inc., Publishers
Jefferson, North Carolina

LIBRARY OF CONGRESS CATALOGUING-IN-PUBLICATION DATA

Green, Paul, 1955–
Roy Huggins : creator of Maverick, 77 Sunset Strip,
The fugitive and The Rockford files / Paul Green ;
foreword by Jo Swerling, Jr.
p.   cm.
Includes bibliographical references and index.

ISBN 978-0-7864-7671-8 (softcover : acid free paper) ∞
ISBN 978-1-4766-1349-9 (ebook)

1. Huggins, Roy, 1914–2002.   2. Television producers and directors—United States—Biography.   I. Title.
PN1992.4.H76G74 2014
791.4502'32092—dc23   [B]   2013048594

BRITISH LIBRARY CATALOGUING DATA ARE AVAILABLE

© 2014 Paul Green. All rights reserved

No part of this book may be reproduced or transmitted in any form or by any means, electronic or mechanical, including photocopying or recording, or by any information storage and retrieval system, without permission in writing from the publisher.

On the cover: Roy Huggins at Warner Bros. in the late 1950s
(courtesy John Huggins)

Manufactured in the United States of America

*McFarland & Company, Inc., Publishers
Box 611, Jefferson, North Carolina 28640
www.mcfarlandpub.com*

Acknowledgments

I would like to thank the following people for taking time to contribute extensively to my book. Roy Huggins' long-time production assistant Jo Swerling, Jr., and Frank Price, former president of Universal Television and Columbia Pictures, provided valuable information and insights into Huggins' working methods, personality and television shows.

His daughter, former actress Katherine Crawford, kindly shared her memories of growing up and supplied many family photographs.

Thanks to son John and the Huggins family for granting me access to two unpublished memoirs written by Huggins. John also contributed his father's speeches, articles, more family photographs and personal insights.

I would also like to thank: Bonnie Porter, first wife of Roy Huggins, who kindly granted me an interview some years before her passing on June 4, 2012; his daughter-in-law, writer-producer Charlotte Huggins; Karen L. Herman, director of the Archive of American Television; author, lecturer and music critic Jon Burlingame; author and broadcaster Ed Robertson; *The Rockford Files* writer Juanita Bartlett; *The Fugitive* advisor Chris Soldo; Gary Winter, director and post-production executive on *Hunter*; and actress-writer-director Stepfanie Kramer, who starred as Sgt. Dee Dee McCall on *Hunter*.

Table of Contents

Acknowledgments — v
Foreword by Jo Swerling, Jr. — 1
Preface — 3
Introduction — 4

1. Lineage — 7
2. Formal Years — 11
3. Hard-Boiled Huggins — 20
4. The Lady with the Torch — 26
5. Howard Hughes Radio Pictures — 36
6. Paranoia and Discord — 42
7. Transition — 51
8. Shady Dealings — 58
9. Trouble at Fox — 73
10. Guilty Until Proven Innocent — 78
11. Escape from Tomorrow — 87
12. One Step Ahead — 99
13. Fallow Ground — 115
14. Revolving Doors — 121
15. Best Sellers — 132
16. Rejuvenation — 140
17. Denouement — 149

The Works of Roy Huggins — 155
Chapter Notes — 170
Bibliography — 175
Index — 177

Foreword

by Jo Swerling, Jr.

Roy was many things to many people. Those of us who really knew him saw him as a very brilliant, compassionate, nice and generous human being. But Roy could be intimidating to some people, especially directors. He was quite emotional in the way he reacted to bad film. Roy would sit there and look at an early cut of an episode or bad dailies and literally yell at the screen, "This is shit! This is shit!" He would rein himself in and look toward the film editor. "Don't get me wrong ... I'm not reacting to your editing, I'm reacting to shitty film." Certain others might have considered him dictatorial and pedantic. A frustrated professor. He was an academic at heart.

Roy was very skillful at post-production. During the many years I worked with him, we hardly ever re-shot anything. Some producers will look at dailies and if they don't like something they'll put it down on the list to re-shoot, which is an expensive way to do things. Roy could always find a way to cut around the bad shot and make the scene work without the expense of re-shooting.

He was a very creative editor and an excellent writer, and a stickler when it came to the preparation and submission of scripts. If we sent a script to the network that had a typographical error in it, there was hell to pay. I learned under Roy to proofread to the nth degree. He was very literate and flawless in his command of language, grammar and spelling. He wouldn't pull punches with his staff. If I screwed up, he wouldn't just pat me on the head and say, "That's okay." He would let me know I'd screwed up in no uncertain terms ... but never in front of anybody.

Having been in the Navy as an officer, the first rule of leadership I learned is that you congratulate somebody in public and chastise them in private.

Jo Swerling, Jr.

You don't take away someone's dignity. Roy never broke that rule. But if I made a mistake, he'd let me know in a way I'd likely never forget. But having done that, he would always say, "The only reason that I take the time to do this is that I think you have talent and something to offer. If I didn't think so, I'd say nothing and when your option came up, I'd just let it go." I knew that when he seemed to get mad or raised his voice, it was just his way of teaching me to be better at my job.

He was extremely hard-working and dedicated to making the best product possible. In my never-to-be humble opinion, he was a great man, a giant in the television industry, a terrific teacher, and a true and loyal friend. I was his right-hand guy for eighteen years. Getting a chance to work with him was one of the luckiest breaks of my career.

I am delighted that Paul Green has written this first official biography of Roy Huggins. I know Mr. Green to be a meticulous and thorough researcher as well as a very talented writer.

Jo Swerling, Jr., worked for MCA–Universal TV as a coordinator, then associate producer, producer and executive producer on many television series. He worked with such television notables as William Frye and Stephen J. Cannell during a 40-year career and retired in 1997 as senior vice-president, production, for Stephen J. Cannell Productions.

Preface

I grew up watching Roy Huggins' television shows in England. *Cheyenne* had the handsome, athletic figure of Clint Walker, who epitomized the classic Western hero: strong, highly moral and a man of few words. *Maverick* turned the traditional TV Western on its head, added humor and introduced the world to James Garner. *77 Sunset Strip* was "hip" and glamorous with its stylish 1950s automobiles and Southern California backdrop. *The Fugitive* was simply a must-watch show with the charismatic David Janssen pursued each week for a murder he didn't commit. *Run for Your Life* had glamour, beautiful women and exotic locations plus the excellent Ben Gazzara running from his deadly fate. *Alias Smith and Jones* had humor and the talent of Pete Duel, whose tragic real-life fate eventually overshadowed the series. *The Rockford Files* had James Garner repeating his Bret Maverick persona, *Baretta* had the tough, street-wise Robert Blake and *Hunter* had action, adventure, humor and the talents of Fred Dryer and Stepfanie Kramer.

This book aims to give shape and form to Huggins' personal life and his work as it travels through a career spanning six decades. Although he gained recognition for his work in television, his early feature film output placed him alongside major players in the film industry and proved to be a valuable training ground for the hectic pace of work on a weekly television series. In 2001 Huggins was still working on his memoirs. *The Story of My Life* a.k.a. "The Profane Comedy" a.k.a. "Reds, Beds and Feds" covered the period of June 1942 to September 1952 with a chapter on the 1930s. "Tears from a Glass Eye" a.k.a. "The Bloodshot Eye" covered his early years in television. I was granted access to these memoirs along with unpublished speeches. Huggins' personal recollections provide intimate details of his government work during World War II, his days as a novelist and screenwriter for Columbia, Universal-International and RKO leading up to and including the House Un-American Activities (HUAC) hearings, his return to Columbia and his time at Warner Bros and 20th Century–Fox television and beyond.

In the foreword to *The Story of My Life*, Huggins states that his memoir is a "personal history of an extraordinary Hollywood decade" and not "an autobiography." He includes many dialogued scenes and admits, "I do not recall every word spoken in those scenes, but I well recall what the scenes were about, and much of what is said is close to verbatim, which may have helped keep the fictive discourse trustworthy."

Huggins' personal observations from his memoirs, coupled with accounts resulting from author interviews and numerous hours of research, provide an intimate portrait of a complex man.

INTRODUCTION

Roy Marshall Huggins was a writer-producer of major importance, one of only a handful of television producers with name recognition in the formative years of the medium. An intellectual with a common touch who had the ability to engage the average man and woman without undermining their intelligence, Huggins had talent that wasn't localized to a limited, narrow base but spoke to international audiences.

Huggins' literary roots can be traced back to the hard-boiled fiction of Raymond Chandler, whose novels *Farewell My Lovely* and *The Big Sleep* inspired Huggins to write *The Double Take*, featuring Los Angeles private eye Stuart Bailey. That first novel served as his introduction to Hollywood and Columbia Studios. Although Huggins was a reluctant writer with only a passing interest in movies, he soon learned there was more money to be made in writing screenplays and adapting novels for the big screen than writing for New York publishers. Those early years at Columbia and RKO Radio Pictures would eventually lead to television, where he enjoyed his greatest success.

Huggins' political activism at UCLA and early Communist sympathies came out of misplaced idealism which saw Communism as the counter for Hitler's Fascism. The House Un-American Activities Committee hearings were aimed at causing division within the Hollywood creative community. Huggins was subpoenaed and agreed to testify under great pressure. He weathered the HUAC storm but much of his future work would display a general mistrust of authority. His shows often focused on outcasts in society: alienated loners fighting the establishment, attempting to escape their destiny. It was a model based on the classic American Western hero but also owed much to the cynical, world-weary detective fiction of Chandler and the Cold War paranoia of America. One of Huggins' most enduring creations, Richard Kimble, was continually looking over his shoulder, a fugitive from the law fearing the police on every corner. A form of paranoia based on the genuine threat of capture and execution by the state for a crime he didn't commit.

Huggins was a creator who was bored with the stereotypes of network television. TV Westerns of the 1950s were becoming stale and predictable when he went against type to create a self-serving anti-hero played by James Garner in *Maverick*. Years later Garner would take the lead again in *The Rockford Files*. The setting switched from the Old West to contemporary California but the character was essentially the same: a man with a begrudging relationship with the establishment, world-weary and preferring to live independently by his own rules.

In the days before cable television, VCRs, DVDs and the Internet, nobody expected television shows to have a long life outside of a few years in syndication. Here today, gone tomorrow, with only the memories of the viewers preserving their favorite episodes in the warm golden glow of nostalgia. Many of those treasured shows were created by Roy Huggins. *Maverick, 77 Sunset Strip, The Fugitive, Run for Your Life, The Rockford Files* and *Baretta. Cheyenne, The Virginian* and *Hunter* were rescued by Huggins and Hannibal Heyes in *Alias Smith and Jones* transformed into a Bret Maverick–type character under his pen name John Thomas James. Huggins often laid the path and left others to walk it as he moved on to laying new foundations elsewhere. Stephen J. Cannell and Glen A. Larson learned their craft under Huggins, going on to be prolific writer-producers in their own right.

Like all successful men, Huggins wasn't universally liked. His testimony at the infamous House Un-American Activities Committee hearings in 1952 struck a bad chord with those who believed in taking the Fifth Amendment. Decades later, the "Huggins Contract" led to criticism from James Garner, who saw him making millions of dollars for his one-season contribution to *The Rockford Files*. Huggins was no fool when it came to business and knew the importance of creator owner rights on a long-running television show following his early negative experiences at Warner Bros. Never again would Jack L. Warner types claim ownership and profits of a Huggins property.

Although an intellectual, Huggins was far removed from the traditional dry and dusty academic. A man of passion, he demanded perfection both in himself and in those who worked for him. Huggins acknowledged the audience to be the most important factor in television entertainment. He also acknowledged the mass audience of the 1950s and 1960s often felt most comfortable and relaxed with the conventional stereotypical drama where the good guys and bad guys were clearly defined. Huggins was working within a medium that had basically replaced the "B" feature in the movie theater. Complex, subtle storylines or characters were avoided in favor of the mundane and predictable. He agreed with the views of Sir Robert Fraser regarding the state of television who commented:

> Every person of common sense knows that people of superior mental constitutions are bound to find much of television intellectually beneath them. If such innately fortunate people cannot realize this gently and with good manners, if in their hearts they despise popular pleasure and interest, then, of course, they will be dissatisfied with television. But it is not really television with which they are dissatisfied. It is with people.

Huggins never spoke down to his audience. He pushed boundaries and brought a fresh vision to the rigid and predictable world of television, encouraging viewers to think outside of traditional values. He bridged the gap between the average viewer seeking relaxation and entertainment after a day's work and the viewer wanting to be engaged in something beyond passive pleasure. Huggins was working against what he termed "negative television" which sought to create a "socially bland" television, creating a "false picture of the society in which we live." Huggins preferred television that challenged the audience and involved them in looking at subjects from unexpected angles. It is impossible and unnecessary to create meaningful television on a weekly basis but Huggins succeeded in his lofty ambitions and diversified the television landscape over the course of four decades, to the benefit of the viewers. Like all producers, he encountered failure and rejection and not all of his work reached his own high standards, but he didn't go into a decline with age; he turned around the fortunes of the failing *Hunter* when he was in his seventies.

Huggins was a controversial figure to some, a teacher, mentor and creative dynamo to others, and most importantly a loving father and husband to his family.

1

Lineage

> Without doubt, no man with more wickedness ever brought to pass what he desired more wickedly.—Earl of Clarendon, *History of the Rebellion* (ca. 1688)

The arrival of Oliver Cromwell, Lord Lieutenant and General for the Parliament of England, in Dublin, Ireland, on August 15, 1649, with a fleet of thirty-five ships[1] was followed the next day by a speech that made his intentions clear. "We are here to carry on the great work against the barbarous and bloodthirsty Irish. To propagate the Gospel of Christ and the establishment of truth—and to restore the nation to its former happiness and tranquility."

On September 1, Cromwell rode over thirty miles north to Drogheda with his Parliamentarian New Model Army totaling 8,000 cavalry and 2,000 infantry. Royalist Sir Arthur Aston awaited to defend the Catholic medieval fortified city with a meager 2,200 infantry and 20 cavalry as Cromwell's troops set up an encampment outside the twenty-foot-high city walls. Meanwhile two artillery batteries were unloaded from the fleet sailing up the River Boyne. The heavy siege guns proceeded to blast breaches in the southern and eastern walls and the storming of Drogheda began with Parliamentarian troops killing every armed person in their path, including Catholic priests and friars. Aston surrendered to Cromwell with the promise of his life but was murdered in cold blood, his skull shattered with his own wooden leg which Parliamentarians believed was filled with gold coins. The remaining officers were also clubbed to death. An Irish Jesuit priest who survived the massacre described the scene: "When the city was captured by the English, the blood of the Catholics was mercilessly shed in the streets, in the dwelling houses, and in the open fields; to no one was mercy shown; not to the women, not to the aged, nor the young."

Cromwell boasted about the victory of his troops at Drogheda in a letter to the Honorable William Lenthall the Speaker of the Parliament of England on September 17, 1649: "Divers of the Enemy retreated into Mill-Mount: a place very strong and of difficult access; being exceedingly high ... our men getting up to them, were ordered to put them all to the sword. And indeed, being in the heat of action I forbade them to spare any that were in arms in the town: and I think that night they put to the sword about 2,000 men." A little over one hundred Royalist officers and soldiers took refuge in the steeple of St. Peter's Church. "These being summoned to yield to mercy, refused. Whereupon I ordered the steeple of St. Peter's Church to be fired." Cromwell followed the massacre at Drogheda with the fall of

Wexford and another 2,000 deaths. Cromwell was assured in his belief that the slaughter at Drogheda in 1649 had been "a righteous judgment of God upon these barbarous wretches, who have imbrued their hands in so much innocent blood."[2] The innocent blood in question being the massacre of the Protestant Ulster Plantation settlers by Ulster Catholics in the Irish Rebellion of 1641, notably the drowning in freezing waters of over 100 men, women and children at Portadown, County Armagh.

Oliver Cromwell and his New Model Army brought the Irish Confederate Wars to a brutal conclusion in 1653 with the capture and deportation of thousands of Irish Catholics as indentured servants. Cromwell's soldiers had been responsible for the massacre of 504,000 Catholic men, women and children between 1641 and 1652. Following the conclusion of the wars, British Protestant settlers and their supporters succeeded in confiscating land previously owned by the native Irish Catholics. For landowners who hadn't participated in the wars, barren land in the western province of Connacht was the only compensation offered to them.[3] Others were forcibly seized in their homes. "It was the usual practice of Colonel Strubber, the governor of Galway, and other commanders in the said county, to take people out of their beds at night and sell them as slaves to the Indies."[4] Sixty thousand Irish Catholics in total were ultimately sent to the Indies as slaves.

Edward Huggins, identified as "poor man," was among those forcibly transported by the English government to the Caribbean islands in the British West Indies as an indentured servant. Huggins' destination was Nevis. The seven- by five-mile island, dominated by a dormant volcano, was first colonized by the British in July 1628 when tobacco planter Anthony Hilton relocated from neighboring Saint Kitts. The soil and climate of Nevis, combined with an abundance of land, provided the perfect opportunity for the British to divide it into slave-dependent plantations, with sugar cane being the major cash crop. Irish Catholics comprised the largest ethnic group of white servants on the plantations of Nevis, accounting for 22.7 percent of the population.[5] The dominance of Anglicans in West Indies ensured the Irish Catholics were relegated to the lowest social status.

Following seven years of labor, their "masters" had to release the indentured servants by law and usually offered them a small plot of land. If the former servants could work the land successfully, it offered them a way out of poverty. Other freed servants became overseers of plantations in the absence of the owners who often preferred to receive the income while remaining on their estates in England and visiting their plantations on the rare occasion. Once the former servant succeeded as an overseer, it became possible to marry the younger daughter or a widow in a more prominent family.[6]

In the century following the arrival of "poor man" Edward Huggins, the Huggins name became widespread in Nevis as they populated the island. In 1778 a merchant named John Huggins became renowned as the builder of the Bath Hotel. The stone building (originally comprised of three apartments) provided homes and offices for John Huggins and his married sons.[7] The center of the building was eventually transformed into a hotel with the therapeutic thermal springs of sulfur, iron and iodine attracting wealthy and famous people such as Lord Nelson and Samuel Taylor Coleridge. A commentator of the day described the Bath Hotel and its surroundings:

> A building, well constructed of stone, of three stories with a spacious verandah or open gallery in front, erected by a philanthropist, a Mr. Huggins for the use of invalids, adjoins the baths. The middle story alone is now open as a hotel. It is capable of accommodating about 15 persons,

has 11 bedrooms, a large common room and a drawing room. Standing on a rising ground, it commands a pleasant view of part of the island of St. Kitts and of the intervening sea, and is considered healthy.[8]

Another Huggins became renowned in the late 1700s for less uplifting reasons. Edward Huggins, Sr. had been born into poverty and lost his father when he was still an infant. John Richardson Herbert taught him planting and in 1782 Huggins began acquiring plantation estates after marriage into the planter class. He eventually owned Golden Rock (built by John Huggins), New River, Coconut Walk and Mountravers Estates.[9] On February 23, 1810, the *St. Christopher Gazette* newspaper reported a story that would ultimately reach the British Parliament. John Burke, Jr. testified under oath that on January 23 he

> was standing in the street opposite the house of the Rev. William Green; when he saw Edward Huggins [Sr.] and his two sons, Edward [and] Peter Thomas Huggins, ride by, with a gang of negros, to the public market-place; from whence the deponent heard the noise of the cart-whip; that deponent walked up the street, and saw Mr. Huggins [Sr.] standing by, with two drivers flogging a negro-man, whose deponent understood to be Yellow Quashy. That deponent went into Dr. Crosse's gallery, and sat down: that two drivers continued flogging the said negro-man for about fifteen minutes: that as he appeared to be severely whipped deponent was induced to count the lashes given the other negros, being under an impression that the country would take up the business. That deponent heard Mr. George Abbot declare, at Dr. Crosse's steps, near the market-place, that the first negro had received 165 lashes: deponent saith, that Mr. Huggins [Sr.] gave another negro-man 115 lashes; to another 212 lashes; to another 181 lashes; to a woman 110 lashes: to another woman 212 lashes; and that the woman who received 291 lashes appeared young, and was most cruelly flogged. That all the negros were flogged by two expert whippers: that Mr. Edward Huggins [Jr.] and Mr. Peter Huggins were present at the time the negros were punished: that Dr. Cassin was present, when some of the negros were whipped, and when a man received 242 lashes. That deponent understood that Dr. Cassin was sent for by Mr. Huggins [Sr.] That Edward Harris, Esp,' Mr. Peter Bulter, and Dr. Crosse, were present at Dr. Crosse's house a part of the time during the punishment: and that Mr. Joseph Nicholson, Mr. Joseph Laurence, and Mr. William Keepe, were present all the time.

Huggins Sr. was charged with excessive cruelty in the public flogging of thirty-two of his slaves in the marketplace of Charlestown but was acquitted of all charges of mistreatment. Outrage at the verdict resulted in the British Parliament amending the Melioration Act of 1792 which limited the number of lashes given to a slave to thirty-nine. The case highlighted the harsh treatment of black and white slaves who were traded in Charlestown at the slave auction blocks at Crosses Alley and Market Shop.

A conflicting account of the day claimed Edward Huggins was a victim of the envy of the English-born planters who looked down on the native-born Huggins, "Creole" family and resented their continuing success as their plantation ownership increased. The charges of cruelty were viewed as being greatly inflated by envious competitors and those charges fell apart when they faced the light of a courtroom. Huggins Sr. successfully sued the *St. Christopher Gazette* for libel for publishing the "alleged" account of the whippings and received 15 pounds sterling in damages. He died on June 3, 1829, following a fall from his carriage. A son, John Huggins, was killed in a duel with Walter Maynard in 1822 at the age of 32.[10]

Following the abolition of slavery on the island in 1834, the sugar plantations went into decline. A branch of the Huggins family had moved to Trinidad where John Murdoch Huggins was born in June 1840. By 1859 he had left Trinidad for Canada before moving to

Michigan where he found employment in the booming lumber industry. Following his marriage to 16-year-old Irish immigrant Helen F. Hickey in 1865, they moved to Wisconsin. A son, Edward Francis Huggins, was born on May 22, 1877, in Eau Claire, Wisconsin. Work took the family to Minnesota where Edward met his future wife, Maybelle Therina Crawford. Her mother, Elizabeth Emeline Whittier Crawford, was related to the renowned abolitionist, editor and poet John Greenleaf Whittier and was descended from several pilgrims located in Plymouth Colony in 1620.[11] Episcopalian minister Henry M. Green performed the marriage ceremony between 26-year-old Edward Francis Huggins and 23-year-old Maybelle Therina Crawford on December 12, 1903, at Crookston, Polk County, Minnesota, with Mrs. H.M. Green and Minnie Dravant serving as witnesses.[12]

2

Formal Years

"Youth is easily deceived, because it is quick to hope."—Aristotle (384–322 BC)

Following the 1904 birth of their first child, daughter Marvel, Edward Huggins and his wife moved to Washington state to find work in the flourishing timber industry that fed off the surrounding pine forests. In 1870 the announcement of a transcontinental railroad crossing the northern states by the Northern Pacific Railroad Company was followed by construction on a western line at Kalama in Washington Territory and an eastern line beginning in Duluth, Minnesota, in 1871. Attacks from Indian tribes and financial troubles resulting in bankruptcy stretched the construction over twelve years before the line was completed at Gold Creek, Montana Territory, in September 1883. With the completion of the Northern Pacific Railway, timber companies saw an opportunity for growth and began to build small sawmill towns along the railroad.

Littell in Lewis County, Washington, was one of those new towns. Founded by logging company manager Harold J. Syverson,[1] the town site was platted by brickmaker and merchant Charles Littell on October 19, 1891.[2] Two sawmills and a brickyard attracted workers from afar including the Huggins family, who were soon joined by another daughter Eva in 1906 and son Jack Whittier on August 4, 1911.

Almost three years later, Roy Marshall Huggins became the final addition to the household on July 18, 1914. The young Huggins favored his mother's attractive features with his high forehead and prominent eyes and inherited his father's blond-sandy-colored hair. Edward Huggins worked as a saw filer, maintaining the large saws at one of the local sawmills on the banks of Columbia River near Mill Creek. It was a skilled craft that required calm nerves and expertise based on experience in metalworking. At six feet two inches, the blue-eyed Huggins was a handsome and charming man with a great sense of humor. He would tell his son Jack, "Always be your own person, be original, one of a kind."[3] Unfortunately Huggins had a weakness for alcohol and during periods of heavy drinking he would be assigned other, less exacting duties at the sawmill. The drinking eventually undermined his health and on a trip to Tacoma, Washington, he contracted pneumonia and died on April 5, 1917.[4] He was only thirty-nine years of age. After her husband's death Belle decided to put her knowledge of the hotel industry (gained through her mother who had owned the "New Duluth Hotel" in Minnesota) to good use and bought a boarding house in nearby Chehalis. However, her hopes of prospering were curtailed when the uninsured property burned to the ground in the middle of the night following the end of World War I. The fire had a lasting impression on Huggins, who recalled, "I remember being held in someone's arms, watching it burn. I have never forgotten how it looked and could paint an accurate picture of it today."[5]

Belle was forced into changing direction to find a way to support her children. The "Permanent Wave" was coming into vogue and Belle decided to train as a beauty operator in Portland, Oregon. For a short period of time Roy, Jack, Marvel and Eva moved in with Belle's brother, Frank Crawford, his wife Sadie and their two young daughters Pauline and Ione in Doty, Lewis County. Roy was only five years old. As the youngest member of the family, the fatherless Roy Marshall became the object of his sister's loving affection and his uncle's unwanted attention (the uncle stole money from his piggy bank).

Roy Huggins' father Edward Francis Huggins in the early 1900s (courtesy Katherine Crawford).

The young Huggins became particularly attached to a young married woman named Stella. She took care of him while Belle was still away from home. By the time Belle returned from her training, the young Huggins mistook Stella for his mother. He would never see Stella again after the age of five but kept in touch by letter.[6]

Despite his mother's forced periods of absence from her family, Huggins later stated, "I was a very happy little kid, adored by two much older sisters who thought I was the best-looking kid alive. So did I. I always felt secure and well-loved: and Jack, only three years older, did his best to stand in for our missing father."[7]

Belle made good progress with her new profession and opened a shop in Portland named "Marvel's Permanent Wave." The 1920s saw the popularity of short-hair styles continue with "the bob" becoming fashionable with the addition of curls and permanent waves also

Huggins' mother, Maybelle Therina Huggins, ran a successful beauty parlor in Portland, Oregon, in the 1920s and 1930s (courtesy John Huggins).

known as the perm. Spiral rods were wound tight to the scalp of the wet, washed hair and attached to pre-heated clamps which in turn were attached to overhead cables connected to a machine. Young women in particular were willing to put up with the inconvenience of sitting for long periods of time attached to rods, clamps and cables so as to look fashionable. Belle was also discovering a new talent as a palm reader. Although raised a Protestant, Belle found herself attracted to spiritualist practices that offered many women a sense of purpose and empowerment. Her talent proved to be popular and she soon gained a following as people sought advice about their lives and attended her séances. Granddaughter Katherine Crawford recalled, "Whenever Daddy told me about it (many times) he would say she was a lot like me. Very loving, and that she had a talent for it, and that people all wanted her to read for them. They trusted her and were drawn to her loving. It was clearly something that impressed him about her, even though he didn't believe in any of that."[8]

At the tender age of six, Roy Huggins was introduced to the Military Academy, in effect a boarding school teaching children within a strict military structure. At Hill Military Academy the young Huggins and his older brother Jack had to adapt to rigid and often harsh discipline, respect authority and learn teamwork. Founder Joseph Wood Hill modeled the respected private school after other popular American military academies of the early 20th century. When Huggins attended the Academy in the 1920s it was located on Marshall Street in northwest Portland, Oregon, and consisted of a four-storey wooden building with a donjon tower. Belle agreed with the popular wisdom of the day that stated military schools were good for fatherless boys. The young Roy Huggins complained regularly to his mother about how much he hated the Academy but Belle had little choice. She had to work, and thought it best that the boys learn discipline in a strong male environment.

Finely built, with blond curls, the young Roy Huggins wasn't a tough kid and, being the youngest boy at the Academy, he became the target

Roy Marshall Huggins as a Bealey Military Academy student, Troutdale, Oregon, in the 1920s (courtesy John Huggins).

of bullies. Jack genuinely cared for his brother's welfare and did his best to protect him from bullies but they would still pick fights, make him clean the toilets and carry the heavy pails of water from the well to the sleeping dorm in freezing temperatures at night with the wire handles cutting into his bare hands. Huggins' spirit remained unbroken and the constant bullying taught him a valuable lesson. Not to fight but to charm with the knowledge he was safe in himself.

The time spent in military schools would be the only blight on Huggins' happy childhood. He was all too aware of the hard life his mother endured. He said, "She worked long hours and had four kids to worry about. She was kind, understanding, but stern too. She was intelligent and had a circle of women friends who adored her all her life. I don't know how close I was to my mother, but I loved her very much. She had tremendous strength and charisma. And great insight into people's characters."[9]

The Depression forced Belle to take Roy out of the Military Academies[10] and put him in a public high school. Huggins found the classes dull and tedious and was placed one year back in class for his lack of effort. After five years he finally completed high school. The principal offered Huggins what he considered to be good advice given his weak grades, when he said, "Roy, don't ever try to do anything with your life. You should be a plumber or maybe you could get a job as a gas station attendant."[11] The 18-year-old Huggins, unsure of his direction and having always enjoyed some natural artistic ability, decided to explore his untrained talent. Following his departure from high school, he attended art classes at Oregon University.

Elsewhere in Portland, Belle's business continued (with a change of name to "Marvel Beauty Shop") throughout the 1930s with daughter Eva in charge. It was at the beauty shop that a teenage Huggins had first crossed paths with Bonnie Porter through her mother Bessie, a regular customer. But it wasn't until one fateful day while attending the same art class at Oregon University that they actually noticed each other as if for the first time and Huggins started a conversation with the pretty girl with blond hair and blue eyes.

"We met at a summer art class at the University," recalled Bonnie. "He was quite charming and walked the three miles home with me. We just kept walking and talking and didn't bother to get on the street car. I had never done anything like that before. From that moment I was mad about Roy. He would always want to walk in back of me when we were downtown and would say, 'I do that because I like to watch everybody looking at you as they pass.'"

When Roy left high school he focused on getting into college. He had to prepare for the entrance exams so he began reading everything. His mother didn't want him to read in dim light at night, thinking it was bad for his eyes which were bad to start with, so he went into hiding and holed up in the closet reading with a flashlight during that year! Roy never had to study. He could read a book overnight and get As the next day.

Huggins in 1933 (courtesy John Huggins).

But Roy never paid attention at high school. Bonnie continued, "For my art studies I found an empty room on the third floor of the University, put up an easel and started drawing portraits of everyone including the Dean of Women and the University President. I spent three years at Oregon University and never graduated. I didn't care for the art teacher I'd been assigned to so I skipped classes that I didn't like and the University let me do it."[12]

Roy Huggins was known as Marshall to friends, including Doris Bailey, who described him as "Jack's little brother, a tousled headed kid usually slouched in a chair reading." Bailey was a close intimate friend of Jack at the time. Although Bailey was only three years older than "Marshall," she commented, "He seemed a generation removed."[13] Huggins' artistic ambitions resulted in him asking Bailey to pose for him for a pastel portrait. It was during these sitting sessions that Huggins first described the plot to a novel he intended to write. Bailey saw similarities to his brother Jack in their shared enthusiasm for life and intellectual curiosity but Jack's personality was more focused and his career path more defined. He intended to teach literature in a university whereas his younger brother wanted to be an artist one week and a writer the next. A brother-sister relationship developed and they were often joined by Huggins' older friend Don Giesy in heated discussions about literature.

These discussions resulted in Bailey coming up with the idea for *The Dilettante, A Bi-Monthly Literary Review*, a magazine devoted to the arts. Jack Huggins thought the project impractical and refused to contribute but Bailey, Roy Huggins and Giesy moved forward. It took time to arrange, but the Metropolitan Press agreed to a limited print run of one hundred copies for a thirty-eight-page periodical with a cover price of thirty cents. Contributors to *The Dilettante* included poets Howard McKinley Corning, Ted Joyner, Ben Botkin and local author Roderick Lull. Bailey, Huggins and Giesy got their revenge on Jack for his refusal to contribute by publishing his letter criticizing Doris Bailey's plans for *The Dilettante* on the editorial page:

> Your choice of a title is full of ironic humor. I don't think you really know all the implications of the word dilettante and if you intend to make your magazine live down to it, your plans are nothing short of criminal premeditation and there is no hope for you. Youthful enthusiasm for the arts is natural and healthy. Youthful cynicism and aloofness can be dignified by no better a name than ludicrous. To speak truth, you are a walking antinomy; I never saw so enthusiastic a dilettante in my life.[14]

The publishing hopes of Bailey, Huggins and Giesy came to a premature end when *The Dilettante* failed to attract readers in August 1934. The second issue was cancelled due to lack of financing and interest. Huggins took the failure in his stride and looked to a new future at Pasadena Junior College where he attended as an English Major at the advice of a friend. A number of earthquakes in the Long Beach area in 1933 had undermined the structure of various college buildings to such a degree that the Horace Mann, Louis Agassiz and Jane Adams buildings were demolished down to their steel frames before being rebuilt. This forced students and faculty to take lessons in fifty temporary steam-heated wood-and-canvas tents for the next three years. Rules for acceptance were temporarily lowered and Huggins was accepted despite poor grades. Tent City as it came to be called offered little protection from the weather. An observer recalled,

> At times there was not enough light and at other instances there would be too much light and glare; and the tents were often too cold, too hot or too drafty. During the rainy season, students splashed around in mud and water and were compelled to sit through lessons with wet feet....

The tents were very close together, consequently, a student could very plainly hear what was going on in the neighboring tent. This was very annoying to the teacher and proved to be a distracting feature for many students.[15]

At Pasadena College, Huggins was a member of the local chapter of Phi Rho Pi, a national forensic fraternity that recognized outstanding work in the fields of student debate and oratory, and he took part in their debating team under the leadership of Earl Davis. Huggins and fellow team member Phillip Cartwright won second place in the Los Angeles Junior College invitational tournament and a team composed of Huggins, Cartwright, Bruce Jessup and Jean Valentine also placed high in the Redlands Invitational Tournament.[16] Huggins graduated in 1937, receiving A grades, before applying to UCLA where he eventually majored in Political Science.

In between studies Huggins was regularly returning to Oregon to continue his courtship of Bonnie. She said, "We had planned on getting married but never told anyone we were engaged. We had a party at my house with our friends. My father had supplied half a pint of bourbon. Roy said, 'Why don't we get married now? That will give us something to do.' So that's what we did on August 28, 1938, in Vancouver, Washington. Everybody followed us to the church. Roy's friend managed it so that by the time we arrived, there was a minister. As neither of us owned a car we just stood on the steps of the church after the wedding wondering what to do. We had no plans. A friend took us to his mother's house that night. The next day we saw an advertisement in the newspaper asking if somebody would like to help a woman drive to California. Roy called

Huggins reflects on his past as he departs for Pasadena Junior College, California, in 1935 (courtesy John Huggins).

her and we drove down to California together. My father found out and cried. He didn't see that this was going to go anywhere. Roy had no money and was going to UCLA, but I hated Oregon and wanted to get out. I came to California and never went back."

The rise of Fascism in Europe and the threat from Adolf Hitler prompted Huggins' political activism on UCLA campus. Said Huggins, "Hitler's apparent readiness to plunge the world into a second world war seemed beyond madness. And when Martin Heidegger, one of the most influential philosophers of the century, proclaimed to the students of Germany that 'No dogmas and ideas will any longer be the laws of your being. The *Fuhrer* himself, and he alone, is the present and future reality for Germany and its law,' I turned in dread from the study of English literature to political science, and registered to vote."

Huggins saw Communism as a remedy for German Fascism and was an antifascist activist on campus, calling for a halt to German rearmament and aggression before the Associated Student's Peace Council at Royce Hall. His activism brought Huggins into contact with two Communist Party "organizers" on campus, Celeste Strack and Bernadette Doyle, but attempts at recruiting him to the party failed. The turning point for Huggins occurred when he was refused a graduate fellowship on the grounds he was a member of the Communist Party. His professor of political theory, Eric Beecroft, who had been accused of being a Marxist, was fired shortly after department chairman J.A.C. Grant and Charles H. Titus met with Huggins. In protest, an outraged Huggins joined the Communist Party in June 1939, the same month he graduated UCLA Phi Beta Kappa and *summa cum laude* and went into the UCLA graduate school of political science.

On August 23, Huggins' faith in Josef Stalin was proven to be badly misplaced when the Soviet Union agreed to the Nazi-Soviet Non-Aggression Pact, thus paving the way for German dominance in Europe and neutrality for the Communist Party. The pact stated that the two countries would not attack each other. In effect the Soviet Union would allow Germany to invade Poland and any other country in Europe without intervening. On September 1, 1939, Germany followed through on its plans to invade Poland and two days later Great Britain declared war on Germany.

Meanwhile the Soviet Union occupied Poland beginning September 17, followed by their invasion of Finland in late November while Germany moved across Europe. It had been predicted by Charles Titus, but Huggins had dismissed Titus as being reactionary. An "obscene notion" had become fact and Huggins' youthful idealism had been compromised but he remained politically active. He wrote an article for the UCLA newspaper *The Daily Bruin*, "We, the Rabble," in response to a campus group called "Organization Control Board." Celeste Strack was impressed. She said, "I know you went through a period of shock after the pact, we all did, but when I read that piece you wrote for the *Bruin* I knew you were still with us."

Prior to enrolling at UCLA, Strack had been expelled from the University of Southern California in 1934 for her political activities. In 1935 playwright Clifford Odets had accompanied Strack to Cuba as chairman of the Communist-created "American Commission to Investigate Social Conditions in Cuba." They spent the majority of their time isolated in jail before deportation. Odets considered her a "quick, smart girl." Huggins thought Strack "had a solid intelligence and a sensual intensity."

Strack was excited about the upcoming anti-war rally on campus and asked to see Huggins' speech. Huggins replied he would simply take a few notes in his head and talk. It had worked with his previous speeches for the Peace Council. Only this time Huggins was feeling less than confident because he was uncertain on his own views about "the war-peace problem." Strack sensed a change in Huggins and asked, "Are you still with us?" Huggins brushed off her question but Strack's intuition was correct.

That Friday Huggins stood before his fellow students alongside fellow speaker and future editor of *The Nation*, Carey McWilliams. *The Daily Bruin* published part of Huggins' speech:

> We must not forsake our position of observers and become the observed. I voice a plea for student action, action that will make our stand known. Our lives and liberties are at stake. American can stay out of the war if the people, and especially the students and young workers, make up their minds to stay out of war.

Huggins claimed he remembered "almost nothing about the meeting except my extraordinary state of anguish. I have no recollection of what I said." Reading the newspaper account, it felt as if he was listening to the speech of a stranger. A weekend of reflection in Palm Springs with friend and roommate Stuart Bailey resulted in Huggins making the decision to abandon the Communist Party. "I concluded, after painful deliberation, that I had never come to terms with the Nazi-Soviet pact.... It was not possible for the Communist Party to take a neutral stance on the war: The USSR had been pouring great quantities of food and industrial material into Germany for almost a year.... Given my intellectual turmoil since the signing of the Nazi-Soviet pact I thought my decision was an epiphany."

Huggins' UCLA days came to an end on December 7, 1941. In 1942 he applied for an army commission following the bombing of Pearl Harbor by Japanese forces but a kneecap that had a nasty habit of falling out of place made him ineligible for active duty. "I had seriously damaged my knee playing soccer at the Bealey Academy, a military school in which the instructors were retired army men, from whom I learned all the ways to exploit military customs, bents and biases. I had the makings of a happy soldier and resented the army's rejecting me," recalled Huggins.

Instead he found himself stamping and signing civil service personal certifications (known as 57s) in room 1001 at the Tenth Region of the Office for Emergency Management (OEM) located on the corner of 10th and Broadway in Los Angeles. It was June 1942 and 27-year-old Huggins was beginning work at his new job as Special-Representative-in-Charge-of-Recruitment, National War Agencies (West Coast). A week later he would have his own office and personal secretary. The OEM's mission was to recruit 80,000 men and women for the National War Agencies by executive order of President Roosevelt, Pearl Harbor being the motivating factor.

Huggins' short-time affiliation with the Communist Party had repercussions in his job at the OEM when his boss E. Ross Hoyle told him to ask for a transfer within two weeks or be removed "for deliberate obstruction of this agency's wartime responsibilities." Huggins stood his ground. Hoyle was transferred to Washington and Huggins continued to work a seven-hour day as an OEM recruiting officer and Civil Service representative. But with the 80,000 positions filled, the workload was declining and Huggins was looking elsewhere for employment opportunities.

Meanwhile on October 9, 1941, Bonnie had given birth to their first child, Bret Huggins, at Santa Monica General Hospital. Three years later, on March 2, 1944, a daughter, Katherine, was born in Hollywood. At the time the Huggins family were living in a condo in Baldwin Hills, located in south Los Angeles. Katherine recalled,

> When I was born, Mom got peritonitis and was hospitalized for a couple of months, so Daddy and I bonded. And it always remained that way. Mom has always told me how she would get Bret, at 3+ years old, and the stroller and me onto a bus to go to the market to shop. And then she had to get us and the groceries all back onto the bus again and then walk back to the apartment. When we got home Daddy, would still be swinging in the hammock. It drove Mom crazy! And when she'd say something he'd defend himself by saying, "Bonnie, I'm thinking!" And of course he was right. That is how writers work. Writing requires a lot of thinking. But mostly what I remember of him when I was a child was that he was the Pied Piper. He made everything fun. Being with him was always a grand adventure, a show, an event ... full of fun and love.
>
> Daddy would sing me to sleep every night. He'd carry me in to the bed, tuck me in, then sit on my bed with his guitar and sing the most beautiful songs like an angel. His voice was smooth, pure and soft. I used to close my eyes just to please him. And he'd stay for a while, still singing, until he believed I was really asleep. Ahhh. So beautiful. English and Irish folk songs. "*Greensleeves*," "*Molly Malone*," "*Black Is the Color of My True Love's Hair*," "*Danny Boy*," "*My Bonnie Lies Over the Ocean*," and more.

3

Hard-Boiled Huggins

> I was sitting in his paneled office on the top floor of the Security Building looking at him across a desk that was as bare as a mannequin's mind and large enough for a pair of midgets to play badminton on.—Roy Huggins, "The Double Take" (1946)

Bookstore manager Joe Whalen was a surly and cynical Irishman whose only published novel had failed. He had been introduced to Huggins by his brother Jack, who was now a professor of English at the University of Arizona. In his spare time at the OEM, Huggins had been exploring the idea of writing a novel with commercial appeal as a means of making money to continue his education at UCLA. Whalen suggested Huggins read mystery-detective novels as he noted there was an insatiable market for them. But Huggins was unimpressed with the rigid, formulaic stories and considered them to be boring puzzles rather than well-constructed novels. Stories took place against a static, uniform backdrop with the murderer intruding into a stable world. Neither Rex Stout, Dorothy L. Sayers, Clifford Knight, Michael Innes, Ngaio Marsh or John Dickson Carr failed to stimulate Huggins into wanting to imitate their style of writing no matter the potential financial rewards that a best-selling novel might bring.

But when Whalen introduced Huggins to Raymond Chandler's *Farewell My Lovely*, his interest peaked. The themes explored in *Farewell My Lovely* and Chandler's first novel, *The Big Sleep*, appealed to Huggins. Private detective Philip Marlowe was a loner with no attachments, living by his own rules within a corrupt system peopled by shady individuals. The detective relied on his own ingenuity in a cynical world where trust and honor often didn't exist. Huggins recognized the Los Angeles that Marlowe inhabited. He said, "Chandler's writing engaged me from the opening page with its style and wit and intelligence, its sense of place and its sardonic attitude toward the rich and powerful and their public servants. His hard and pure protagonist, Philip Marlowe, traveled many of the same Los Angeles streets I had traveled, and he missed nothing, not even the 'tomcat smell' of the eucalyptus trees in spring. Chandler's world was the one Americans actually lived in."[1]

Huggins decided to write a novel in the manner of Chandler. Although Dashiell Hammett was the writer credited as the creator of the hard-boiled detective genre, Huggins was of the opinion that Chandler was a better stylist with sharper humor. He began by copying *The Big Sleep* by longhand to get a better understanding of Chandler's style and approach. But the task of writing didn't come easily to Huggins and he re-wrote over fifty percent of his 167-page manuscript titled *The Horizontal Man* before approaching Joe Whalen to hear his honest opinion of his work. Huggins had drawn on his own background in Portland and UCLA in a complex story about blackmail and the mysterious, hidden and often sordid life of the young and attractive Mary Bleeker Johnston. A real-life event (a female friend of Huggins failed to graduate from high school but succeeded in enrolling at UCLA using her friend's name) served as the main inspiration for the story.

After reading Huggins' manuscript, Whalen exclaimed, "It's a hell of a lot better than I thought it'd be—in fact, if I hadn't read Chandler, I'd think you had some talent.... It's almost scary how you bagged his style, but he's gutsier than you, he doesn't give a damn about plausibility—that's his real secret, not those repetitious poetry-manqué similes you caught all too well ... your scenes are all scrupulously credible."

Despite Whalen's reservations, Huggins mailed the completed 70,000-word manuscript to Howard Browne, editor of the pulp detective magazine *Mammoth Detective*, under the pseudonym Bret Whittier, after his son and maternal grandmother.

> Dear Sir,
>
> I have just completed a 70,000-word detective novel in the "hard-boiled" tradition. The unkind might say that I had written it with a pen in one hand and a copy of *The Big Sleep* in the other and emerged a kind of Poor Man's Raymond Chandler.
>
> However, it has a fairly tight plot with more integrity than the usual whodunit, and it is almost as good an imitation of the Chandler type as *Halo Round My Dead* was an imitation of Cain.
>
> I tell you this by way of giving you something to go on in answering this question: Would you be interested in seeing the novel with first American serial rights only offered? And how long would it be before you could consider publication if you decided to like it? The novel was read by my aging grandmother, who's a connoisseur of detective novels. She didn't like it.
>
> Very truly yours,
> Roy Huggins
> (Bret Whittier)

Huggins eagerly awaited Browne's response in the mail. When it finally arrived, his expectations were high as he opened the envelope to read the letter.

> The writing is excellent, in fact parts of it are downright spectacular. But ... the plot itself has flaws. For one thing, murder is incidental. Both killings are off-stage and do not seem to touch either Bailey or the reader. Another: you build and build toward a magnificent climax ... and that climax never comes off.
>
> It seems to me that confusion seeps in after page 180. Personally, I did not care about that, at least not very much—because I so enjoyed the style itself that plot weaknesses seemed irrelevant.
>
> Unfortunately I must consider the readers of the magazine and I'm pretty sure that not enough of them to count are as spellbound by Chandler's style as you or I.

A disappointed Huggins accepted Browne's constructive criticism and re-worked the manuscript before sending it to William Morrow & Co. under the revised title *The Mare's Nest*. The rewrite was comprehensive. Huggins decided,

> I should not write from a fixed outline or with any clear idea of what was going to happen next; that had created the "plot" problems of the first, failed draft. I must write each chapter with nothing but that chapter in mind unless I knew with great confidence what should happen next. It was generally better not to know, to allow things to *happen* within a chapter, things with much more promise than had been imagined before the writing itself had created its own direction.

> It helped to have a premise and a general sense of where I was going, but it was fatal to work toward a scene a chapter or two away that would force the writing of interim scenes that are not being written for themselves but to service some idea that had not emerged from the writing itself.

On August 14, 1945, he received a telegram telling him his manuscript had been accepted for publication. Huggins' joy was amplified when he learned Morrow had sold the story and rights to the Detective Book Club for $4,000. Morrow editor Helen King, who Huggins later described as "a young woman with honey-blonde hair and a Virginia accent," was intrigued with Huggins' work: "You must sit right down and tell me something about yourself because if this is your first mystery it is a remarkable accomplishment and I'd like to know how it happened." King was so impressed with Huggins' novel she originally thought it was written by Raymond Chandler using a pseudonym and bypassing his agent. She had sent a telegram to Morrow's West Coast representative Jesse Carmack telling him to find out if a Roy Huggins actually existed at his stated address and had written the novel.

In January 1946 *The Mare's Nest* was published under its new title *The Double Take*. *Mammoth Mystery* magazine adapted the novel in March 1946 under the editorship of Howard Browne, who had originally rejected the story. The original rejection had worked in Huggins' favor with Huggins discussing his writing in the *Mammoth Mystery* section "The Author Confesses" (March 1946):

> How did I happen to start writing at thirty? Several people have asked me that. The answer is that I am a mystery fan, and like most fans, I am disappointed in nine out of every ten detective stories I sit down to read. I decided to try to write a detective novel that would commit none of the more egregious sins against us readers, such as detectives who are "hard-boiled" because they have a strident delivery and are nasty to old ladies and children; "cute" detectives who solve their cases casually between rolls in the hay; plots without integrity, based on accident, coincidence, unmotivated behavior; long explanations, with the characters suddenly turning stooge while the detective reels off two chapters of double-talk that only the author understands; saboteurs, spies, big shots who have the mayor, the city council, and the state legislature in various pockets.
> I don't know how well I succeeded, but William Morrow is bringing the book out later this month, and there have been two bids from the studios, on the basis of galley proofs. But my agent says no sale until after publication. As he cryptically puts it: "Let's look this gift horse in the mouth."

The Double Take quickly went into a second edition in 1946. The dust jacket blurb played to its "hard-boiled" readership: "Ralph Johnston was afraid it was blackmail—he knew surprisingly little about his wife's past. Stuart Bailey thought it was a gag—but why sneeze at $40 a day and expenses. So Bailey started digging and what he turned up was definitely not small potatoes."

Insecurity and anxiety replaced Huggins' joy when he realized he must follow his debut novel with another book. Bonnie Porter recalled, "Every time Roy finished a story, it took him a couple of days to get over it. He was certain he wasn't going to write another word or ever have another idea. He was insecure about his work and in general. Many successful men are. He didn't show it to people. Everything had to be right. Because if it isn't they won't like him. It was early into the World War II era and had a job with a government bureau, and of course had to change his career goals. This experience probably contributed to his outlook."[2]

Mystery writers, jealous of Huggins' success, contacted Raymond Chandler to tell him about *The Double Take* in the hope he would put a stop to Huggins imitating his work. Huggins received a phone call from Chandler and dreaded the worst as Chandler introduced himself, but to his relief Chandler told Huggins that he wished him luck and commended him on doing something that he recommended to new writers: find an author you like and imitate their style.

Huggins began work on a proposed follow-up novel titled *Now You See It* after a meeting with chemist Perry Landis, who presented the basis for the story. Landis told Huggins that certain plastics had a "memory" whereby the original mold could be heated and remolded into a different shape. When the plastic was heated again, it returned to its original mold. Although it sounded like magic it was hard science. Huggins saw possibilities with the plastic with a "memory" gimmick but knew he didn't have a story that he could turn into a novel. After 20,000 words it was complete.

New York literary agent Paul Reynolds was far from impressed, but still managed to secure a sale with *The Saturday Evening Post* with the proviso Huggins could get a "reputable chemist to affirm facts about plastic with memory." Landis provided the proof and received $200 as thanks from Huggins, who in turn received $3,500 minus agent fees for *Now You See It*. Huggins was aware his reliance on gimmicks rather than character-based ideas for stories was failing to meet the requirements of a novel. His latest story, "Gladly, Said the Fly," was yet another 20,000-word novelette.

While writing his novels and short stories in the evenings and on weekends, Huggins was employed full-time in private industry as an industrial engineer in partnership with a civil engineer from Stanford University named John Pettker. He had recently completed his time at the OEM and met Pettker while attending pilot courses devised by "Training Within Industry," a division of the War Manpower Commission. Pettker was monitoring the three courses Huggins attended and was impressed enough to offer him one-half of a two-man civil-engineering partnership providing consulting services to small firms engaged in war-related work. Huggins would be in charge of the

Huggins and Bonnie Porter enjoying their new married life in Los Angeles in the early 1940s (courtesy Katherine Crawford).

administrative, personnel government relations work within the partnership. Despite feeling unqualified for the work, he accepted the offer of the short-term partnership which would be dissolved when the war ended. "I still wasn't thinking of becoming a writer. I was thinking about earning enough money so I could go back and earn my Ph.D.," declared Huggins.

Despite his reservations about writing, Huggins was working on an idea that he was confident could be stretched to his second novel-length book. It began with the premise of two related people with different temperaments coming across a large amount of money from an unknown source that should be handed over to the police. The moral dilemma lay in one of the two people wanting to keep the money. The new novel would rely less on the sardonic wit of Chandler and lean more to the suspense thriller genre. Huggins also decided to begin the novel in the third person with private detective Stuart Bailey making his appearance later in the story. The preliminary working title *Break the Wild Wind* was changed to *Nothing But the Night* but Huggins was experiencing serious doubts about the third person narrative suddenly switching to the first person with the introduction of Stuart Bailey. The problems would have to be resolved after the manuscript was completed.

Meanwhile, *Now You See it* had undergone rewriting at *The Saturday Evening Post*. Huggins' style was seen as too reliant on Chandler and the editors feared Chandler's approach might not appeal to the readers. Huggins was told by Paul Reynolds it was unlikely that *The Saturday Evening Post* would purchase another novelette from him. According to Huggins, "They know that Raymond Chandler has a lot of appeal in the book market and they want to see if his type of stuff will have appeal in the *Post*. They can't use Chandler because they can't clean his material up. I have often said to authors that they should be more afraid of success than of failure.... Things rarely go as regularly and smoothly as they have for you."

The news depressed Huggins. To add to his self-doubt about his future as an author, his novel *The Double Take* was being ignored by Hollywood studios. The words of Paul Reynolds came to mind: "There's no money in writing thrillers unless you can sell to Hollywood and to the serial market." His depression was relieved when *The Saturday Evening Post* bought "Gladly, Said the Fly" for $3,500. But it required revisions and wasn't considered as good as the first novelette.

Huggins continued to be displeased with the structure of his novel *Nothing But the Night*. *The Saturday Evening Post* shared his displeasure and rejected it. Huggins removed Stuart Bailey from the story along with the confusing third person-first person narrative. The revised version was submitted to William Morrow through Paul Reynolds, who Huggins was now referring to as "the Great Pessimist."

Despite his early success with *The Double Take*, Huggins was making arrangements to return to his studies at UCLA for the 1946 fall semester. He saw little security in writing for a living and was forced to borrow $800 against royalties on an unpublished novel to pay the bills. But his fortunes would soon take a dramatic upward turn with one phone call. Agent Ray Stark was calling on behalf of his Hollywood producer-director client Sylvan Simon. Simon had read *The Double Take* and wanted to meet Huggins to discuss it further. Stark concluded the phone call with, "Do you have a motion picture agent?"

An excited and somewhat incredulous Huggins agreed to the meeting at Simon's home on Sunset Boulevard. To Huggins' surprise, not only did Simon want to buy his novel, he also wanted him to write the screenplay. Simon offered him a deal totaling $25,000 but Huggins still had reservations. He had no experience writing a screenplay. Simon gave him a test.

Write a twelve-page screenplay for $2,000. If Simon liked it, Huggins was to complete it for an extra $5,000.

Huggins wasn't even that familiar with Hollywood movies and here he was writing a screenplay. He was a novice and knew it. The first 24-page draft was written in ten days. Simon liked it enough to pick up Huggins' option to complete the screenplay in six weeks. But first Huggins had to eliminate camera directions and concentrate on the story. Simon was so pleased with Huggins' work he offered him a seven-year contract at Columbia for $1,000 a week, rising to $2,500 by the final year. Paul Reynolds was less than enthusiastic about the Columbia contract and felt it would destroy his career as a writer. "I will stake my reputation that learning to write screenplays will make it more difficult for you to write good books or good serials. Writing for the screen in nine cases out of ten hurts a man's ability to write for any other medium."

Reynolds' letter was followed by a letter from Thayer Hobson, the president of William Morrow & Company:

> You're a damn fool and shouldn't be allowed out on the streets without a nurse to hold your hand. But I suppose it is too much to hope that anyone with your very real creative gifts should have any sense about his own affairs. The trouble with you is that you have had it much too easy since you first started to write. You've been much too successful and you are plain rotten spoiled.... And don't think for a moment that the reason for my rage is any financial disappointment. I think I can honestly say it is just a case of having discovered someone with real ability, having twelve months' experience prove [my] judgment was right, and then seeing the rocket go "phut."

Editor Helen King added her voice: "Of course my first reaction was to nickname you 'Mortimer'—you know, 'Mortimer, how can you be so STUPID!' But after seeing that correspondence you've been receiving lately, I want to extend my heartfelt sympathy instead."

Although Bonnie agreed it was probably unwise for her husband to work as a screenplay writer, she knew the money was too big a temptation to ignore. She said, "They kept telling him back east not to work in the movies. Roy kept saying no. Finally one day a couple of men came over from the studios. Roy took them outside for about one hour. Roy had agreed to work for them. They offered him a lot of money even though he was making decent money with the books. That was the big change."

Huggins' response to Thayer summed up his feelings about his work: "My largest point of disagreement was in your assumption that I really consider myself capable of turning out creative literature. I have never demonstrated any talent for it, and so far the things I have done had but one value: They made me a living. When I signed the Columbia contract, I thought that would assure me an even better living."

All thoughts of returning to UCLA were abandoned. Although Huggins was now an official Hollywood screenwriter on a huge salary, he was to discover success was an ongoing process and not to be taken for granted. Huggins' business upgrade also meant a change of agents. The young and dynamic Ray Stark replaced the negative and sarcastic George Willner, who had once asked Huggins, "You thinking of trying to make a living as a writer?" Meanwhile, *Nothing But the Night* had been accepted by William Morrow, who sold the serial rights to *The Saturday Evening Post* where it was published from April 19 to May 24, 1947 under its new title *Too Late for Tears*. Huggins' career as a novelist was put on hold as he looked toward Hollywood and the movie industry.

4

THE LADY WITH THE TORCH

> The secret to creativity is knowing how to hide your sources.—Albert Einstein (1879–1955)

Huggins first reported for work at Columbia Pictures in January 1947. His second floor office in the writer's building located on Gower Street in the Gower Gulch neighborhood of Los Angeles overlooked a two-story apartment building. The early history of the area saw production companies come and go due to lack of financing. One of the shoestring companies renting studio space was CBC Film Sales. When the company president Joe Brandt sold his stake to Harry Cohn, CBC was renamed Columbia Pictures Corporation. The year was 1924. By the time Huggins arrived, Columbia was on the verge of becoming one of the "Big Five" film studios with contract stars that included Rita Hayworth, Glenn Ford, William Holden, the Three Stooges, Larry Parks and Lucille Ball.

Across from Gower Street, working cowboys looking for fame or just a day's wages would hang out on the street corner known as "Gower Gulch."

One day Huggins' attention was caught by the sight of a young blonde woman passing one of the second floor windows overlooking his office. He felt something was familiar about her. Rita Hayworth flashed into his mind and then he connected the dots. Back in 1941 his friend Delmer Daves had invited Huggins on the set of *You Were Never Lovelier* and Huggins hoped to see Fred Astaire and Rita Hayworth dancing together. He didn't, but he did notice a pretty sixteen-year-old girl speaking to the director in "the pure Spanish of a Madrilena." She was playing Hayworth's younger sister. Her hair color had changed from brunette to blonde in the intervening years but there was no mistaking it was the same girl. She held a certain fascination for Huggins but in the meantime he had a new job to attend to and new skills to perfect. And he soon discovered the contracted screenwriter occupied a lowly place in the studio pecking order.

As a novelist, Huggins was in control of his creation. As a screenwriter, he was at the mercy of the studio where the director was king of the hill. This was evident in the dailies for *The Double Take* where a scene had been added, without his consent, for sexual titillation. Huggins complained about a scene where the protagonist Stuart Bailey leers at two large-breasted women passing him in the corridor as he keeps his appointment at the office of a homicide detective. Huggins' dislike of film directors was given birth. He said, "The scene was not in the script. It was a cliché, a defamation of the character of Stuart Bailey, and an offense against the author of the script. It was also an offense against women but this was 1947 and nobody noticed. The striking thing about the exchange was that my opinion was not something Simon felt compelled to deal with or give much thought to, and I understood for the first time that Hollywood writers were not expected, and certainly not encouraged, to influence a director's interpretation of their work."[1]

His next assignment was a Red Skelton comedy-mystery, *The Fuller Brush Man* (1948). Huggins was told to create a story. It occurred to Huggins to incorporate the plastic-with-memory gimmick from *Now You See It*. The Fuller brushes would be made of plastic. Huggins sent Sylvan Simon the *Saturday Evening Post* story with the intention of being excused from writing the script on the grounds of not feeling competent to write a Red Skelton comedy. Simon arranged a meeting with Columbia boss Harry Cohn and failed to mention Huggins' novelette but he assured Huggins he would be paid $5,000 for use of the plastic memory gimmick and receive sole credit on *The Fuller Brush Man* even though Devery Freeman would be writing the screenplay.

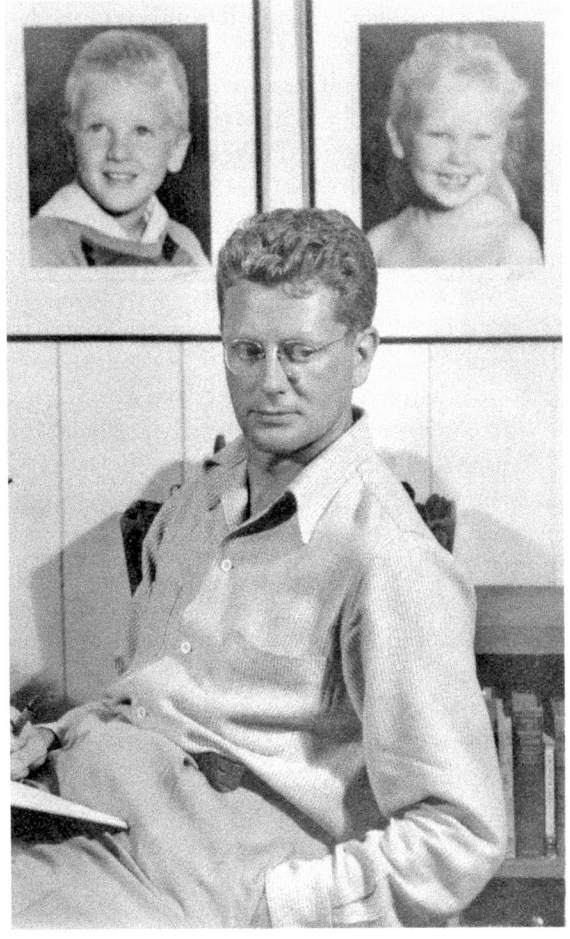

Huggins at Columbia Pictures (with photos of son Bret and daughter Katherine on the wall behind him) in the 1940s (courtesy Katherine Crawford).

Huggins found no room for complaint but wasn't as happy when he was told the title *The Double Take* was being changed to *I Love Trouble* for the film release. He thought the new title was "lousy" and protested that Stuart Bailey did his best to avoid trouble but Simon stood firm and blamed the sales department. Huggins also learned that Devery Freeman had polished his script, adding inventive humor. Once again Freeman's work wasn't credited on the film and Huggins received the praise from critics. Freeman, a fellow Columbia contact writer who occupied the office next door to Huggins, had become good friends with Huggins and accepted that being a hired hand meant the writer's ego had to be put on the back burner. Credits in the movies didn't always accurately depict the creative process and writers at work on the script. "In Hollywood, writers are treated like tailors, appreciated while the work is in progress but forgotten when it is finished. Tailors actually have it better than writers, their clients don't take the suits home and alter them," said Huggins.

In *I Love Trouble*, Stuart Bailey (Franchot Tone) is hired by wealthy politician Ralph Johnston (Tom Powers) to investigate threatening letters addressed to his wife. Bailey soon discovers that Mrs. Jane Johnston was formerly a night club dancer working out of Portland, Oregon, under her maiden name of Breeger. With Bailey getting too close for comfort, the night club owner (Steven Geray) sets his gangsters on him in the hope of making him abandon the case. But Bailey's curiosity is aroused further when Mrs. Johnston's sister Norma (Janet Blair) arrives on the scene and fails to recognize a photograph of Mrs. Johnston as her sister. When Mrs. Caprillo (Janis Carter) attempts to bribe Bailey to stop probing into the case, Norma recognizes her as her sister Jane.

The plot takes another twist when Mrs. Johnston's body is found under a pier and Bailey is framed for her murder. Bailey finally solves the case when he learns of Mr. Johnston's plans to frame him and thus absolve him of the murder of his wife. The convoluted tale comes to a conclusion with Bailey and Norma planning their marriage.

The general tone of the film was lighter than the novel but the stolen identity storyline was just as complex. The film received modest praise from critics including *Box Office* (February 28, 1948): "It will even please [viewers] not especially given to mystery dramas, for it is literally crowded with lovely girls who keep screen private eye Franchot Tone guessing for an hour and a half of clue seeking...."

Writers at Columbia worked to a clock: nine o'clock in the morning until six o'clock in the evening with one hour for lunch. But an unwritten "Screw Harry" rule between writers saw them using the afternoon hours for recreation and their own projects. Huggins was introduced to gin rummy and the gossip mill that concentrated on Harry Cohn.

When *The Fuller Brush Man* was released, Huggins felt a certain sense of embarrassment seeing his name on billboards towering over the small credit for Devery Freeman. The story may have been partly based on his *Saturday Evening Post* novelette but he acknowledged that Freeman was responsible for transforming it into a box office hit for Red Skelton.

The New York Times (May 15, 1948) review was mildly enthusiastic:

> *The Fuller Brush Man*, for all its limpness, especially at the start, is a pretty good sample of slapstick in the latter-day Keystone style. Mr. Skelton is a clown with obvious talent for the moments of frantic distress, and he gives a good show of hysteria in the ultimately concluding chase.

Box Office (May 15, 1948) stated:

> Mounted with the opulence characteristic of producer Edward Small, the vehicle was hand-tailored for Skelton's sizable and diversified bag of tricks.... It's a Harold Lloydish story with the title roler a lovable goon getting into jams.

Huggins failed to share even the mild enthusiasm of the film critics: "I saw *The Fuller Brush Man* and loathed it." Sylvan Simon, realizing Roy Huggins was gaining name recognition with the public, sought to associate him with the follow-up: *The Good Humor Man* would be another Skelton mystery comedy with a loose connection to Huggins' *Saturday Evening Post* novelette "Gladly, Said the Fly" which had been published as *Appointment with Fear*. Simon wanted it for $5,000. After some thought, Huggins agreed. However, Skelton had second thoughts about the project and was replaced by Jack Carson. Huggins took the money and the credit and moved on.

During the Easter holiday the idea for the next Huggins novel took shape. Huggins requested a three-month leave of absence from Columbia in the summer of 1947 to work on *Point Doom*. John, the protagonist, meets a beautiful woman in Palm Springs and learns that she is Ann Melville, married to a wealthy man thirty years her senior. John finds himself attracted to Melville as his own marriage falls apart. But when John discovers the body of his murdered wife, Ann Melville refuses to support his alibi even though she was with John when the body was discovered.

Away from the typewriter and office, Huggins was a regular visitor to Palm Springs with his wife and children Katherine and Bret. Katherine Crawford recalled,

> Palm Springs is something I still remember quite well. We went many times, and it seemed quite often, usually to a place called "Smoketree Ranch" at the base of the hills, which I loved. They had horses which was nirvana to me. Bret and I were occupied for hours every day so Mom and Daddy could have time for themselves. In the dining room they had your name on a clothes pin and it would be ceremoniously clipped onto a cord on the wall when you came in. It was a wonderfully happy place always.
>
> Mom told me stories in later years of dancing there in the evenings with Daddy. He would tell her how beautiful she was and how he would always love her. She imitated his exact words every time she told the story, and her eyes looked off into the distance as if seeing it all in detail. She'd become almost breathless and tears would come to her eyes. She would say "Ohhh ... he was so romantic." It was during this period that Mom and Daddy loved to go to the drive-in theater. Probably because they didn't have to get babysitters. But we had a wonderful time there too. An adventure in your pajamas. And in the snack store, many of the kids were in pajamas as well. Daddy would make hanging the speaker onto the window of the car seem like great fun. And when we came home, I always pretended to be asleep and Daddy would carry me from the car in to my bed.
>
> He was very loving and fun. Never rushed or irritable during those times when we did things together. It always seemed his total attention was happily and completely on us. He was having

Huggins helping with the pool construction at his Van Nuys home, circa 1948 (courtesy Katherine Crawford).

fun and we were having fun, and he would never "ignore" us. He built a study at our house in Van Nuys where the garage had been. He would work in there. It had a television when they first came out. Daddy was very proud of it. Bret and I watched *Beany and Cecil the Seasick Sea Serpent*, and *Space Patrol*. It was one of the first TVs there were. And it worked!

When we had the pool in the Valley, I ignored it for a long time since I wasn't interested in swimming. I was an artist. Pencils and crayons made my life blissful at three years old. So I missed this whole event of building the pool although Daddy always told me he built it. And I believed him ... for awhile. One day, clever Mom said that Bret was going to be in a swimming competition and I wasn't going to be part of it because I couldn't swim. Oh! A week later I had taught myself to swim. I liked competition, and couldn't let Bret win. I became a real water baby.

Daddy loved the pool. Someone built an eight-foot-high diving board and Bret and I never stopped diving off it. Belly flops were a regular event and we didn't even mind. Daddy was very encouraging and supportive. Gentle. He encouraged with charm. Never got tough. He left that to Mom.

They had many weekend pool parties. Friends would bring their kids and swim. Daddy was very social and seemed to love those gatherings. Sometimes the men played poker or chess. Sometimes he played the guitar and sang by the pool, standing in his trunks. He seemed to be having a very happy time back then. We had many parties including one in which Marlon Brando and Tony Curtis preferred to go to the "study," away from the noise of the party, and play Blind Man's Bluff with Bret and me alone, in the quiet. I also had great fun dancing out in the main party by standing on Tony Curtis's feet and he did the dance steps for me, for many dances, before we all went in to the study. I remember it vividly so both of them must have had charisma even with four- or five-year-olds. I thought they were both simply wonderful. And I had no idea who they were.[2]

Bonnie recalled,

We went to Palm Springs often. We would dine at The Tennis Club in Palm Springs once or twice a month at the weekend It was a beautiful place. Roy was a very romantic man who liked going out at night. He was a gambler. My mother was as well. They got along beautifully. Roy would gamble at anything but he wasn't addictive. Whenever we went out with Bob and Dorothy Van de Grift, Bob and Roy would gamble over who should pay for dinner. It was fun. After dancing and dinner Roy and Bob would take Dorothy and me home to the hotel. Then they would spend all night gambling and come home in the early morning hours.

When I first met him he was poor. He was wearing old white leather shoes. They were polished so much there were cracks where the shoe polish was thicker. He was always proud of his appearance even when he was poor. And he was proud of being successful and knew that appearance mattered.[3]

Katherine elaborated on her mother's comments:

People rarely get over their roots. So a watchfulness was there, and a demand on himself, people, work, clothes and houses. He knew what quality was. Quality was never to be overstated. That was the number one rule. Never overstate. That's crass. Understate. His theory was that true quality never had to prove itself. It was simple and real, not contrived. It simply was. Never elaborated on, or gilded. He came from the bottom with no father that he ever knew. But he knew quality and good taste and demanded it from himself. He never lost that demand. He had the highest values, and his family reflected that as much as he did, so we were all very aware of genuine quality versus everything else. And I am grateful to him for that."[4]

Huggins took time out on one of his trips to Palm Springs to research material for his latest novel. At night he intended to explore the gambling scene at The Cove and 139 Club but discovered, for reasons unknown, they were no longer in business. Back at The Tennis Club where he was staying, he was introduced to a Mr. Crespi who provided valuable

Huggins types as his wife Bonnie relaxes poolside at their Van Nuys home in the late 1940s (courtesy Katherine Crawford).

background information on the hard-core gambling scene, including a real-life craps table dealing in cash, run out of the brightly lit double garage behind his Spanish bungalow. The craps table came complete with two "stickmen" who were switching dice. "I had done my share of crap-shooting, and I had never seen dice handled during a roll by anyone but the shooter," recalled Huggins.

As soon as Huggins noticed the switch, he left the game and the garage behind him. But it was all great material for his novel. Sadly for Huggins, a recurring problem presented itself. His "novel" only ran to 35,000 words. *The Saturday Evening Post* rejected it. Not due to length or style but due to the subject matter of infidelity. Huggins was told that cheating husbands wasn't a good fit for their readers. When Huggins turned down an offer from *American Magazine* because they wanted him to cut 15,000 words, he had no choice but to expand his story to novel length.

Meanwhile, Hunt Stromberg wanted to buy the screen rights to *Too Late for Tears*. Joan Crawford was interested in playing the lead. Stromberg had been one of the "Big Four" producers at Metro-Goldwyn-Mayer and produced Greta Garbo's first American film *Torrent* (1926). Huggins had confidence in Stromberg given his impressive track record with *The Great Ziegfeld* (1936), *Night Must Fall* (1937), *Northwest Passage* (1940) and the *Thin Man* series, among others. With Huggins still under contract to Columbia, the screenplay would have to be written by another screenwriter, but Huggins liked the terms offered which included five percent of any profits. He signed on the dotted line and hoped for a hit.

On his return to Columbia, Huggins was effectively sidelined with no assignments to work on. He filled his time with a new story titled *Death and the Skylark*. He decided to approach Cohn about it on the advice of Sylvan Simon. The story was set on board the yacht *Skylark* as it traveled between Los Angeles and Honolulu. Huggins pitched his story as Cohn was getting a haircut in the barber shop down the hall from his office. He was unimpressed. "Forget it. It's a fuckin' B movie," yelled Cohn.

Huggins refused to be defeated and added Stuart Bailey to the cast of characters. With adultery as a theme in the story, Huggins wasn't surprised when *The Saturday Evening Post* rejected it. He had better luck with *Esquire*. It would later find a new life on television but in 1947 television was a medium that had zero interest for Huggins.

Huggins' problems with Cohn were just beginning. Cohn wasn't happy with his output. "Harry Cohn's office was large and it was a long, cold walk to his slightly elevated desk," described Huggins. "I have no idea how tall Harry Cohn was or how much he weighed, but he looked big and he was packed with interest. Cohn's eyes, the blue of copper-sulfate, were what caught your attention first, the quick and watchful eyes of an auctioneer, set in a head that looked large and round and hard."

As he slapped his leather swagger against his desk, Cohn shouted, "I'm payin' this schmuck a fortune and I haven't seen a fuckin' dime. Got one lousy picture out of him, the one you wrote, and it's doin' shit at the box office," Cohn shouted to Sylvan Simon as Huggins stood to one side and took the verbal abuse in his stride.

Cohn looked to Huggins with the swagger stick firmly grasped in his palm. "What in hell are you doing playing gin rummy with all those other fuckin' bums and hacks?"

"I'm thinking while I play. I have some good ideas but none are good enough to waste your time," replied Huggins.

"Let me worry about my fuckin' time! I want something from you before I go to Phoenix on the 18th. I don't care if it's a Western or a fuckin' South Sea romance, as long as it's not ersatz Chandler like that shitty novel you sold Simon here. If you gotta steal from somebody, why don't you steal from a writer with a little class, like Maugham?"

"Moon over the South Seas" was the result: a fourteen-page screen treatment in the style of Somerset Maugham, written to a very tight deadline. The story involved Tahiti-born Jacques Bonnet who, after marrying a beautiful native girl, sells his paintings of native women to tourists. But following the birth of his fifth child he undergoes a mid–life crisis and leaves his wife, children and Tahiti for Paris, where he finds a new life and success as a banker.

The story read like the life of acclaimed painter Paul Gauguin in reverse. Cohn hated it and fired Huggins by long distance phone call from Phoenix with four-and-a-half weeks still left on his option. He was told to vacate his offices immediately. Huggins' period of unemployment lasted less than a week. At Universal, William Dozier was interested in developing an original story into a screenplay for Barbara Stanwyck. The story failed to interest Huggins but writing for Stanwyck was too good an opportunity to pass on. Huggins decided to come up with an alternative story about a compulsive gambler. Dozier was intrigued enough by the basic premise to hear more. Huggins sold him on the story which became *The Lady Gambles* (1949) and Huggins moved into his office located in building C at Universal.

The film opens with Stanwyck being badly beaten in an alley for gambling with loaded dice. It is a shocking introduction to Stanwyck's character Joan Phillips Boothe. Her husband (Robert Preston), in the presence of an unsympathetic and jaded Dr. Rojac (John Hoyt), recalls her decline from a happily married woman living in Chicago to a compulsive gambler. While working on a speculative magazine article about Las Vegas, Mrs. Boothe comes to the realization that gambling excites her and soon she prefers the company of gamblers in Vegas casinos to that of her husband. Soon she is forced to pawn her camera to cover gambling losses, but a winning streak at the dice table only serves to encourage her gambling addiction. Mr. Boothe returns home while his wife stays in Vegas and becomes involved with shady Horace Corrigan (Stephen McNally).

Realizing she has a serious problem, Mrs. Boothe takes a second honeymoon with her husband in Mexico. But a chance meeting with old friends leads her to an underground gambling den and a return to her addiction. In Las Vegas, Corrigan offers her a job in horse racing. But her life continues to crumble around her as divorce papers from her husband are followed by her being fired from her job. Discarded by Corrigan and her husband, she finds work as a hostess in a seedy gambling club and ends up in a hospital following her beating in the alley.

Mrs. Boothe blames herself for the death of her mother and feels self-destructive and worthless to the point of attempting suicide by threatening to jump off the ledge outside the window of her hospital room. But she is pulled back by her husband and they attempt to rebuild their lives away from the temptation of the casinos and gambling dives of Las Vegas.

Reviews complained about the lurid content and melodramatic finale. Publicity for the film with the headline, "You're not even a woman anymore ... just another dame with the 'fever!'" only served to enhance the pulp fiction mentality. Bosley Crowther of *The New York Times* (May 21, 1949) commented: "[F]or all the solemn moralizing in the script, this passionate disturbance over gambling seems completely contrived and ludicrous."

Meanwhile, "Point Doom" (a play of words on Point Dume) was now titled *Lovely Lady Pity Me*. Publisher Duell, Sloane and Pearce accepted the manuscript after minor revisions. Prior to its acceptance, Huggins had been working on the screenplay for *Too Late for Tears* at Republic Pictures. The script by Jay Dratler didn't work. The casting for the film had taken a turn for the worse when Joan Crawford dropped out of contention for the lead role and Kirk Douglas decided he preferred the lead as struggling boxer "Midge" Kelly in *Champion* (1949). Lizabeth Scott and Dan Duryea stepped in. The story centered on Jane Palmer (Scott), wife of Alan Palmer (Arthur Kennedy). Their lives are turned around when a suitcase of laundered money is thrown into their automobile from a passing car. Jane's passion for a wealthy lifestyle convinces her to say, against her husband's wishes, they should keep the $100,000 in cash for themselves.

Palmer's greed leads to her involvement with gangster Danny Fuller (Duryea) who promises her half the cash if she returns it to him. Seeing her husband as an obstacle to her newfound wealth, she murders him while boating on a lake. But the suspicions of Alan's sister Kathy (Kristine Miller) and the appearance of Don Blake (Don DeFore), secretly the brother of Palmer's first husband who was also murdered by Jane, eventually leads to the truth being revealed.

Huggins was far from pleased when the film was previewed in early 1949 in Inglewood,

California. "I hated the movie Stromberg made from my script. It was intended to be a suspense movie and it had all the suspense of a two-hour ride on a merry-go-round. It was a bad movie because it was badly directed—and possibly badly written, but in view of the lethargic direction, how could you tell?" When it went into general release, it died at the box office despite some favorable reviews.

The New York Times (August 15, 1949) commented:

> Despite an involved plot and an occasional overabundance of palaver, none of which is bright, this yarn about a cash-hungry dame who doesn't let men or her conscience stand in her way, is an adult and generally suspenseful adventure.

Box Office (April 16, 1949) was impressed:

> This is a powerful melodrama which pulls no punches and makes no effort to create a sympathy for its heartless heroine who is almost a modern Lucretia Borgia. The hard-featured blond Miss Scott is ideally cast as the ruthless female and Duryea is his usual sneering self as blackmailing crook... The "Crime Doesn't Pay" finale is theatrical but highly effective.

Huggins had sold his five percent interest from Republic Pictures to Bobbie Newman, in return for a cashier's check. Newman had wrongly predicted *Too Late for Tears* would succeed. Stromberg was forced into bankruptcy by the Bank of America.

The failure of *Too Late for Tears* was bad news for Huggins and soon the phones became silent. One film assignment came along from producer Milton Sperling in the form of *Murder Incorporated*, later released as *The Enforcer* (1951). Humphrey Bogart starred as assistant District Attorney Martin Ferguson, seeking to prosecute Murder Inc. boss Albert Mendoza (Everett Sloane). An article in the *Los Angeles Daily News* (November 11, 1949) reported that John Higgins had been assigned the screenplay with Martin Rackin. John Higgins alias Roy Huggins failed to receive a credit on the released film.

Huggins' final freelance assignment was the screen adaptation of James Webb's *Saturday Evening Post* story "Fugitive from Terror." Oscar Saul provided the screenplay. *Woman in Hiding* (1949) starred Ida Lupino as Deborah Chandler Clark, who after falling for the charms of Seldon Clark (Stephen McNally) discovers she may have married the man who killed her father. Fearing for her life, she fakes her own death and adopts the identity of Ann Carter. But her husband, convinced she is still alive, continues to pursue her and offers a $5,000 reward, which attracts the attention of drifter Keith Ramsey (Howard Duff).

Box Office (December 17, 1949) gave a favorable review:

> [The approach] is sufficiently original to circumvent any stigma of formula; and the film's appeal is further enhanced because performances and direction take full advantage of a tight, suspenseful, fast-moving script.

Other projects weren't progressing well. A lengthy treatment written in collaboration with Lieutenant Commander Harold M. Auerbach, former director of flight operations for the Israeli Airforce, about the war that established Israel as a nation, failed to sell as a screen project. A fictionalized version of the life of Howard Hughes titled "Show Me a Hero" was abandoned and Huggins' relationship with his agent Ray Stark was terminated under disagreeable circumstances.

Stark had agreed to share commissions with Paul Reynolds on the sale of any Huggins story sold by Reynolds to a magazine or publisher. But unknown to Huggins at the time, Stark had written to Reynolds claiming full commission on the sale of *Too Late for Tears*, claiming he had sold it in manuscript form before publication. Reynolds sent Huggins a copy of Stark's letter. Huggins set up a meeting with Stark.

Huggins decided not to tell Stark about Reynolds forwarding his letter. He was protecting Reynolds, who Huggins knew was entitled to his share of the commission because he had sold the story to *The Saturday Evening Post* before book publication. Stark argued his case but Huggins had heard enough and walked away from any future dealings with Stark. But once again Huggins didn't stay down for long and soon found himself working for Howard Hughes at RKO.

5

HOWARD HUGHES RADIO PICTURES

> Audiences don't know somebody sits down and writes a picture. They think the actors make it up as they go along.—Joe Gillis in *Sunset Blvd.* (1950)

A letter to Howard Browne, dated April 3, 1950, explained how Huggins found himself hired at RKO operating out of a rundown office on the Samuel Goldwyn lot: "By October of 1949 I was getting really desperate. I had borrowed five grand altogether and had gone through half of it. I was just getting a novel about Hollywood underway (the Hughes novel) and had written an original about the air war in Israel. I told the Israel story to the story editor at RKO, who couldn't use the story but liked me for my wholesome and lovable personality and gave me a job. I rewrote a bad screenplay called *Eyewitness to Murder* and came out with a script that nobody liked including me. But was I fired as I should have been? They fired the producer, put the director on layoff and gave me a new assignment."[1]

Following his inauspicious start on *Eyewitness to Murder*, Huggins was given the assignment of re-writing a script by Frank Fenton and Jack Leonard. *Smiler with a Gun* was a vehicle for Jane Russell and Robert Mitchum that eventually became *His Kind of Woman* (1951). Fenton's well-written dialogue was to remain but the basic story had to be revamped. "What it needed was more credibility, less predictability, more suspense, and more drive, but trying to match Fenton's hard and lyrical dialogue was a tough task," declared Huggins. Seven weeks later the script was completed and accommodated suitable moments where Russell's character could break into song.

As *His Kind of Woman* approached the end of production, Paramount producer Hal Wallis offered Huggins a job at his studio. Huggins turned him down, preferring to work on Roberto Rossellini's *Stromboli* (1950). The adulterous affair involving Rossellini and Ingrid Bergman served to promote interest in the film in Europe where it had been released. But RKO's head of production Sid Rogell knew the film about a displaced Lithuanian woman (Bergman) adapting to life on the harsh Italian volcanic island of Stromboli wouldn't play well with American audiences. Huggins was asked to write a narration to make the film easier to follow. After viewing *Stromboli* twice, Huggins thought it "a paralyzing bore" and a "turgid picture." He met with Renzo Cesana, the actor portraying the priest in the film and co-writer of the original story, who agreed to read the narration. Huggins found him to be a charming man with a pleasant Italian accent and was pleased with his completed narration. But a furious Howard Hughes claimed he couldn't understand "a damned word the priest said" and demanded an American-sounding narrator and a rewrite from Huggins. When the completed film previewed in Huntingdon Park, Huggins fearfully awaited the narration. Huggins was relieved it didn't make the final cut and he wouldn't have his name attached to a critical and box office failure.

Josef von Sternberg was best known for directing *The Blue Angel* (1930) starring Marlene Dietrich. Huggins expected to hear a thick German accent when he reported to the set of von Sternberg's latest film *Macao* (1952) but encountered a 58-year-old man speaking perfect English, having spent his childhood in America. Huggins was told to be available to change Jane Russell's dialogue where necessary. He used his time on the set to watch von Sternberg at work in the hope of learning something about directing.

Russell never asked Huggins change one word of dialogue. She was a grounded actress who had a good relationship

Huggins the successful screenwriter in the early 1950s (courtesy John Huggins).

with Huggins. This gave Huggins more time to concentrate on von Sternberg during the long hours on the set. Von Sternberg told Huggins, "We're both writers, you know. The director happens to write with a camera." The assistant director offered sober advice: "Don't hesitate to take the first chance you get to direct, there's nothing special you have to know." Von Sternberg failed to complete the picture after refusing to direct retakes and was replaced by Robert Stevenson, Nicholas Ray and Mel Ferrer late into production.

Meanwhile *His Kind of Woman* was going over-budget thanks to Howard Hughes insisting Vincent Price's scenes be expanded. Director John Farrow was replaced with Richard Fleischer and the comic wit of Price took center stage over the original dramatic storyline. When production was finally completed, Jack Leonard objected to Huggins receiving a screen credit. Leonard insisted that Huggins had only been hired to write "intros" to Jane Russell's songs. He was successful in removing the credit for Huggins. The film lost $850,000 at the box office and once again Huggins was glad to have no official connection to the film.

In 1950 Huggins moved into an apartment in Beverly Hills following his separation and pending divorce from Bonnie. Shortly after moving in, he embarked on a short-lived relationship with Franchot Tone's former wife Jean Wallace. Huggins was a good friend of Tone and had known Wallace for many years. Following her divorce, Wallace had attempted suicide in 1949 with a self-inflicted knife wound to her abdomen. This was followed by a marriage that only lasted a few months. Huggins was someone to talk over problems with and for a short time he listened. She would later marry actor Cornel Wilde and enjoy a marriage that lasted until Wilde's death in 1989.

With Huggins unattached, he explored the Hollywood party scene in the hope of meeting attractive, unattached females, but he was a poor fit. It wasn't a social scene he enjoyed. He was gaining a reputation for being self-important, reclusive and shy. Actress Coleen Gray stopped seeing him after she decided she didn't care for his liberal views.

Huggins' next project for RKO was an adaptation of the World War II adventure novel *The Gaunt Woman* by Edmund Gilligan. Released as *Sealed Cargo* (1951), the film starred Dana Andrews as Grand Banks fishing boat captain Pat Bannon, who rescues a stricken schooner not knowing it contains a cargo of torpedoes destined for a German U-boat. Bannon must attempt to stop an impending submarine attack as he tangles with Nazi spies.

While working on *The Gaunt Woman*, Huggins received a phone call from Abigail "Tommye" Adams who lived nearby. Huggins knew her briefly from a screen test that he wrote and she filmed in 1947 where he recalled her Southern accent, charming personality and beauty. The test was a success and Adams was placed under contract to Columbia although she never appeared in a movie and her option wasn't picked up. Her on-off relationship with 20th Century–Fox producer George Jessel (twenty-four years her senior) was just one aspect of a troubled personal life.

When they arranged to meet again, Huggins found her to be "sweet, ingenuous and more than pretty" and began to see her as often as five times a week at her apartment. As well as having a liking for alcohol she also enjoyed sex, although Huggins noted it was more of a desire for affection and intimacy rather than passion and a need to please. It wasn't long before Huggins noticed she was mixing sleeping pills and prescription drugs (including Phenobarbital) with alcohol. He warned her of the dangers to no avail and slowly their relationship died during the summer of 1950. "For over a year I called her once or twice a month to see how she was. She said she was 'getting by,' and now and then she said in little-girl tones that she missed me. One Saturday morning I called and the phone was answered by a man who sounded half asleep. I hung up, but the incident freed me: there was someone in her life. I hoped he would look after her."

Five years later, his fear for her well-being proved to be valid when she died from an accidental overdose of barbiturates mixed with alcohol at the age of 33. Huggins said the news "stopped me like a glass wall." Despite press reports that her death was suicide, the official verdict was accidental—a verdict Huggins agreed with.

In late November 1950, Huggins finally found the perfect reason to stop the merry-go-round of the Hollywood party scene when he met Adele Mara. Huggins was having dinner with Leo Guild and his wife Hazel at "Don the Beachcomber." On their way out they stopped at the table of Jerry Herman. Seated with him was a brunette and his date, a blonde woman. Huggins was introduced to the blonde by Hazel. Huggins immediately recognized her as the girl he had admired from afar at Columbia. The next day Huggins asked Hazel for Adele's phone number so he could invite her to a November 28 preview of Warner Bros.' *Storm Warning* (1950), starring Doris Day and Ronald Reagan, at the Warner Theatre in Hollywood. Adele accepted his invitation to a pre-preview dinner at the Sportsman's Lodge in Sherman Oaks near her new home in Stansbury. It marked the start of a relationship that would last for 54 years.

In April 1951 Huggins was assigned to *The Las Vegas Story* (1952) after Paul Jarrico's first draft based on *The Miami Story* by Jay Dratler failed to please Howard Hughes. On March 23, Jarrico had been refused entry to RKO Studios without explanation. The underlying reason behind Hughes' rejection of Jarrico's draft lay in his affiliation with the Communist Party and his imminent appearance before the House Un-American Activities Commission (HUAC) on April 13 where he would take the Fifth Amendment. The film would be another starring role for Hughes' favorite actress Jane Russell, here playing a former Las Vegas lounge singer who becomes mixed up in robbery and murder. Huggins tweaked the script and saw ten days of work ahead of him to complete his task. When he turned up for work Monday morning, Huggins received the same greeting as Jarrico by the guard at the gate: "I've been instructed to inform you I can't let you in." Huggins gave the guard his script and drove away. Screenwriters Harry Essex and Earl Fenton would eventually complete the screenplay. Neither Jarrico or Huggins were credited when the film was released on January 30, 1952. An incensed Jarrico demanded screen credit or $5,000 in payment. Hughes refused to give in to his demands and took him to court. Jarrico in turn sued RKO for $350,000 in damages. Hughes remained stubborn and eventually took the case to the California Supreme Court where they decided Jarrico had violated a morals clause in his contract. Hughes declared, "It is my determination to make RKO one studio where the work of Communist sympathizers will be impossible."[2]

Huggins arranged to meet his agent M.C. "Mike" Levee. The paper trail led back to Huggins' former agent George Willner. He had worked for a magazine published by the Communist Party in New York. *New Masses*, the Communist magazine, led to Hollywood and agency work with Nat Goldstone. "The Reds pulled off a power play. It was a small-time power play to get a Red into an agency," commented Levee. Huggins had no knowledge of Willner's connection to the Communist Party and had no idea Willner was aware of his political background. Huggins later learned that the American Legion was feeding information to the studios via HUAC and the FBI.

Huggins was in trouble. The official story was that blacklisted writers were having to adopt pseudonyms on a new black market born out of necessity. Huggins knew it made little sense. If an experienced screenwriter adopted a new name, nobody would buy the script without having to meet them to discuss various drafts. Either the producer knew the writer and was in collusion with him or a friend was posing as the writer. But that would involve fooling the IRS and a tax agreement between the genuine writer and fake writer friend that would have to be worked out between them. Given the intricacies involved, Huggins decided collusion was the most likely method of working under the blacklist.

As his name hadn't been mentioned in any HUAC hearing to date and as far as he knew wasn't on any published list, Huggins decided he could take a chance trying to sell his new script *The Outsiders* to Warner Bros. or Columbia. He also specified he wanted to direct the film. Warner made the first offer of $25,000 but wouldn't allow him to direct. Columbia would let him direct but only offered $17,000. Huggins went with Columbia because he had an itch to direct. Huggins was back at Columbia, in the executive office building. But it was a one-off deal. No seven-year option. Cohn made it clear this was a business deal with no love lost. Before filming began, *The Outsiders* became *Hangman's Knot* with a cast that included Randolph Scott, Donna Reed, Lee Marvin, Richard Denning, Jeanette Nolan and Claude Jarman, Jr. Huggins and Marvin became friends during the shooting, with Marvin referring to Huggins as "my fellow pinchbeck."

Scott played Matt Stewart, the leader of a detachment of Confederate volunteers who successfully ambush a Union cargo of gold bullion in Nevada Territory. To their dismay they discover the Civil War has been over for a month and they find themselves and their loot the target of renegades.

Huggins was learning as he went along. Directing required certain laws to be followed. including the principle of crossing the proscenium. Cinematographer Bud Lawton explained the principle to Huggins. As Huggins explained "The camera is the audience, and what the camera is photographing is the stage. In staging a scene there are multiple shots. What is put on film between 'action' and 'cut' is a shot, and after the camera is 'cut' it is usually moved, or at least turned to a new angle." He continued,

> The most common error committed by tyro directors is to cut, then move the camera to a position that in effect takes the audience on to the stage: The camera crosses the proscenium. The move has altered (for the audience, but not the director) the geographic relationship of the actors. An actor may be looking camera right, delivering a line to an off-scene actor the audience thinks should be at his left. The failure to apply this principle can lead to more confusion, it is distracting and can fatally disrupt the flow of a scene.

Lawton also taught Huggins the importance of the camera lens in transforming, distorting, modifying geography, altering contours and the speed of actors and horses and stage-

Huggins (white shirt, sunglasses, right middleground) on location making his debut as a film director on *Hangman's Knot* (1952) (courtesy John Huggins).

coaches in motion. Huggins decided, "If you have a good script and a clear understanding of it, the good fortune to have a talented cinematographer, the good sense to leave the actors alone when you can, and the judgment to know when you can't, it's hard to go wrong."

Reviews for *Hangman's Knot* (1952) were generally positive. *The New York Times* critic (December 11, 1952) stated:

> The Western, a movie staple often misused and maligned through stereotyped production, is given handsome, credible and edifying treatment in *Hangman's Knot*, a taut, action-filled adventure sensibly designed to keep the devotees—especially the older ones—from yawning.... Credit, of course, must go to Roy Huggins, who not only wrote the yarn but directed it without being patronizing toward it.... Mr. Huggins has centered his cast in plausible situations... [I]t is a tight little entertainment which does justice to this film form.

Adele Mara's association with the left-wing and anti-capitalist Actors Laboratory founded by Roman Bohnen, J. Edward Bromberg, Morris Carnovsky and Phoebe Brand placed her on the blacklist in 1951. At the request of her agent, Adele wrote the following letter:

> To Whom It May Concern:
>
> I am not now, nor have I ever been, a member of the Communist party. I have never had any sympathy for the Communist party nor any conscious contact with Communists or their sympathizers.
>
> I did attend the Actors Laboratory for about one year in 1946 or 1947. I did so because I was under contract to Republic Studios and needed training as an actress. Also, at that time, several major studios were officially sending their young contract players there and others were attending under the G.I. Bill. I was never given a scholarship at the Actors Laboratory, nor any special treatment. And when Republic Studios provided me with a full time dramatic coach I quit the Actors Laboratory.
>
> No one, during my attendance at the Actors Laboratory, ever tried to influence me to favor Communist causes or principles, perhaps this is because I am a devout Catholic and attend mass at least once each week. I believe this fact was known to the administrators of the Actors Laboratory. In any case, politics were not a part of my activities there.

The atmosphere in Hollywood had become toxic with careers put on hold based on nothing more than being in the company of a Communist. Huggins would soon be a person of interest for the HUAC.

6

PARANOIA AND DISCORD

> By union the smallest states thrive
> By discord the greatest are destroyed.
> —Sallust (86–35 bc)

On March 21, 1947, President Harry S Truman issued Executive Order 9835: "Whereas maximum protection must be afforded the United States against infiltration of disloyal persons into the ranks of its employees...." In September of that year the House Committee on Un-American Activities under the leadership of J. Parnell Thomas (R–New Jersey) investigated Communist infiltration of Hollywood. Out of 41 witnesses subpoenaed, the group of screenwriters later known as "Hollywood Ten" remained silent about any alleged Communist Party membership and were sentenced to one year in prison for contempt of Congress, fined $1,000 each and blacklisted in the film industry.[1]

In an increasingly paranoid environment, any viewpoint that seemed critical of the political establishment in America was viewed with suspicion. In 1949 the American Legion distributed a list of more than 100 names suspected of Communist affiliation to film studios. Columnists Walter Winchell and Hedda Hopper jumped on the "Commie-bashing" bandwagon and readers of *The Hollywood Reporter* were bombarded with the anti–Communist rants of W.R. Wilkerson, who had a specific dislike of screenwriters and the creation of the Screen Writers Guild. In May 1947, three former F.B.I. agents founded Counterattack, a private, independent anti–Communist organization that published a small four-page newsletter. On June 22, 1950, *Counterattack* published *Red Channels: The Report of Communist Influence in Radio and Television*. In an attempt to purge radio and television of Communists and their sympathizers, it listed 151 names including major figures working in Hollywood. The Hollywood studios offered no resistance or refuge for the accused. In the "land of the free," careers were being destroyed for holding a left-wing political belief.

In September 1952 Huggins was working on a screen treatment for another Randolph Scott Western, this one titled *The Burning Sky*, when he was interrupted by the ringing of his doorbell. He opened the door to be greeted with, "Are you Roy Huggins?" followed by a pink subpoena shoved into his hand. He was to be a witness in the latest HUAC hearings.

The hearings were taking place against the backdrop of the Korean War. The People's Republic of Korea had invaded South Korea on June 25, 1950. U.S. troops were deployed to come to the aid of South Korea under the authorization of President Truman, and war with the Soviet Union was a genuine possibility.

6. Paranoia and Discord

On Monday, September 29, 1952, Huggins parked in the parking lot of the Federal Building in Los Angeles and was immediately escorted to the fifth floor by two deputy marshals. The entire fourth and sixth floors had been blocked off. Roped off areas in the fifth floor elevator lobby and along the corridor to the hearing room allowed for the screening of spectators before they were allowed into the hearings.

On his arrival at the fifth floor, two federal guards escorted him into a holding room where he patiently and nervously waited to be called. Huggins had time for thought as he sipped his coffee. To name or not name names. Huggins reflected, "In the five days I wrestled with the problem, I had reduced it to a single question: How to state my aversion to the American Communist Party, refuse to name names, and not be found in contempt of Congress and sent to prison. I had what sounded to my untrained mind an irrefutable legal case: HUAC was violating its Congressional mandate when it demanded that cooperative witnesses 'prove their sincerity' by naming names the Committee already had."[2]

Huggins had met with the former president of the Writers Guild, Emmett Lavery, who was now a practicing lawyer. Lavery told Huggins that HUAC was a committee of Congress and had a right to ask him anything they wanted if he didn't invoke the Fifth Amendment. Huggins responded that he intended to answer all their questions but wouldn't name names. But despite outward assurances he was still in conflict:

> I had resolved to ask no one's advice on the course I ought to take. If I came to regret my choice, I wanted to fault no one but myself. I was probably alone in declining to seek psychiatric advice: My opinion of Freud resembled my opinion of Marx. If I had elected to seek moral advice, there were only two people I'd have turned to: Adele and my brother Jack. I hoped one day to ask Adele to marry me, but not when my future was incalculable. I learned later that Jack and Adele would have given me almost identical advice, not to be "sucked into the Communist Party's con game," as my brother put it. Both Adele and Jack avoided offering advice on principle. I understood and approved. Adele was a Catholic for many reasons besides being born one, one of her primary reasons being a rejection of intellectual hubris. That my brother was also a Catholic who abhorred intellectual hubris was a coincidence.
>
> I had compelling reasons for accepting HUAC's subpoena: One was that I did not want to decline the national platform I was being provided to state that case against communism as powerfully as I knew how. In doing so I would be triggering Rogers vs. U.S., which would require that I play that "symbolic role in [HUAC's] surrealistic morality play" or spend a year in prison.
>
> In irrational, or perhaps bathetic, moments I tried to minimize the gravity of putting in a year behind bars, but my children, their mother and my own mother would be damaged emotionally and economically, which forced me to face it: Going to prison was not a decision that was unintended and unanticipated. As a consequence of that misjudgment, the Communist Party abandoned its 1947 dogmatism and turned to the Fifth Amendment. Loyal Party members themselves had demanded the change on the grounds that a year-long separation from wives and children was a toll they were unwilling to pay. In the entire HUAC era only two Hollywood witnesses took the risk of going to prison.
>
> Several witnesses appeared before HUAC twice. They had left the Party after being attacked by cultural commissars and fellow members for failing to apply due Marxist diligence in their creative work. They left the Party in anger and loathing, but in their first appearance before HUAC they asked to be excused from naming the names of men and women who had once been their close friends and comrades. Their problem was not about informing—they knew HUAC had the names and their friends would be subpoenaed—their problem was one of intense private and personal import and reluctance to betray the sincerity and depth of feeling they had felt for their former comrades. The strength of the HUAC conspiracy was revealed when such men as Dmytryk, Kazan and Rossen appeared before HUAC, made uncompromising anti–Communist

statements, but remained blacklisted because they declined to name names. Each made a second appearance before HUAC and named names. It was something they would rather not have done, and their antagonists truthfully said, "They hurt no one but themselves," not realizing that being honest was a tactical error in view of false claims that people named were grievously injured. Those who we named were injured by HUAC and the keepers of the blacklist. As Dalton Trumbo said later, the enemy was HUAC, all the others were "only victims."

Huggins testifying before the Congressional Committee on Un-American activities on September 29, 1952, with committee member Morgan M. Moulder in the background (courtesy Katherine Crawford).

Huggins appeared before the United States House of Representatives, Subcommittee of the Committee on Un-American Activities, in room 518 with Honorable John S. Wood presiding over the public hearing. Committee members present were Francis E. Walter, Morgan M. Moulder, Clyde Doyle, James B. Frazier, Jr., and Donald L. Jackson. Staff members present included Frank S. Tavenner, Jr., counsel, Thomas W. Beale, Sr., assistant counsel, Louis J. Russell, senior investigator, William A. Wheeler, Charles E. McKillips, investigators, and John W. Carrington, clerk. Tavenner opened the questioning.

Tavenner: Mr. Huggins, this committee has been engaged for some time in the investigation of Communist Party activities in the field of entertainment, especially in that field which relates to the moving picture industry. The committee has information that your connection in the past has been such that you could enlighten the committee on some of the Communist Party activities in that field. So, I wanted to ask you, first of all: Are you now a member of the Communist Party?

Huggins: No; I am not.

Tavenner: Have you ever been a member of the Communist Party?

Huggins: Yes; I have been.... Marxism has a wonderful thing about it, in that, being a closed system of thought, if you feel great despair about the world or are having difficulty understanding it, Marxism does something for you. It suddenly allows the whole universe to fall into a nice simple pattern. There are no unanswered questions once you become a Marxist. It is a nice feeling, particularly if your field is political philosophy, and you like to feel that you do know all of the answers.

I became a Marxist, I guess, sometime in 1938 or 1939, and I was a very hard-working Marxist, and I did a lot of reading, not in Lenin and Stalin; I was not particularly interested in Lenin and Stalin, but I did a lot of reading in Marxist theories, and especially in his methodology, his approach to all phenomena, in which he had an answer for everything.

About that time of course, I was also interested in politics, as everyone was in that day, and my politics, I guess, were just democratic, and I was in favor of Roosevelt's foreign policy of "quarantining" the aggressors as he stated it in 1937, and I was often asked to speak at big student meetings. There is a yearly peace meeting in UCLA, and I was chairman one year, and the chief speaker another year. I did not know at the time, but I suspect now that the people who asked me to speak and the people who had organized and sort of taken over these things were members of the Communist Party. But I knew no Communists, and I was stating my beliefs which were pro–American and anti–Fascist and pro–Roosevelt.

... Now, all through 1939 I had been getting little hints from people that I really ought to become a Communist. I don't know whether it was Miss Celeste Strack, who was a well-known Communist, who was talking to me at that time, or not, but I know whoever it was, they kept saying, "Look, you are a Marxist, and therefore you should belong to the Communist Party." And I remember that one of my answers was that Sidney Hook was a Marxist, and he did not belong to the Communist Party and, in fact, he wrote articles every week condemning it.

Well, he was a different kind of Marxist, Well, at that time I had discovered the differences, and I read Sidney Hook right along with all of the other Marxists, and found them to be, as far as I could see, in basic agreement about what Marxism was all about, and so I did not join the Communist Party and I knew no Communists, and I didn't associate with Communists, and my friends were all fraternity brothers, or fraternity boys, at least, who lived with me down at the beach. But I was a Communist to the faculty of UCLA, and I was refused a fellowship on those grounds.

I was already fairly despairing of democracy at that time, but I did not do anything about it, but in 1940 history had moved also, and I think every democracy in any large industrial nation, except England and America, had now fallen to fascism, and I began to despair of the thing that I had felt so deeply about, the democratic system. I had been a victim of undemocratic treatment, and I was just naive enough to believe that it was impossible that this could not really have happened, but it did happen, and I knew it. So, when I got back to school in 1940, the campaign took up again, and, through Celeste Strack working on me to join the Communist Party, I joined the Communist Party sometime in 1940. I think that I attended three meetings. I can't remember the meetings very well, but I do remember that I was being asked to picket war plants and being asked to engage in other activities which were hindering our preparedness program and to do what I could to oppose draft laws, and so on and so forth.

While I began to wonder perhaps if I had gotten into the Communist Party and gotten out without giving it a chance, it looked to me as if I was wrong about their attitude toward democracy and the rest of it, and so I rejoined the Communist Party in 1943. As far as I could see, there had not been any changes, except that they were now, at least—I could not oppose what they were doing and saying because they were selling war bonds, and they were talking about how to prevent strikes in the factories, and they were a very patriotic group.

I attended a couple or three meetings, and then stopped attending meetings, because I think that I felt, as a Marxist, I really ought to get into this thing and see what was happening, and it seemed to me being a Communist was a part of being a Marxist, and this I think was my motivation; but somehow or other, after doing it, I couldn't stay with it, and so I attended very few meetings. In fact, I suppose not more than five or six meetings in the next two or three years. I suppose I retained my membership accordingly.

In 1946 ... I became a member of the steering committee of the Authors' Guild here on the coast, and the chairman of that committee was Albert Maltz.

After a meeting one night, after a meeting of the steering committee of the Authors' Guild, Albert Maltz asked me to have a drink with him in the bar of the hotel, and we talked for a while, and it came out that he understood that I was in some way still a member of the Communist Party, and not attending meetings or anything, and why didn't I. I gave him my reasons: that it didn't mean anything to me; that I saw no reason why I should. He asked me if I were a Marxist, and I said "Yes," and he asked me if I would allow him to transfer me to the Hollywood group. And I said I didn't think so. We had meetings, I guess fairly regularly, of the Authors' Guild, and after each meeting Albert Maltz would ask me if I had changed my mind, and he gave a glowing picture of the stimulation ... and the new understanding I would have of Marxism if I came into this group, which was made up of highly intelligent people, and finally, sometime toward the end of 1946, I said: "All right; tell me where to go, and I will come to one of your meetings."

Well, he said, "It will take a little time," and so I think it was a few weeks later I was told to attend a meeting of the Communist Party in Hollywood, which I did, and for the first time in my connection with the Communist Party I started attending meetings fairly regularly. I think in the period of nine months or so that I was a member of the Communist Party in Hollywood I must have attended a dozen or two dozen meetings. It was sufficient to know something about the Communist Party at last.

I discovered the usual things: That there was certainly no democracy in the Communist Party; decisions were brought down and rendered or you found out about them by having to read the [Communist] press, which I could not bear reading, and I was supposed to read the *Daily Worker*, and I think I took it for a while, but I do not read it, and I was also supposed to read *Political Affairs*, or something like that, which was on a little higher level, but still was opinionated and without much force, I felt.

Discussions in the group seemed to be or to consist of restatement in slightly different wording of things that were appearing... Any difference of opinion was immediately pounced upon with name-calling and all of the rest of the things that you have heard about so many times before. But no one ever disagreed really. They might tentatively disagree, and then immediately withdraw it ... when they got pounced upon by the chief intellectual of the group. At the same time history was moving forward, and I was making a big change in my basic philosophy.

In 1947 a lot of things were happening; the Cold War had started; the U.N. was a total loss because of Russian vetoes, and I think that by the time I got out of the Communist Party they had used the veto about two dozen times on crucial issues, and I had great faith in the U.N. It looked to me as if it were being destroyed. Russia was refusing to have anything to do with control of the atomic bomb, which appalled me, and then sometime late in 1947 they suddenly reformed the Communist Internationale, and I quit the Communist Party.

This time I quit, no longer a Marxist, for reasons both that I could have found in the first place if I had read with less of an eager eye, and for reasons of history. The historical reasons were now it became pretty obvious that the Soviet Union was not the hope of the world or the hope of democracy or anything else, but was an imperialist power. I used to believe in the early days, in 1943, when I went back in, that the only reason that the Soviet Union was not democratic was because it was surrounded by enemies like Germany and Japan, and so on, and it was on a wartime footing, and that was the reason for it. But it got worse as we all know after the war was over, and it had no enemies surrounding it at all. Its attacks on every kind of freedom of thought increased, its attitude toward other peoples became clear in its dealings with all of its border nations, Poland, Yugoslavia, and Hungary, and the six so-called satellite states, and it had moved in and destroyed all freedom and had shot several leaders of those nations.

There were a good many things happening at that time, all of them seemed to be building up and I can't even remember them all, but it was obvious to me that there was no hope that the future was held in the hand of the Soviet Union. It is a terrible thing when you finally realize the great gap between the grim realities and your vision of an ideal future. It is hard to realize it, and it takes a little time. But I did finally realize it, and when I realized it on a historical level, I also realized it on a theoretical level, and I realized finally what the basic flaw in the Marxist philosophy was, and it is simply this. I think it might be important to get this on the record, and I think it is clear.

... Marx sets up a methodology which is fairly sound and he made a lot of predictions which came true. Then Marx gets into the way of the future, away beyond his time, with statements about the nature of the Communist state, and the foundation stone, the moral foundation of Marxism was the Marxist theory which I believe was scientifically founded, and I believe that Marxism was a science, and that Marxist theory called the withering away of the state, was founded on scientific principles, which Marxism I thought was.

Well, it is obvious to anyone who wants to look that the state is not withering away, in the Soviet Union, that it is getting more tyrannical every day, and it seemed obvious to me then finally in 1947 that Marxist theory of the withering away of the state was just a mystical and metaphysical thing, and had no foundation whatever in scientific fact. It seemed, too, if you accepted all of his *a priori* conclusions about the economic determination of history and the reason why there were states, and Marx said the reason why there are states is because there are classes, and when there are no more classes there cannot be more states, because there is no need for a state, and all of this, if you accept it, then you go right on and say that it must be true, and the Soviet Union will someday be a great democracy. But it is obvious that it is not. It is obvious that Marx's statements are simply unfounded, and that it isn't true and it isn't proved that if you have no classes that you won't need a state, and, in fact, the contrary has been proved by the Soviet Union, where I don't believe they do have any classes, they have just one class, but they have a state in the Soviet Union, and that state is getting more and more powerful and more and more tyrannical every year.... So I left the Communist Party in 1947 finally, no longer a Marxist nor a Communist.

Tavenner: Let me interrupt you there a moment. Do you attribute your present disagreement with Marxist theory to your experience within the Communist Party?

Huggins: No; it is partly that, because certainly the fear and the complete absence of any kind of integrity was made clear to me in the Communist Party. A man cannot think for himself in the Communist Party. He must abrogate that privilege, and do it willingly on some theoretical ground. They seldom state it so coldly as that; but actually that is what is behind it.... But it was not the experience in the Communist Party that convinced me or made me cease to be a Marxist. It was history, and I suppose it is just the fact that one day I woke up and decided to think about something else, you know. Once you get into a closed system of thought it takes more than fact to get you out of it, and it takes something else, and it takes a real jarring experience of some kind to get you out of it, and then once you are out of it a lot of things become obvious that should have been obvious in the first place.

Tavenner: Then from history and from your experience in the Communist Party you concluded that there were flaws in the Marxist theory, which finally resulted in your disillusionment on that subject?

Huggins: ... I realize, like all closed systems of thought, once you find a hole in it, then you realize that it is all wrong, because that is the nature of a closed system of thought. You must either accept it all without question, or you do not accept any of it, and this is recognized by the Communists.... So I think it is in the nature of the things that once you find one big flaw, then you suddenly realize that that is just a resultant flaw of other flaws.... I think in 1948 and 1949 and 1950 it is becoming ever more clear that democracy has a heck of a lot more vitality and strength than a lot of people thought in 1940, when so many nations had fallen to fascism. I am now of the firm belief that we have just witnessed the first act in the history of free democracy, and that it has a long way to go.

Tavenner: Your views, then, with regard to your former despair for democracy have changed materially?

Huggins: Yes; because of what has been happening in the world.

Tavenner: Did you observe during your experience in the Communist Party that the Communist Party program or line followed that of the Soviet state, or was dictated by the Soviet state?

Huggins: Yes; I think it is obvious. Every change of the party line has always come immediately after a change in foreign policy of the Soviet Union ... when the Soviet Union signed a pact with Nazi Germany, the non-aggression pact, the line immediately changed overnight. I was not a member then, either, but I can remember very well I was studying in summer school up at Berkeley, and I remember very well that some of the people that I had met up there were busy running around trying to pick up pamphlets that they had laid on doorsteps calling for a third term for President Roosevelt, and they were trying to get them back again. The line had changed as they put them on the doorsteps.

Tavenner: Is it not correct to say in the line of what you have just stated that if a person were a devout member of the Communist Party he would sooner or later have to take a definite stand on behalf of the Soviet Union and against the United States?

Huggins: Well, I think that is obvious now. When I joined, in 1940, it seemed to me that that is what I was being asked to do, and that is why I quit, after such a very short membership, because I was unwilling to make that choice, or even to grant that that choice was necessary.

My feeling about Marxism was that it was a great methodology, but as far as any revolutions went, I thought they would come when my grandchildren were around, if they came at all, and I didn't look upon it as a thing that was going to happen tomorrow on Seventh and Broadway. I was interested in Marxism as a methodology, and when I went into the party and I was asked to make what I felt was to take a position that I felt was contrary to the best interest of this country I quit. Of course, it was their position then was—"Let us not help anybody, and, in fact, let us help the Germans," and I had a vision of our being left alone to fight the Nazis.

I think today that same thing exists, and in fact I would say that with the reestablishment of the Comintern in 1947, which is the part where I got out, I would say from that point on membership in the Communist Party automatically constituted a subversive position.

Doyle: What year would that be?

Huggins: In 1947, that is the year they re-established the Comintern, and they called it the Cominform.

Wood: Membership in the Communist Party means enmity to the United States government?

Huggins: I think that that is obvious. I don't think that there is any question that the Communist Party line is dictated by the needs of the Soviet Union, and history proves it all along the line. If that is true, then it seems to me that today you cannot be a loyal American and be a member of the Communist Party. It is impossible.

Tavenner: We have heard a great deal said by the Communist Party about a so-called form of democracy within the party, that is in the way of procedure. They call it democratic procedure, and freedom of thought, notwithstanding these hearings have developed many, many instances where it has been demonstrated that thought control is a speciality of the Communist Party. What are your views on that subject from your experience in the party?

Huggins: Well, they claim that there is in the Communist Party a thing called democratic centralism, which means that discussion takes place about a problem and reports are made, and I suppose on up the line, that is the theory, and as a result of those discussions a decision is made, and once the decision is made, there is no more discussion or argument. You accept the decision. I didn't see it work. I imagine altogether I attended 30 meetings of the Communist Party in all of my membership in it, and in none of those 30 meetings did I ever hear anything discussed before it became a policy. It was only after it became a policy, and then it was a matter of being sure everybody understood it right. That is all. So I would say that there is no semblance of this so-called democratic centralism in the Communist Party.

Tavenner: Were you familiar with any instances such as that which occurred to Budd Schulberg, when Charles Glenn published the very complimentary article that this is the novel that Hollywood has been waiting for, and then within a week was compelled to reverse his entire line, and destroy all that he had builtup?

Huggins: No; I know the Maltz situation was similar to that, but that was before I went in there. By the time I got in, no one was talking about that any more. They did seem to be a little displeased with the sort of thing I wrote. As a matter of fact, I think one of the members implied once that my stuff was sort of Fascist writing, and I wrote hard-boiled novels, so-called hard-boiled novels, which they did not like very well, and they wanted to know why I didn't write something good. I said, "Well, you bring me into this thing, you know, and then you ask me to write something good, and it is like recruiting a house painter and then handing him a palette and some oil paints and saying, 'Here, paint canvases now'" That is about how I felt about it.

My writing, I felt, was a commercial type of writing, and I didn't consider myself to be an artist, and so they gave up, but there was a good deal of propaganda within that Hollywood group about the time I was there, to get all of the members to write proletarian novels, and this seemed to be the line. They took no political stands on anything in the Hollywood group, and the other groups that I belonged to during the war were just interested in selling war bonds and stuff like that. The Hollywood group was interested only in Hollywood, and they never, as far as I know, had a discussion of world politics.

Doyle: Three or four times you stated that the Communist Party in America is such that you cannot be a loyal American and a member of the Communist Party in America. I am not sure that I grasp the ultimate conclusion yet. Why can you not be?

Huggins: Well, it is based on two things. One, I think it is abundantly proved that the Communist Party line always reflects Soviet foreign policy. If you accept that, as I do, that is the basis for the assumption. Now, there are other bases for it. A member of the Communist Party must take discipline and must do as he is told to do, and this is another clear-cut fact about Communism.

Doyle: Then you mean that the Soviet foreign policy is contrary to the best interests of the policy of the United States. Is that why you cannot accept it and still be a loyal American?

Huggins: Soviet foreign policy turns about, or Soviet propaganda, let us say, which is the basis for the Communist Party line here, turns everything that this country does upside down. We aid democracy in Europe, and it is called warmongering. We come to the aid through the United Nations of the South Koreans, and we are called again warmongers, and the world is even told that the South Koreans started the war, and not the North Koreans at all, and we are just trying to put a yoke on the peoples of Asia. This is the line of the Soviet Union.

Doyle: Was there any act or omission which you participated in, directly or indirectly, as you look back at it, which in your judgment should have labeled you as a Communist at the university, and caused you to be denied a fellowship?

Huggins: None at all; not one.

Doyle: You certainly were, according to your Phi Beta Kappa record and other statements of scholarship made by you, you were a diligent thinker and an intellectual.

Huggins: I was what is known as a premature anti–Fascist.

Doyle: Have you any suggestions to make to this committee in the functioning of our responsibilities to the American people, through the United States Congress—do you know what our responsibility is? It is to uncover wherever possible subversive activities of people who would advocate or use force and violence to overthrow the Constitution of the United States. Have you any advice for us or suggestions or criticism, even? I have never talked with you, sir. I have never talked with you, have I, and I realize in asking you this question I am doing it right out of a clear sky to you.

Huggins: Yes, that is true.

Doyle: And yet I feel that if you have a statement, I would like to get it.

Huggins: I think that you are in a spot, because there isn't any question in my mind at all but there is a great need for democracy to do something about the subversive drives which intend to overthrow it. This is one of the things that disturbed me deeply about the Communist Party, is that they do not believe in individual freedom, and yet they shout to the housetops in defense of individual freedom in all of the democratic countries in which they exist. They become champions of complete political freedom. The moment they get power, they will destroy political freedom. It seems to be one more evidence of their complete lack of integrity or scrupulousness or anything else. So I think that to the Communist, capitalism is going to be in a sense an easy thing to overthrow, eventually, I suppose, because we do have a tendency to fail to fight our enemies properly, but I suppose one of the reasons for that is that it would be a terrible thing if we were to fight tyranny by becoming a tyranny ourselves, isn't that so? This would be a terrible thing if we are anti–Communist because we feel that Communists destroy individual freedom and liberty, and in fighting communism, we destroy individual freedom and liberty. This would be a fight in vain.

So I think that is why I say this committee is in a terrible spot, because I think that subversive elements must be fought, and I think democracy has to fight for its life, and it can't just sit back and say, "Well, history will take care of us." It has got enemies and it has to fight those enemies but it has to fight them within the framework of the democratic system, or it might as well not fight at all, because it loses the battle in the means it chooses to use to fight that battle. I don't know whether that answers your question or not.[3]

Threatened with a jail sentence or internment in a concentration camp, separation from his wife and children and long-term blacklisting, Huggins had named Communist Party members. Although the majority of the people Huggins named were already known by the HUAC after being listed in the *Red Channels* booklet (among other sources), Huggins would later admit, "I was ashamed of myself.... I was caught unprepared and had a failure of nerve. I don't think there's any question about it.... To cooperate in that respect, even though the names had already been mentioned, was, I believe, the wrong thing to do. And that's the only part of my part in this thing that I really regret."[4]

He continued, "I was not about to take the Communist Party tone which was to take the Fifth Amendment. I decided I would do two things. I would give them the names that they already had.... I was also going to state what they were doing was wrong."[5]

Doris Bailey found it difficult to forgive Huggins for naming her friend Ben Barzman, who had been part of a circle of friends during Huggins' politically active years. She asked Huggins why he chose to name him. "They already had Ben's name. I only confirmed what they already knew," replied Huggins.

"What if I had joined in those days before I met Joe?" enquired Bailey. "What if I had listened to your theory about saving this country from the evils of capitalism, what then? Would you have named me?"

"Ah, but that is a specious argument. You were smarter than we were. You didn't join," replied Huggins.

While Doris Bailey considered the naming of Barzman regrettable, perhaps more depressing to her was what she viewed as Huggins' betrayal of "our youthful high-mindedness."[6]

7

TRANSITION

> Does the imagination dwell the most
> Upon a woman won or a woman lost?
> —William Butler Yeats

The Huggins' 13-year marriage had been over for a little over two years before the divorce was finalized on April 4, 1952. Katherine, Bret and their mother traveled to Mexico in 1953, and stayed for almost four years. Katherine reminisced,

> Mom was exceptionally beautiful. Five-foot-two, blue eyes, dark blondish hair, strong, outspoken and very independent. A dedicated artist who worked every day of her life. She was an artist first, she liked to say, but in fact she put my brother and me first. She was a great mother. I never challenged her premise, though. She believed it. Her most successful early work was in wax. Mom had a unique product. They were very similar to the old wax miniatures that have been done through the centuries of royalty and other dignitaries. Very fine, delicate and detailed wax portraits in profile, with lace collars at the necks and details in the hair. She created the formula for the wax by trial and error and made the tiny wax portraits of various stars and placed them in shadow box frames lined with velvet.
>
> Mom literally walked the streets in Beverly Hills, ringing the doorbells of the big houses to show them around. She sent one that she had made to William Powell's house unbidden. He finally called her after being out of town, to her relief and joy, and sent a car to pick her

Bonnie Porter's bust of Roy Huggins. It was later accidentally destroyed (courtesy Katherine Crawford).

up and bring her to visit him and his wife to thank her for it. Commissions quickly poured in after that and never stopped. Red Skelton was also one of the first.

They were all very wonderful to her and admiring.

She could live anywhere since her art wasn't limited to any location. Mom was strong and unafraid and believed in herself and worked constantly because she loved it. An extraordinary woman. When the three of us moved to Mexico in 1953 she continued doing wax miniatures of the business and political leaders there. These fine little historic works of art were her trademark and her support until she changed to bronze and porcelain in later years.

Mexico was immeasurably unhappy for me, because I wanted to be near my father, and a couple other reasons too, having to do with the actual conditions of Mexico. Very dangerous, everywhere. It was apparent to me every day, every minute. Daddy was never in Mexico so we wouldn't see him for six months at a time. It was very hard for me. Bret was fine and Mom had moved on and was so happy there.

We returned to Los Angeles for a couple of weeks a year to renew our visa to Mexico. Bret and I sometimes stayed with Daddy during those times. We finally returned to Los Angeles for good at the end of 1956. Our kitchen table always had clay dust and figures and tools on them. We'd eat around it. The smell of clay was a constant and very pleasant.

Confidence was one of Mom's gifts. In that way she was perfect with Daddy. She was unafraid, self-motivated and driven, vivacious and smart, and created her own success from nothing. Their problem was they were both dynamic creative stars who each needed an assistant. Mom handled responsibilities but she didn't baby anyone and Daddy needed someone whose focus was much more on him. They both got that in their next marriages.[1]

In January 1953, on the Day of Epiphany, Adele Mara accepted Huggins' offer of marriage delivered in a note buried in a bouquet of roses. "Early on, when she was about 15 or 16 and dancing with Xavier Cugat she went by the name Adel Maria," said her son John Huggins. "My mother was stereotyped as a Latino in her early career and spent a lot of time in Argentina making Hispanic movies. Of course she was Spanish and could speak it fluently and she could dance the Flamenco. She dyed her hair blonde to try to escape the typecasting, dropped her maiden name Delgado and replaced Maria with Mara."[2]

Following the HUAC hearings, Huggins was approached by Columbia Pictures vice-president Ben Kahane, who offered him a new seven-year contract. *Hangman's Knot* had been a critical and financial success and Harry Cohn wanted more of the same. The job description on the contract read, "Roy Huggins, hereinafter referred to as the director."[3]

Huggins had no intention of becoming a full-time director but for the time being he remained quiet as Cohn sent him to Sedona, Arizona, to watch a master director at work. *Gun Fury* (1953) was a western adventure set in the post–Civil War era starring Rock Hudson and Donna Reed and directed by Raoul Walsh. Huggins had been busy working on the adapted screenplay, based on the novel *Ten Against Caesar* by Kathleen B. Granger, George Granger and Robert A. Granger, out of an office in the Executive Building at Columbia. Hudson starred as pacifist Ben Warren, the fiancé of Jennifer Ballard (Donna Reed); she is kidnapped by Frank Slayton (Phil Carey) and his gang during a stagecoach robbery.

The newlyweds mixed business and pleasure with a honeymoon on location in Sedona with Raoul Walsh as the entertainment. Walsh had a solid reputation as the director of tough action movies including *The Roaring Twenties* (1939) and *White Heat* (1949), both starring James Cagney. Walsh also became Errol Flynn's favorite director on such films as *They Died with Their Boots On* (1941), *Gentleman Jim* (1942) and *Objective Burma* (1945). His early life saw Walsh employed as a cowpuncher in Texas and Mexico, a gravedigger in Montana and bronco buster for the U.S. Cavalry. His career as an actor was cut short when he lost an eye while filming *In Old Arizona* (1929) and his trademark black eye patch was born.

On location, Huggins and Adele were amazed to find Walsh directing scenes with his back to the action. Adele offered the suggestion that Walsh turned his back on scenes that relied more on verbal than visual cues and listening to the actors gave him a better feel for their performances. Huggins had a more practical answer. Walsh was simply not interested and already thinking of the next scene. Although Huggins had no intention of resuming the role of a film director, he admitted he "had learned more about directing on *Gun Fury* than I had on *Hangman's Knot*."[4]

During leave from Columbia Pictures, Huggins joined Richard L. Bare as story editor on *The Joe Palooka Story* (1954), a television series based on the popular Ham Fisher cartoon strip about a heavyweight boxing champion. Unknown to him at the time, working on the twenty-six-half hour shows would serve as good training for his future career in television. However, writing two half-hour shows a week didn't make Huggins warm to the relatively new medium and he was glad to return to writing features for Columbia.[5]

Gun Fury was followed by *Pushover* (1954) with a screenplay by Huggins based on the novels *The Night Watch* by Thomas Walsh and *Rafferty* by William S. Ballinger. The twenty-year-old Novak introduced herself to Huggins and informed him, "Mr. Schermer told me you'll be directing *Pushover*, so I looked at *Hangman's Knot*. I don't usually like westerns, but I liked yours." On hearing this, Huggins told Cohn he wasn't interested and suggested that he find somebody more suitable. Huggins considered Novak "too young and too anonymous for the lead role, although she seemed right enough if she could get the idea that body language and silence outweighed dialogue in the role."

Huggins told Cohn, "If you've got me in mind to direct it, I think it's bad casting. Kim Novak's a beginner. She needs an actor's director, not a writer with only one credit and a western at that." Cohn required little persuasion and agreed that Huggins was the wrong choice. Instead he hired the man who shot Novak's successful screen test for Cohn, former actor Richard Quine. Cohn was convinced Novak would be "the next fuckin' Hayworth!"

The film was notable for introducing audiences to a sexually charged performance by newcomer Novak as Lona McLane, who becomes romantically involved with police detective Paul Sheridan (Fred MacMurray). His initial aim is to trap her boyfriend who has stolen $200,000 in a bank robbery. But his sexual attraction to McLane is immediate and soon he is trapped in a downward destructive spiral of lust, betrayal and murder to secure his share of the money. The story featured themes evident in Huggins' *Too Late for Tears* (1949): the destructive lure of claiming stolen money out of greed and the promise of shared wealth with the murder of a loved one. This was Novak's first starring role as Kim Novak, rather than her birth name Marilyn Novak.

Box Office (July 24, 1954) found fault in Novak's performance.

> Miss Novak is a striking looking young actress, but her portrayal of a "bad girl" is on the obvious side. Much better is Dorothy Malone, who gives a sincere performance as a nurse....

Huggins' final screenplay produced by Columbia was the Western *Three Hours to Kill* (1954), based on a short story by Alex Gottlieb. Gunslinger Jim Guthrie (Dana Andrews) narrowly escapes being lynched by an angry mob accusing him of murder. After five years of wandering, the rope-scarred Guthrie returns to the town but is given only three hours to find the real killer by Sheriff Ben East (Stephen Elliott). Guthrie discovers his former sweetheart Laurie Martin (Donna Reed) has married in his absence and he is the father of her child. The finale sees Sheriff East as the killer, and a lovestruck dance hall girl follows Guthrie out of town. *The New York Times* (September 4, 1954) film critic wasn't impressed:

> It's hard to imagine how Dana Andrews and Donna Reed ... got involved in the lukewarm Columbia Western. In this timid, one-dimensional view of a community beset by fear and conscience the actors, as we say, acquit themselves respectively.

The *Box Office* "Feature Review" (September 18, 1954) was more positive.

> Action, mystery, romance, suspense, wonderful settings in beautiful color and sound acting distinguish this Harry Joe Brown production with credit going where credit is due to the direction of Alfred Werker for pace and neat precision in the development of the tricky plot. There are unexpected twists which even the intelligentsia will follow with interest, yet action addicts will never for a moment be bored.

More writing assignments followed but none made it to the screen. *My Dear Children* was a project based on the comedy play best known for being John Barrymore's final stage work. A new executive producer at Columbia, Jerry Wald, informed Huggins he would be producing and adapting a film version of the play and suggested Groucho Marx or Jack Benny for the lead role. Huggins thought the aging Errol Flynn would be perfect in Barrymore's role, but Huggins "could persuade no one that Flynn was still a star" and the project was shelved.

Another project that never made it to film was a remake of *Gilda* starring Kim Novak. Wald told Huggins to watch the original film starring Rita Hayworth. He struggled through the film in the projection room and concluded it was an "awful movie." Despite his reservations about a remake, Huggins produced a 46-page treatment based on the original script in one week. There would a change of locale to 19th century Montana for the remake and a backstory of a con game that cost Amalgamated Copper a fortune as described in a book Wald had presented to Huggins titled *The War of the Copper Kings*. (Wald told him, "Read this tonight—and keep quiet about it too—the legal department says it's in the public domain, but Warner Bros. paid good money for it and you can't be too careful.") Director Vincent Sherman had been the catalyst for pairing a remake of *Gilda* with the Montana copper wars as a backdrop when he first suggested it to Harry Cohn. But it soon became evident the idea of a remake of *Gilda* was going to be hampered by the fact that the original was considered a classic of its genre.

On November 18, 1954, Louella O. Parsons' column headline declared, "Kim Novak Picked by Wald to Star in Huggins' *Antonia*." There was no truth to Parsons' headline or story that listed Huggins as both writer and producer. Ideas for other projects for Columbia's rising star Novak were thrown around in internal office memos between Wald and Huggins for the next three months. The comedy play *Time Out for Ginger* would see Novak cast as a fourteen-year-old schoolgirl in a story about "the transition from confused girl-child into unconfused womanhood." Huggins was convinced that Novak never looked fourteen years old. Huggins considered *A Woman Called Fancy* nothing more than a dated soap opera and the "strong, good woman" character too strong and good for the sexually charged but insecure Novak persona. Next came a Garson Kanin story, *Do Re Mi*. Huggins was an admirer of Kanin but unimpressed with the story of "quaint gangsters and jukebox proprietors who make their own records." *Vanity Row* and *Past All Dishonor* also met with disapproval from Huggins. It was obvious that Wald and Huggins were on different wavelengths.

Huggins' career was at a turning point. Despite the fact Ben Kahane at Columbia had told him he had a future as a writer or director, Huggins wanted to be a producer. "Huggins doesn't look like a producer, smell like a producer, or think like a producer," exclaimed Harry Cohn. His second period with Columbia would prove to be short-lived. Due to a mixture of average performing features and an inability to move more projects into production, Huggins had not produced one picture in the final seven months of his time at Columbia. He had little choice but to clear his desk at Columbia on May 28, 1955.

The following day he applied for a producer's job at Warner Bros. but was met with rejection due to strong opposition from actor and director Paul Stewart. The intervention of director and friend Richard L. Bare (who had been signed to direct TV's *Cheyenne*) led to a meeting with executive William T. Orr and a change of heart. Huggins gladly accepted the terms offered even though he would be receiving one hundred dollars less per week than Harry Cohn had been paying him.

Meanwhile Katherine Crawford was adapting to the new family dynamic:

> Mom and Adele were not alike. Adele's focus was completely on Daddy, and she ferociously protected the peace, serenity and comfort of the home. Adele made sure everything was beautiful and right for Daddy, who was not easy to please, and had a creative critical eye. But as I see it, Daddy's charm, charisma, incredible mind, and the magic of his utter delight in what he saw, whether it was you, or the sea, or an idea, made him worth the trouble and more.
>
> Adele was beautiful and strong and took care of Daddy like a Spanish wife. Determined and fierce in her focus on him and the family. She was perfect for him and Mom wasn't. Mom and Daddy were both artists. They both needed a "wife." So Daddy married Adele and Mom married her next husband Jack, who doted on her, helped with the heavy lifting of her molds, 25-lb. bags of clay, boxing and shipping of the larger pieces, and handled all house emergencies, repairs, put in light bulbs, fixed the furnace, locked the doors at night and thoroughly took care of everything. He was easygoing yet successfully ran his own business, but as her father had, he adored her and did as much as he could for her. She had been the oldest and the favorite by far, of her father during her childhood, and he handled the money and security of the family. That's what she expected from a man.
>
> Daddy wouldn't do that. And she couldn't be the impeccable wife for him. Mom and Daddy never showed any anger toward each other after the divorce, or spoke ill of each other that I ever saw. They remained adoring. I don't think they ever fell out of love completely. They had great sentimentality for each other. Never argued, or spoke with anything other than great affection for each other. They were both wonderful, unique people. Just not right for each other, sad as that was, and neither showed noticeable sadness outwardly afterwards. They were each just not the types that would. Or maybe neither was sad. I have never been sure. Mom only looked forward in life. That was her way always. Even when it was tough. Never had a negative thought. Life was an adventure. Daddy was the same. He accepted what was with a quietness then would come up with a solution that was better. Always positive. No victims here.
>
> After the divorce, Bret and I saw Daddy on weekends at the little beach house with Adele. He didn't live there. It was a weekend place. Tiny. Almost a shack or cabin. But it had a balcony on the beach. And he would put on his "aqualung" tank and go deep sea diving for the abalone every Saturday. He loved nature adventure. All marine life was wonderful to him. He would take us mussel-hunting in the tide pools and the craggy rocks or fishing in a little lake. We used to go for fun to a restaurant where we fished first from the stream that was there, then supposedly would be served the same fish for dinner. It was great fun even though I always suspected they didn't actually cook us the very same fish.

Huggins (right) and William T. Orr celebrate Huggins' contract with Warner Bros. Television in 1955 (courtesy John Huggins).

Huggins and second wife Adele Mara pose in his MG automobile in the 1950s (courtesy John Huggins).

He took us to see the phosphorescence of the waves at night. Everything in nature was fun when he was with you. But it was the most fun for him. He felt such joy in sharing it all with us and awakening in us the fascination of it all. The storyteller in him made it all simply wondrous as he led us through it all. Learning, teaching, showing, sharing. Life was a great adventure of discovery and he usually had that little smile on his face. He was happy about something, and you really wanted him to share it, and he always would. It was sort of like opening a good book and reading the first words: "Well kids, I'm going to tell you what we're going to do today!"

8

SHADY DEALINGS

Never have a companion that casts you in the shade.—Baltasar Gracian y Morales, *The Art of Worldly Wisdom* (1637)

Huggins was turning to a medium on the rise. Movie theaters were losing their audience at an alarming rate: from 80 million in 1946 to less than 40 million in 1955. When the Federal Communications Commission lifted its three-and-a-half year ban on new television stations in April 1952, the number of stations rose from 108 to 2,053. A huge new market was unleashed. Jack Warner remained unimpressed until the head of ABC Leonard Goldenson told him there were 40,000,000 television sets in American homes and the same number of opportunities for Warner to promote its product. Warner signed on the dotted line and agreed to deliver thirty-nine hours of film per year for Tuesday evening broadcast on ABC.

When Warner ventured into television in 1955 he wisely employed people who had some knowledge of working in the industry, including Oren Haglund who became production manager for the new TV department. But Warner's decisions sometimes worked against him. Gary Stevens, who came from a background in advertising and publicity, was employed as head of the studio division. When an ill-advised article in *Daily Variety* criticizing Warner Bros. came to the attention of Warner, Stevens was out. Warner's son-in-law William Orr was brought in as a temporary replacement. Orr hired Hugh Benson as his personal assistant and set about producing *Warner Brothers Presents* (1955). The weekly one-hour show would highlight Warner Bros.' new theatrical productions and releases under the ten-minute segment *Behind the Cameras at Warner Brothers*. The major portion of each episode revolved around three alternating shows, *Kings Row*, *Casablanca* and the western *Cheyenne*.

His first assignment on *Kings Row* was a disappointing start for Huggins as he considered the show to be nothing more than soap opera. Based on the 1942 film starring Ronald Reagan, the series featured the community of small town Kings Row, including Jack Kelly who would feature in one of Huggins' greatest successes a few years later. Huggins' contract had a ten-week option which provided a safety net for Warner Bros. From his new offices in an off-the-lot, rundown two-story building, Huggins encountered the hostility of Paul Stewart face to face. Huggins recalled that Stewart "received me with cool disdain."

By the end of his first week, Huggins was doubting his decision to move into television. "I had read the three *Kings Row* scripts, looked at the episode in production, and studied the one already shot. It was a chastening experience. If *Kings Row* was the best of the three series, Warners, ABC and television itself were in serious trouble and so was I."[1]

Huggins found himself in a daily struggle working alongside the disagreeable Stewart, who went out of his way to be negative about all of Huggins' suggestions. Huggins knew he was in trouble and seriously considered resigning before he was fired—yet again. Returning to work after a refreshing weekend break, he feared the worst when Bill Orr summoned him to his office. Seated across from Orr was Richard L. Bare. *Cheyenne* was in serious trouble with the Monsanto Chemical Company threatening to withdraw sponsorship and a lawsuit for recovery of monies.

"We want you to leave *Kings Row* and take on the task of salvaging *Cheyenne*," declared Orr.

"I need time to think it over," responded Huggins.

Ten minutes later he phoned Bare to tell him what a relief it would be to make the move from *Kings Row* to *Cheyenne*. The following morning Huggins had more trouble to contend with, in the form of Paul Stewart. In front of Bill Orr he demanded Huggins' name be removed from *Kings Row*. "The only contribution you made to the first show was to sit in on the dubbing," exclaimed Stewart.

To his surprise Huggins said he agreed with him. "The series is yours. You and Bill cast it, you're directing it and it represents your style, not mine."

Stewart had nowhere to turn. There would be no confrontation or argument and soon Stewart would be without a show when *Kings Row* was cancelled mid-season. Orders on *Cheyenne* increased to fill the gap.

The basic premise saw Cheyenne Bodie as a frontier scout raised by Chief White Cloud after Bodie's parents were massacred by Cheyenne Indians. The role called for a strong, handsome actor with a commanding screen presence. Illinois native Norman Eugene Walker was working as a deputy sheriff at the Sands Hotel in Las Vegas when actor Van Johnson suggested he contact agent Henry Willson. Johnson was struck with Walker's good looks and muscular 6'6" physique. Walker moved to Hollywood where her made an inauspicious start in a cameo as a Tarzan type in the Bowery Boys comedy *Jungle Gents* (1954). In June 1955 he was testing for the lead role in *Cheyenne*. A long-term contract and a change of name (to Clint Walker) followed.

The first four episodes had proved unsatisfactory to the studio, who wanted an adult approach. The September 28, 1955, review by *Variety* calling *Cheyenne* "almost strictly kideo fare" with "standard desperado Injun fighting," didn't help raise spirits. Huggins decided to dismiss L.Q. Jones as Cheyenne Bodie's humorous sidekick Smitty, place an emphasis on action and adventure and humanize the hero. "We've made him more real, more honest and more human. For instance we've got Clint walking in a girl's bedroom in an upcoming episode. Some people think we'll be kicked off the air, but I think we'll get a better rating than ever. We've taken the cowboy out of the rut," stated Huggins.[2]

The first episode of the season, "Mountain Fortress" (1:01), had been a remake of the western *Rocky Mountain* (1950) starring Errol Flynn. *The Treasure of the Sierra Madre* (1948) starring Humphrey Bogart became "The Argonauts" (1:03). When Huggins took control, the film adaptations continued with "West of the River" (1:10), an adaptation of *The Charge at Feather River* (1953), and "Fury at Rio Hondo" (1:12), a thinly disguised adaptation of *To Have and Have Not* (1944). But Huggins was also contributing his own original scripts beginning with "Decision" (1:07), followed by "Quicksand" (1:11), "Star in the Dust" (1:13) and "Johnny Bravo" (1:14).

"Decision" (1:07) was a standard U.S. Cavalry vs. Indians tale focused on a commanding officer (Richard Denning) who is so afraid of confronting the Arapaho he is prepared to let his unit and their wives and children risk dying from thirst in a lengthy southerly route to Fort McKay that avoids Indian territory. The episode was notable for featuring an early appearance by Michael Landon and introducing Huggins to an actor who would play a major role in his future: James Garner.

In "Quicksand" (1:11), Cheyenne Bodie acted as a guide to a group of settlers who come under attack as they pass through Comanche territory. After they take shelter in a derelict way station, the story explores the various conflicts forced upon them by the stress of their situation as they confront their own failings and come to realize what's important to them in the face of possible death. Bodie seeks a resolution to their problems when he purposely calls Comanche Chief Yellow Knife (Norman Frederic) a coward, inciting a challenge of bravery in the "swallowing sand." If Cheyenne Bodie calls for help first he loses the challenge and forfeits the life of himself and the settlers. But as they sink to their necks, both refuse to call for help and are rescued from death. Cheyenne has won the freedom of the settlers and the respect of the Comanche chief.

The story by Huggins and N.B. Stone (a.k.a. Norris B. Stone) contained overly familiar situations but remains memorable for the concluding test of courage in the quicksand. The episode also featured an early performance by Dennis Hopper as the immature and ill-fated Utah Kid. N.B. Stone would later write the Sam Peckinpah classic *Guns in the Afternoon* (1962).

Huggins cast his wife Adele Mara as a money-hungry opportunist in "Star in the Dust" (1:13). Cheyenne Bodie decides to stay in Three Forks as deputy sheriff after the town's deputy is killed in a shootout with Sheriff Wes Garth (Don Megowan). Desperate to win the love of Claire Du Pas (Adele) and marry her, Sheriff Garth sees an opportunity for an easy fortune when he kills a bank robber and decides to keep the $55,000 for himself. Although she's attracted to Cheyenne, Clara accepts Garth's offer of marriage and a fresh start in New Orleans with the help of the stolen money. When Cheyenne suspects their motives, he confronts Sheriff Garth and is forced to shoot him dead in self-defense. The theme of the lure of stolen money has strong similarities to Huggins' *Too Late for Tears* (1949).

Huggins final story of the first season, co-written with Dean Riesner, was "Johnny Bravo" (1:14). Cheyenne accepts a job as foreman of the Circle M Ranch, unaware he has been hired as a potential husband for the daughter (Penny Edwards) of ranch owner Matt Crowley (Harry Shannon). Crowley hates Mexicans after the murder of his son and when his daughter Molly declares her love for Mexican ranch hand Johnny Bravo (Carlos Rivas), Crowley states he would rather see him dead than married to Molly. An intensifying range war over a parcel of land results in Bravo attempting to save Crowley from a burning building. Cheyenne rescues them both from certain death and Crowley finally gives his daughter his blessing for her upcoming marriage to Bravo.

With the first season successfully concluded, Huggins commented, "*Cheyenne* managed a few weeks before the season's close to rise to the top ten, but all my genes seemed painfully incompatible with the conventions of the traditional western. I didn't hide how I felt from Dick Bare, we were having fun with it, and at season's end Orr asked if I would be interested in producing an anthology series to alternate with *Cheyenne*."

Huggins' final *Cheyenne* writer-producer credit appeared on the season two premiere, broadcast September 11, 1956. "The Dark Rider" (2:01), a story about murder on a cattle drive, was co-written with Howard Browne, the man who initially rejected Huggins' first work. It is best remembered for introducing the female confidence trickster Samantha Crawford, played by Diane Brewster. The character would later make appearances in four *Maverick* episodes. Huggins left behind a solid framework for future producers and writers on *Cheyenne* to build on. Writing for the Associated Press (October 30, 1956), Charles Mercer commented:

> All supermen eventually become bores—and that's the trouble with the heroes of too many westerns. But Cheyenne, as portrayed by Clint Walker, is more human ... he simply doesn't know all the answers. As a literary type he's as old as a ballad character of the Middle Ages. He is the perfect counterpoint to the evil and chicanery of the American frontier. Besides being marked by superior story-line ... *Cheyenne* has superb camera work.

With the cancellation of *Kings Row* and *Casablanca* on *Warner Brothers Presents*, a short series of stand-alone anthologies took their place. Huggins produced the final segment before *Warner Bros. Presents* transformed into *Conflict* in 1956.

"The Deadly Riddle" (1:36) was Huggins' adaptation of Geoffrey Chaucer's *The Wife of Bath's Tale*. It featured a sixteen-year-old Natalie Wood in the process of making the transition from child to adult star. She was still under contract to Warner Bros., who would incorporate their feature film actors into the anthology series as a means to promoting their upcoming theatrical releases. Huggins was opposed to casting Wood for one simple reason: The part called for a flawless English accent. He said,

> Not that I doubted her ability. She was a good actress, and beautiful, and the right age for the role. But I intended to cast the picture with English actors, and a single specious accent would make a bad film. Mixing accents in oblivious disregard of cultural and ethnic factors is a tradition in Hollywood, so the studio persisted.
>
> I was prepared to shelve the script rather than use Natalie, but a never-before-tried solution occurred to me and I put the episode into production. I had learned from Bill Orr that the real magic of film is in post-production, in what can be done with sound and picture after the shooting stops.
>
> Natalie was bewitching and altogether right, except for that American accent surrounded by accents of the British cast. When the film was finished and edited, I brought an English actress onto our looping stage and had her re-record all of Natalie's lines. A looping stage is a place where short pieces of film (loops) are run repeatedly, allowing actors to re-record in flawless synchronization any dialogue over which there is unwanted noise or any other flaw, including a bad reading.
>
> I had the English actress's lines looped in turn and brought Natalie to the looping stage. She listened to each line of dialogue and repeated it, imitating the accent but making the reading her own. She was reluctant to do it at first, but before we were through she thanked me warmly and with honest enthusiasm. The result was a film in which Natalie's original performance was still there, probably improved, but dressed now in a felicitous English accent.

Conflict offered Huggins opportunities to experiment with different genres and also presented the challenge of trying to maintain the interest of an audience showing a preference for continuing weekly series with familiar characters and formats. Huggins tried to push the limits of television drama, producing stories that offered a slice of life based in reality only to have his efforts curtailed by the strict television censorship code. "The Velvet Cage" (2:20), based on the play by Eva Greene and Richard Blake and starring Joanna Barnes as Laura

Ferris, offered divorce as a solution to marital problems. The TV censors wouldn't allow the episode to air until the ending was re-written. Huggins was understandably frustrated. "But this same taboo is violated in an old movie, *In Name Only*, that's now playing on TV—and in many other old movies. I don't understand this double-barreled standard of morality."[3]

During his time on *Conflict*, Huggins worked once more with James Garner. A chance meeting in "The Rondelet Room" on the Sunset Strip between director Richard Bare and struggling actor Jim Bumgarner (Garner's real name) would lead to bit parts on *Cheyenne*. Initially Bumgarner was hired for his good looks. But after watching the dailies of his first day of filming as Lieutenant Rogers, Orr offered Bumgarner a seven-year contract and a change of name. Garner showed few signs he could handle comedy or even interest audiences with his bland performance. His talent was still waiting to emerge.

A small role as a con man and gambler in the *Conflict* episode "The Man from 1997" (2:06) introduced Huggins to a side of Garner that hadn't been evident in his mediocre *Cheyenne* performances. In this story of a young Polish immigrant (Jacques Sernas) seeing his chance for a fortune and love after discovering an almanac from 1997 in a bookshop, Garner delivered his few lines with a dry humor and charm that Huggins found appealing:

> On the second day of production I went to the regular run of the dailies to see how Garner was doing. One of Garner's scenes came on, Garner read a line, and the whole room burst into laughter. I wanted to think I had stumbled onto hidden treasure. I knew for certain the reading hadn't come from the director. That kind of purity can only come from the actor. I had talked with Garner at length more than once. He looked and sounded like an amiable cowboy, and I had never heard him say anything remotely funny, but as the scene went on, other lines that had been written with only a forlorn hope that they might evoke a slight chuckle were being made funnier than they had any right to be by Garner's skewed and underplayed delivery.

Huggins cast Garner in a new comedy western that would define Huggins' time at Warner Bros. Garner's dailies in *Sayonara* (1957) added to Huggins' conviction he had chosen the perfect actor. In late November 1956 Huggins presented the concept of *Maverick* to Bill Orr, his executive story editor Jack Emanuel and Robert Lewine, who was in charge of program development for ABC on the West Coast. It featured a self-centered anti-hero—a "gentle grafter."

It was greeted with enthusiasm by everyone present and Huggins began work on the pilot episode "The Third Cross" a.k.a. "The Saga of Onyx O'Neill"—Huggins' early name for the character of Bret Maverick. In an internal Warner Bros. memo sent by Emanuel to Bryan S. Moore on December 18, 1957, he made claims on the creation of the Bret Maverick character. Emanuel states he was inspired by source material such as *Aces and Eights* by L. P. Holmes, *The Gentle Grafter* by O. Henry, the *Get-Rich-Quick Wallingford* stories by George Randolph Chester, *Sucker's Progress* by Herbert Asbury and *"Yellow Kid" Weil* by Joseph R. Weil and W.T. Brannon. "I concluded that it would be a good idea for us to do a series about a gambler after a quick buck from the South during the period 1876–1886—the basic theme being that he cheats cheaters.... [A]pproximately the first part of December 1956, I suggested that we try to use the title *Cameo Kirby*."

When it was discovered that the Booth Tarkington character was copyrighted by 20th Century–Fox, Emanuel continued, "Roy Huggins suggested the title *Onyx O'Neill* which as I recall Bill didn't care for. Roy subsequently made an oral submission of a story based on *Onyx O'Neill* to Finlay McDermott for a feature."

As stated earlier, this was the original pilot that underwent three changes in title before being broadcast as the second episode. According to Emanuel, the name Maverick was first mentioned in a phone call he received from Orr asking for the definition of the word. He admitted, "I'm not exactly sure who thought of the name Maverick for our central character."

Emanuel concluded his memo with the bold claim, "It is my contention that the protagonist, Bret Maverick of our *Maverick* series, is the same young unmarried gambler that roamed the west in the period of 1876–1886 that I originally conceived and described to Bill Orr under the name of 'Cameo Kirby.'"[4]

Emanuel's claim falls apart based on the dateline. Roy Huggins first presented the then unnamed *Maverick* concept in late November 1956 with Emanuel present. Emanuel, by his own admission, gives a date of early December 1956 for the "Cameo Kirby" title. This was after Huggins' presentation and was clearly based on Huggins' character.

Maverick introduced Huggins to Bill Orr's practice of avoiding paying the $500-per-episode royalties to its writers by insisting pilots be based on existing Warner Bros. properties. The pilot script "The Third Cross" (later broadcast as "Point Blank" [1:02]) by Huggins was ditched in favor of an adaptation of the Warner Bros. property "The War of the Copper Kings" by C. B. Glasscock—the same property Huggins had been introduced to a few years earlier at Columbia. Huggins substituted Bret Maverick for Augustus Heinze, who uses an obscure law to snatch a fortune from the Amalgamated Copper Company. But Warner Bros. and ABC both insisted Maverick play the good cowboy and give his financial gain to a group of small miners the company had driven into bankruptcy. From the outset Huggins had his hands tied. Not only had Standards and Practices dictated the conclusion of his story, Orr had succeeded in snatching creator rights from Huggins. Huggins had learned a hard lesson. Unfortunately it would be repeated at a later date. "Point Blank" with the added creative talents of Howard Browne ultimately served as the second episode of the first season.

Meanwhile, James Garner wasn't pleased with the thought of being stuck in a TV western but as a Warner Bros. contract player he had no choice and soon found himself committed to a weekly series named *Maverick* when ABC sold the pilot to the Kaiser Steel Company. *Maverick* was distinguished from other TV westerns of the era by the fact the main character was a sheriff who was more interested in protecting his own interests than those of the townsfolk. The anti-hero (a person working outside of the system and living by his own moral code) would be a continuing thread throughout much of Huggins' future work.

Huggins had firm views on his TV westerns in general and his new approach. "People are willing to laugh at westerns. But you can't make a direct frontal attack on them. You must do it in an amiable way so that the western buff will enjoy it as much as the person who detests westerns. Above all you have to tell a good story. You can't satirize anything without a strong story."[5]

Huggins introduced a brother for Garner's Bret Maverick early into the first season to insure that episodes were produced on time and avoid being pre-empted. A 39-episode season required that episodes be filmed with two production crews at approximately the same time to meet the deadlines. Bart was named Ben in the first draft of the original presentation to Orr before the series went into production. Huggins described the brothers and basic concept as "Rhett Butlers with boyish smiles. Bret and Bart were raised in Texas by their father, a retired Mississippi River gambler from whom they earned every trick of the gambler's trade and something more: a hatred for cheaters and a respect for honesty in gambling. The father is dead now and since the war the brothers have been making their living as gamblers.... [B]oth of them love to "cheat a cheater."[6]

Kelly's acting style resulted in Bart coming across as a little more serious than Bret. "Jack Kelly was very funny but as soon as someone said 'action' Jack Kelly would deliver a funny line like a load of coal. Jack would become a different person," commented Huggins.[7]

Kelly's wife May Wynn was critical of her husband's status on the show despite his rotating the lead with Garner. The casting of Kelly was never a problem with Garner and the ratings showed little difference between Kelly and Garner episodes. Audience share began with a modest twenty-six percent in September 1957. Adding to Huggins' problems was a disgruntled sixty-five-year-old Jack Warner who didn't care for the show. In a rare staff meeting, producers, directors and executives sat before Warner in an office in the new television department building located on the Warner Bros lot. He began the meeting by telling everyone that he had watched *Maverick* last night and he thought it stunk. "It's slow and dull with no action, gunplay or any hero and sure as hell is no western."

Huggins decided to hold his tongue in the meeting and arrange an appointment with Warner where he could discuss his problems with the show in privacy.

"What you saw last night was a typical *Maverick*. The show isn't going to change or get any better. Hugh Benson asks me each week to put a fight in the script and every week I decline to do it. *Maverick* is an anti-western," explained Huggins to Warner.

"What the hell kind of animal is that and what the hell kind of audience wants to watch it?" replied a puzzled Warner.

"I thought last night's episode was good but if you want to be let off the hook you can release me from my contract as soon as I finish the shows I have in production."

"I'll talk it over with Bill Orr."

Huggins never heard back from Warner or Orr as the ratings continued to climb. Huggins reflected on the mentality of the "men sitting around trying to guess what the audience wants": "Personally, I've never tried to guess what the audience wants. I think you can only do what you want yourself and hope that the audience finds you.... The problem with 99 percent of the thinking in this business is that it isn't dynamic, it's on a superficial level ... they think there aren't enough fights in a certain program when they should be thinking what's the matter dramatically and structurally with this program."

"Shady Deal at Sunny Acres" (2:10) proved to be one of the most popular episodes of the entire series. Garner was offered the choice of roles and preferred sitting on the porch of the Hotel Sunny Acres whittling his piece of wood while brother Bart arranges to retrieve Bret's $15,000 in gambling money from crooked bank owner John Bates (John Dehner). Bart, posing as businessman Bartley Mansfield II, entices Bates with the prospect of making easy money from the Nevada Empress Silver Mine. While most shareholders think their stock worthless, Bart tells Bates that a rich vein has just been discovered and the stocks will soon be worth a fortune. The money-obsessed Bates falls for the bait thanks to a complex counter-swindle involving the many recurring characters featured in the series including Gentleman Jack Darby (Richard Long), Dandy Jim Buckley (Efrem Zimbalist Jr.), Samantha Crawford (Diane Brewster), Big Mike Macomb (Leo Gordon) and Cindy Brown (Arlene Howell).

Huggins' wife Adele Mara made her second of three *Maverick* appearances in "The

Spanish Dancer" (2:13) playing saloon dancer Elena Grande in a story featuring Bart Maverick (Jack Kelly), charged with the murder of Gentleman Jack Darby (Richard Long), who may or may not be dead. The role saw Adele return to dancing after a lengthy break. "It was 104 temperature on the Warners lot the day we shot the dance. Then, too, I hadn't realized how rusty I had become. My legs swelled up like balloons during rehearsal and I developed a fever to match the temperature. One thing I know now. You just can't quit dancing for years and then casually go back to it."[8]

"Gun-Shy" (2:16) was a successful parody of the popular *Gunsmoke* series starring towering James Arness as Marshal Matt Dillon maintaining law and order in Dodge City. Although Marion Hargrove was responsible for the idea and is credited as the writer, Huggins re-wrote his story and removed what he considered farcical scenes, replacing them with comedy arising out of natural situations.

Six-foot-six Ben Gage, who played the role of Marshal Mort Dooley, described his role to UPI correspondent Vernon Scott (December 26, 1958): "I think the show is a riot. We open up the same way *Gunsmoke* does with the marshal pulling a quick draw on the heavy. Only on our show I miss. Matter of fact, I shoot six times and still don't hit my man."

Maverick's retort to Dooley, "Shall I stand a little closer, marshal?" is a highlight of the episode which features Maverick searching for buried Confederate gold in Ellwood, Kansas, home of Marshal Dooley. Gage's towering physique, deep voice and stern, unsmiling manner effectively parodied James Arness. Walter Edmiston as Clyde Diefendorfer stood in for Dennis Weaver's Chester and Marshall Kent as Doc Stucke mimicked Milburn Stone's Doc.

In an article for *Life* (January 19, 1959), Hargrove called *Maverick* "a retarded adolescent. Its 'hero' a lazy, sneaky, poker-playing vagrant.... If the average western is a reaction against the realities of modern life, *Maverick* is a reaction against the unrealities of the average western.... The *Maverick* operation is one of the few places in Hollywood where a writer can escape from westerns."

Without naming Huggins, Hargrove hinted that his original ideas for *Maverick* episodes were often radically changed by the time they were broadcast. "It often happens that the finished story is a pole away from the original idea."

Huggins admitted he re-wrote Hargrove's scripts. "He must have written ten or so scripts in the two years he worked with me on *Maverick* and I always had to re-write them because Marion's writing was always three feet off the ground." Despite his reservations about Hargrove's writing, Huggins later admitted, "Marion Hargrove had a unique kind of humor that I loved."

Huggins explained the relationship between the writer and the audience on *Maverick* at the Jonathan Club in Los Angeles on October 23, 1958:

> The story-tellers, by fully realizing the common daydreams, can and do reinforce and direct attitudes of the audience which are vague and inactive. There is, for example, a good deal of conscious effort to influence attitudes in *Maverick*, the television show that I produce.
>
> The suspicion is growing that we have become a nation of security-seeking, contented conformists, meriting only scorn from those steely-eyed forebears who looked to themselves for rules, and who prized venture over security. The old ideal of rugged individualism is having a rough time and it needs all the help it can get just now, so Maverick's protagonist is the self-reliant, freedom-loving individualist of our still-visible past, and we try to give those qualities such excitement and glamour that any other way of life will look downright ridiculous.
>
> Maverick's irreverent, highly individualistic attitude is frequently too strong meat for some of

our audience, so I allow him to attribute his more acerb remarks to his old "Pappy." In every *Maverick* episode you will hear things like the following: "Marriage is the only game of chance I know where *both* parties can lose." "It isn't *how* you play the game, it's winning that counts." "Friendship is the only thing in life that you have to earn. Everything else you can steal." "You can fool all the people some of the time, and some of the people all of the time, and those are very good odds."

In the final outcome, any effort of a producer to influence aspirations and goals is fruitless if the basis for it does not exist in the audience. It is the audience that ultimately points the way and forces the producers of filmed drama to change their product.

Huggins' relationship with James Garner, which had been polite and even included the occasional poker game at Huggins' home, took a turn for the worse at the Emmy Awards on May 6, 1959. Garner had been nominated for Best Actor in a Continuing Dramatic Series with *Maverick* nominated for Best Dramatic Series for the second consecutive year. To Garner's surprise he failed to win. Instead Huggins collected the Emmy for *Maverick*. If that wasn't enough to displease Garner, Huggins' speech tipped the balance. Because of time constraints caused by Jack Benny delaying the announcement of *Maverick* as the winner and then pulling the statuette away from Huggins on stage while going into a five-minute comedy routine about not being able to give the Emmy to the man who beat his show in the ratings, Huggins couldn't deliver the speech he carefully prepared which acknowledged Marion Hargrove, Douglas Heyes, Leslie Martinson, James Garner and Jack Kelly. Instead he accepted the award with a "few mumbled words I can't recall." Garner, not aware of the time constraint, was furious he didn't get a mention from Huggins. Their relationship was placed under severe strain that evening with Garner a no-show at the after-show party.

The next morning Huggins left by train for New Orleans on his way to a much-needed vacation in New York with Adele. On his return Huggins developed what he thought was a bad case of bronchitis. But a visit to a doctor in Buffalo ended in a journey to Meyer Memorial Hospital where he was treated for double pneumonia. During his two-week stay he was given daily blood tests and cardiograms and impressed the nurses with a telegram from *Maverick* fan Cary Grant. Grant had met with Huggins and Hargrove for dinner a few months earlier to suggest they work on a film together but the plans came to nothing.

Huggins' hospital experience made him realize he had been working too many eighteen-hour days over too long a time and needed a break from the weekly schedule of *Maverick*. He had enjoyed working on the show during "the happiest two years of my life" but he needed a change of pace. Huggins' departure from *Maverick* saw its fortunes reverse with Garner leaving the show at the end of the third season in a contract dispute following a five-month strike by the Writers Guild of America. The Guild demanded writers receive a share of the revenue from sales of movies to television. Warner Bros. had refused to pay Garner's salary during the strike due to lack of scripts to produce and he successfully sued them for breach of contract. Warner Bros. got around the strike by recycling and adapting old scripts under the pseudonym W. Hermanos—a slightly veiled Spanish reference to Warner Brothers. Huggins declared, "At the end of the third season ... *Maverick* had become a broad and desperate and unfunny comedy. In the fourth season, without Garner, the show sank even lower, and in the middle of the fifth season a disappointed ABC and a baffled Henry Kaiser cancelled it."

Huggins had a little over two years remaining on his contract and didn't want to work on pilots. Orr suggested moving Huggins to feature films. Huggins wasn't excited with the

Mara and Huggins with his Emmy Award for *Maverick* as "Best Western Series" on May 6, 1959 (courtesy John Huggins).

prospect but accepted. He was just filling in time before he made his final exit from Warner Bros. and their royalty system that screwed writers out of owning any creator-owned rights.

Another example of Huggins being effectively rolled over was *Colt .45* (1957) which featured federal agent Christopher Colt (Wayde Preston) working undercover as a gun salesman to track down criminals in the Old West of the 1880s. Huggins developed the show after watching the 1950 Randolph Scott film of the same name. He immediately decided to keep the title even though he considered it weak, ditch the story and characters and create his own.

Orr and ABC were sold on the idea and told Huggins to produce another pilot. Meanwhile Orr had told the story department to write a half-dozen storylines for a *Colt .45* series and to send them to ABC along with the Randolph Scott movie. Orr wasn't finished in his slippery maneuvers. Huggins received a phone call from his executive assistant Hugh Benson who told him that Jack Warner had suggested *Colt .45* as the basis for a television series over one year ago. Once again Huggins had been stripped of any creator rights. "I lost another round and took a solemn oath to win the next or pick up my pencils and go home," declared Huggins.

Huggins' pilot episode "Judgment Day" (1:01), written with Marion Hargrove, featured Colt traveling to Cottonwood to keep watch on Jim Rexford (Andrew Duggan) only to find himself challenged to a gunfight if he doesn't leave town before noon. The 30-minute series premiered on ABC on October 18, 1957, and would once again involve a troubled leading man in a contract dispute with Warner Bros. In Wayde Preston's temporary absence Donald May replaced him as Colt's cousin Sam Colt, Jr., and stayed on to star with Preston on his return in the remaining episodes of the third and final season. Christopher Colt featured in four cross-over episodes on *Sugarfoot* and was referenced in the *Maverick* episode "Hadley's Hunters" (4:02) when Bart Maverick finds Colt's satchel on a desk and his Colt .45s and gun belt hanging on the wall in a nod to the cancellation of *Colt .45*. Huggins had no connection to any of the *Colt .45* episodes beyond the pilot.

Yet another example of Huggins being outmaneuvered was the pilot *Girl on the Run* (1958), loosely based on Huggins' private eye creation Stuart Bailey and the office he worked out of on *77 Sunset Strip*. Huggins hired Marion Hargrove to write the 60-minute pilot script for a proposed new private-eye series called *77 Sunset Boulevard*. Orr and ABC liked the concept and told Huggins to begin working on the script for the show now titled *77 Sunset Strip*. The sixty-minute pilot was later expanded to ninety minutes at Orr's request. The official reasons behind the decision to expand the pilot was to enable Warner Bros. to release the pilot as a theatrical film should the pilot fail to sell. Huggins sensed the dirty tricks brigade at work yet again. The real reason for a theatrical release, according to Huggins, was to avoid paying the creator and writer royalties. The fact that *Girl on the Run* only ran for one week in a West Indies theater before airing on ABC appeared to support Huggins' reasoning. Telling Huggins to change the private eye's name to Stuart Bailey also ensured they could claim rights on the creation by stating the character was based on the *Conflict* episode "Anything for Money," adapted by Huggins from his *Saturday Evening Post* story "Death of a Skylark" under a work-for-hire agreement. "Anything for Money" wasn't a pilot but also featured Efrem Zimbalist, Jr. as Stuart Bailey. Orr was also planning another move to enforce Warner's ownership of Huggins' creation. His third novel *Lovely Lady, Pity Me* was bought by Warner Bros and a script written that included Stuart Bailey even though there was no private eye in the original novel.

Director Richard Bare completed *Girl on the Run* in ten days. ABC executives were impressed at the screening and the film served as the pilot to *77 Sunset Strip* (1958). Edd Byrnes as the homicidal psychopath "Kookie" was resurrected from the dead for the television series with an introductory epilogue filmed by Bare and tagged onto the pilot. Efrem Zimbalist, Jr. invited Byrnes to join him as he promoted the upcoming series: "You know, Kookie here is not such a bad fellow, so we're keeping him alive for the series."

As the series progressed, "Kookie" became its most popular character thanks to Byrnes' sex appeal, engaging manner and his signature comb-through-the-hair routine. Bare claimed credit for the latter: "While shooting *Girl on the Run*, a scene called for Kookie, as the killer, to be sitting behind an open window, waiting to shoot someone in a building across the street. He would see the target, aim his rifle, then lose sight of the intended victim and lower the gun again. During the lulls, I told Edd, 'While you're waiting, take a comb and run it through your hair.'"[9] The success of the gimmick ultimately led to a hit song in 1960, "Kookie, Kookie, Lend Me Your Comb."

Despite his apparent enthusiasm for the upcoming series, Zimbalist was a reluctant Stuart Bailey. "The fact is, I didn't want any of it. I hated the idea. I didn't want to do television.... And when 'Anything for Money' didn't sell, I was thrilled.... Of course, I came to love the series with all my heart, but in the beginning that was my attitude."[10]

77 Sunset Strip introduced a new genre to network television: the action-adventure series. Private detective Stuart Bailey (Zimbalist) worked out of offices on Sunset Strip with partner Jeff Spencer (Roger Smith), aided on occasion by the parking lot attendant at Dino's Lodge located next door, Gerald Lloyd Kookson III a.k.a. Kookie. Sex appeal came in the form of switchboard operator Suzanne Fabray (Jacqueline Beer).

Huggins played no part in the *77 Sunset Strip* weekly series. "The studio refused to pay me a royalty and I persuaded the Writers Guild to take it to arbitration. I lost. I decided, of course, that I would never again produce a pilot at Warner Bros. But even on that point Bill had the last chortling word. With the success of *77 Sunset Strip* the studio followed up with three clones of that series called *Bourbon Street Beat*, *Surfside 6*, and *Hawaiian Eye*. I had no connection with any of them, all reflecting the style and talent of Bill Orr."

Zimbalist was unhappy when approached by Huggins about a film to star himself and Byrnes. Not only did Zimbalist consider the script lacked any quality but he felt it was exploiting their popularity on *77 Sunset Strip*. Despite Zimbalist's reluctance, Huggins sold him on the film. Happily for Zimbalist, the film project was later abandoned. "Roy could talk an Eskimo into a deep freeze. He was an incredible salesman. Roy always reminded me of David White, who played Larry Tate on *Bewitched*. He had those thyroid eyes and when he started talking, his eyes would come out an inch from his head," explained Zimbalist.[11]

Zimbalist did appear in the political courtroom drama *A Fever in the Blood* (1961) which cast him as a judge opposite Jack Kelly from *Maverick*. Based on a best-selling novel by former Colorado lawyer William Pearson and adapted for the screen by Huggins and Harry Kleiner with direction by Vincent Sherman, the film opens with the murder of an adulterous socialite in her bedroom. Her estranged husband (Rhodes Reason) is arrested, wrongly accused and found guilty of murder. The prosecuting district attorney (Jack Kelly), a Senator (Don Ameche) and a judge (Zimabalist) are all candidates for gubernatorial nomination, each with their own political agendas.

"I was given Efrem Zimbalist," recalled Huggins. "I was, of course, a warm advocate of Efrem as an actor but he was too young for the role and I said so. Warner and his assistant, Steve Trilling, listened, and cast the picture their way, except for one role they didn't think important enough to command their attention. It was the kind of role that gets noticed. A cynical, pragmatic Irish political boss. I chose an actor from New York who had never worked

Left to right: Jesse White, Jack Kelly and Huggins discussing the script for *A Fever in the Blood* (1961) (courtesy John Huggins).

in film before, Carroll O'Connor. *A Fever in the Blood* made a profit for the studio and most of the reviews were favorable, but it could have been a better film. It dealt in a sophisticated way with American politics after World War II, throwing a sharp light in some of the changes in style and attitude that we could now say foreshadowed Watergate."

Huggins was now told by Warner he would be only allowed to select his own future projects with his approval and he demanded "a chance to go over the final cut." Directing every film he produced was also out of the question. According to Warner he had only directed a Randolph Scott western and a top Hollywood star might demand a director with more substantial credentials. Huggins left the Warner Bros. lot in a reflective mood, seeking peace on the sands of Harrison's Landing near Malibu and Encinal Bluffs where he had dived almost daily in his youth:

> I sat on a sun-bleached log and looked at the slate-blue water, remembering the abalone and lobster that had once so abundantly blessed the rocky sea bottom out there beneath that olive-drab stretch of kelp. I thought about how much simpler life had been in the days when I came here to dive for sheepshead or lobster or whatever looked good for dinner that night. Those sweet days seemed to belong to another time.

Huggins reflected on seeing director George Stevens shooting *Giant* (1956) on the Warner lot and at the end of the day carrying heavy reels of film to the trunk of his car. Orr

Huggins prepares for scuba diving on a Santa Monica beach with Adele Mara in the foreground in the 1950s (courtesy John Huggins).

had told Huggins that Stevens was protecting his valuable film from the meddling hands of Steve Trilling in the cutting room. If an acclaimed director such as Stevens didn't have total control over his work, Huggins knew there was no point negotiating. The next morning Huggins told Warner he would be leaving. Warner wasn't pleased and told *The Hollywood Reporter* (September 16, 1960):

The facts are these, Mr. Huggins was asked if he would call his contract off, as the studio no longer desired his services. Huggins accepted the offer. At no time did Huggins ask for, nor did the studio ever suggest that he would have complete creative freedom and authority.

An angry Huggins knew the false account of events leading to his resignation could harm his future career and demanded a retraction the following issue. The September 19 *Hollywood Reporter* featured the retraction but added more false information about Huggins continuing his work on a film where he wasn't allowed inside the cutting room of the editor:

> Exit of producer Roy Huggins from Warners studio has been deferred while he continues supervision of editing of *A Fever in the Blood*. Augmenting his Friday statement J.L. Warner said the studio would have been happy to retain Huggins as a producer under the terms of his contract if he had not made certain demands to which the studio could not agree within production policy.

Away from the pressures of work at Warner Bros., Huggins was keeping busy. A son, John Huggins, was born October 29, 1961, one year after Thomas born May 2, 1960, and two years before James was born March 1, 1963. According to John,

> Soon after I was born, our family moved to Mandeville Canyon and remained there the rest of their life. We lived with my mother's parents Angel and Eloisa Delgado. Although they were born in Spain, they met each other after they had emigrated to Dearborn, Michigan. They lived with my mother and father from the time they bought their first house. Father referred to them as Mom and Dad and got along with them very well. There was no dysfunction. Because they hadn't learned the English language, Father spoke Spanish and me and my brothers can speak fluent Castilian to this day. Adding to our Spanish home was the maid who maintained the household. Mother would pay all their dental and medical bills.
> Father owned five undeveloped acres and raised thoroughbred horses. He had a great passion for them but didn't ride. He loved the idea of breeding them and having them around. They were almost like pets. He would have the brood mares sired until they foaled. If they were male he would auction them but if it was a female he would keep them to replace our thoroughbreds who died for all manner of reasons. We had horses who reared up and fell and hit their heads. They would die in childbirth and the colic would get them once in a while.
> Father loved to take hikes and identify all the plants. He had a photographic memory and read the Oxford dictionary from cover to cover when he was in his twenties. Roy was a social animal and had parties at his house. He met Jacques Cousteau and they became good friends. Cousteau was experimenting with scuba gear and gave father scuba equipment. Father was one of the first people to scuba dive off the coast of California.
> Father would go out into a skiff with dentist Stuart Bailey. Stu would row father out into the ocean and Dad would scuba dive for abalone and lobster from the bottom of the Santa Monica Bay. He would throw large parties on the beach where everyone would eat free lobster. Stu chewed every morsel of food thirty-five times. Eccentric to say the least. Father loved the beach. At the weekends we would gather mussels and go clamming. He would collect barnacles and eat them. I think he was the only person who knew barnacles were edible. They're a delicacy in parts of Europe.
> Father wanted to be a painter at one point and painted canvasses. At the Mandeville house he was also a beekeeper. Everyone in the canyon knew it and when they would get a swarm they would come to Roy. We would put on the bee suits and capture the swarm and create another hive with it. Eventually we had as many as 20 or 25 hives. We would gather the honey once a year. It was a ritual for fifteen years. He would always end up with tons of stings that seemed not to bother him. He would say, "Oh well, you get stung when you get honey." Father would be very matter-of-fact about it.[12]

9

TROUBLE AT FOX

"Failures are finger posts on the road to achievement."—C.S. Lewis (1898–1963)

Huggins' time at Fox as vice-president in charge of television proved to be trying. Despite a contract that included ten percent of the profits of the entire television enterprise and an option to run the motion picture department if asked, Huggins was not happy. On September 21, 1960, over lunch at Lucy's restaurant, he had turned down an offer from Arthur Kramer to return to Columbia Pictures as a producer. Huggins politely declined the offer to a shocked Kramer despite being offered a 50 percent share in the net profits of any film Huggins produced and a salary three times what he had been paid five years earlier. Even the sudden death of Harry Cohn from a heart attack in February 1958 couldn't tempt Huggins back to Columbia. Huggins considered motion pictures to be in terminal decline and television held more promise, both creatively and financially.

Huggins' problems began when he pitched his concept for a new series titled *The Fugitive* to the president of Fox television Peter G. Levathes. An F.B.I. special agent during World War II, Levathes joined Madison Avenue advertising agency Young & Rubicam as vice-president in charge of media and television after the war. Huggins described Levathes as "a tall, dark-visaged man who looked like Pericles in a Brooks Brothers suit. He was literate and amusing and I was not surprised when he told me he had a masters degree in romance languages."[1]

Huggins' future production assistant Jo Swerling, Jr. recalled Huggins' early attempts to sell the *Fugitive* concept:

> Roy originally came up with the idea of *The Fugitive* when he was still at Warner Bros. It was a six-page-long presentation with three pages in script form. It was basically the opening sequence with the train wreck and escape. The remainder of the presentation was just prose describing the premise of the series. Roy showed the presentation to Howard Browne. He was the first person to see it. "I think this idea is so terrible you'll lose credibility if you show this to anybody else," said Browne.
>
> Roy was taken aback by Howard's reaction and decided to show it to his agent to get a second opinion. His agent had the identical reaction to Howard Browne. Roy had a saying, "When seventy-five people tell you you're drunk, you should go lie down." So he stuck *The Fugitive* away in a drawer and forgot about it.
>
> When Roy left Warner Brothers to become vice-president in charge of television production for Fox he reported to the president of Fox Film Corporation Peter Levathes. They were flying back east to New York for a series of meetings at Fox's New York office. On the flight Levathes

said to Roy, "You must have some ideas for series that you have filed away. Have you got anything?" Roy said to himself, "What the hell. I'll tell him about *The Fugitive.*"

Roy told him the idea and he could see the curtain go down in Levathes' eyes. Roy knew Levathes was thinking, "My God, what have I done? I've hired this idiot."[2]

Huggins recalled, "When I finished he sat in stricken silence, staring at me as if I had just turned rancid before his very eyes. He seemed to be giving desperate thought to throwing one of us off the airplane, and he finished his espresso like a cowboy downing a shot of redeye. His confidence in me perished that night, probably somewhere over Nebraska, never to be revived."

Following the rejection, Huggins was set the unenviable task of reviving the *Hong Kong* series which was failing in the ratings opposite the popular *Wagon Train*. Australian actor Rod Taylor played American journalist Glenn Evans, working out of Hong Kong, whose weekly search for stories involved him in the criminal underworld. Huggins added the Golden Dragon nightclub and Chinese hostess Ching Mei (Mai Tai Sing). Ratings improved but the show was canceled after one season. Following cancellation, the network was deluged with 11,000 letters of protest. Erskine Johnson, Hollywood correspondent for the Newspaper Enterprise Association (January 1962), stated the reasoning behind the cancellation:

> A big talent agency, which sold the show to the network, had a falling out with the TV bosses of the 20th Century–Fox Studio, where it was financed and filmed. To continue the *Hong Kong* series, the studio would be required to make $14,000 weekly commission payments to the talent agency. The big studio was so mad at the big talent agency that the show was scrapped in its 26th week.
>
> The sponsor, of course, was howling mad. "Don't worry," said the studio, "we will film a new show starring Rod Taylor." So the new show, *Follow the Sun*, was filmed, but without Mr. Taylor.

An angry Rod Taylor made his thoughts known in *TV Channels* (July 23, 1961):

> We tried *not* to make this just another *Hawaiian Eye*, but to really do a job with a bit of character and reality to it. And what happens? The bleeding rating services say nobody watches us. Nobody?! What about the thousands and thousands of letters that pour in here because we're going off the air.

The pilot *Dateline: San Francisco* (1962) was subsequently filmed with journalist Glenn Evans now working out of San Francisco. It didn't sell.

One day Huggins received a welcome visitor to his office at Fox. Montgomery Pittman first met Huggins while working on *Conflict* at Warner Bros. and soon became a regular writer on Huggins' shows including *Conflict, Cheyenne, Colt .45* and *Maverick*. Pittman had jokingly remarked, "I gotta quit doin' this. It isn't good for my soul. First job I ever had, back in 1936, was pitchman for a medicine show. I just found out I'm right back where I started." Huggins enjoyed listening to Pittman tell his lurid stories of sexual encounters while traveling with his medicine show through the South with a "rural grin that stretched right across his face." "Monty" (as Huggins called him) was also a chain smoker of cigars during his days at Warner Bros.—a habit that he was now regretting. Pittman's unexpected visit to Huggins was his way of saying farewell. He was suffering from cancer of the throat.

"I'm leaving, going to Mexico. There's a clinic down there that claims to have a cure. I know. You think that's stupid. So do I, but when your life's involved you'll believe anything." As Pittman departed, Huggins knew he would never see his friend again. On June 26, 1962, Pittman passed away. He was only forty-five years old.

Huggins' next assignment *Follow the Sun* (1961), the follow-up to *Hong Kong*, was co-produced with Marion Hargrove. The basic concept was similar to *Hong Kong* with two freelance journalists based in Honolulu encountering mystery and their fair share of beautiful women in their weekly Hawaiian adventures. After five episodes of the ABC Sunday night series, Hargrove departed and Huggins decided to make changes. Journalist Paul Templin (Brett Halsey) replaced Eric Jason (Gary Lockwood) in the title sequence. Halsey had come to Huggins' attention after working on the pilot *The Hunters*. Huggins thought Lockwood looked too young for an experienced reporter. Lockwood survived in his role but in a reduced capacity as leg man and scout for the two freelance reporters. Huggins decided to revise the format, separating the two lead characters and giving each their own alternate episodes. Once again the changes had little impact on viewers and the show was canceled after one season.

Huggins hoped for greater success with six pilots filming on the sound stages and back lot. *The Ginger Rogers Show* in which Rogers played twins opposite Charlie Ruggles as their uncle failed to sell. *The Hunters* starring Brett Halsey as a big game hunter in Africa and *The Jayhawkers* starring Jack Betts and Jock Gaynor also failed to spark interest. Created and produced by Huggins, *The House on Rue Riviera* was an hour-long mystery-suspense-adventure set in the French Riviera, about a tourist who blackmails four people to prove his innocence in the murder of a singer. Although primarily filmed on the Fox back lot, special footage filmed in Nice, Cannes, Monaco, St. Raphael and Cap d'Antibes provided the glamorous backdrop to the proposed series. The unsold pilot starring Jayne Mansfield, John Ericson and Richard Anderson later found a home on NBC's *Kraft Mystery Theatre* (1:12) on August 30, 1961.

The only sales from the pilot season were the sitcom *Margie* (1961) starring Cynthia Pepper as Margie Clayton and *Bus Stop* (1961), based on the play by William Inge and the subsequent 1956 film starring Marilyn Monroe. Huggins served as executive producer on the series, which centered on various strangers coming through the Sherwood bus depot and diner in Sunrise, Colorado. Narrator Hank Simms announced the upcoming series on the ABC network:

> Do you know where *Bus Stop* is? Where strangers pass in the night or meet for a brief interlude. The result can be a savage conflict or a tender moment. *Bus Stop* brings to your television screen the forces and power of unforgettable human drama in one of the most outstanding programs of this or any year. The stories you will see on *Bus Stop* explore every level of life. The warmth and the terror that springs from the restless multitudes always pressing on to the next city on the map. *Bus Stop*. Adult entertainment outstandingly produced. *Bus Stop*. Every week on ABC.

Despite ABC's promotion, *Bus Stop* was soon struggling in the ratings and in need of attention. But when the attention came, it was for all the wrong reasons and marked the beginning of the end for Huggins. Swerling recalled, "It was a disaster at Fox. His experience was something he wish could forget. *Bus Stop* was cancelled because of an episode featuring Fabian. It was notorious at the time."

The episode in question, "A Lion Walks Among Us," (1:10) resulted in a Congressional hearings on violence on television. With a teleplay by Ellis Kadison based on Tom Wicker's novel "Judgment" and directed by Robert Altman, the episode was broadcast December 3, 1961, to an audience not accustomed to watching realistic violence in contemporary dramas. The story starred Fabian as sadistic drifter Luke Freeman who takes a perverse delight in disturbing the peaceful community of Sunrise. Freeman's psychotic personality results in the cold-blooded murder of an elderly grocery store owner and an affair with the district attorney's (Richard Anderson) alcoholic and mentally unstable wife (Dianne Foster). Arrested for the murder of the elderly man by the sheriff (Rhodes Reason), the young Freeman is found not guilty after the wife's testimony is undermined by her mental condition.

Even before the episode aired, attention was drawn to it when sponsors withdrew and over two dozen ABC affiliates reacting to a screening refused to broadcast it. "However, the withdrawal of the sponsors resulted in the kind of unsought publicity usually associated with scandals," declared Huggins.

Huggins decided to ditch the original *Macbeth*-inspired title "Told by an Idiot" and tweak the script after objections by the ABC Continuity Acceptance department. A cynical press viewed the events as a publicity stunt with the aim to boost ratings. Huggins reacted by stating, "The show was finished before *Bus Stop* began the season, long before ratings problems were known to exist."

When "A Lion Walks Among Us" aired, the reaction by the majority of critics was scathing. Jack Gould of *The New York Times* (December 4, 1961) referred to the episode as "[a]n hour of dark and sordid ugliness—cheaper than anything yet seen in television...."

It quickly became yet another target for Senator Thomas J. Dodd, a Democrat from Connecticut serving as chairman of the Juvenile Delinquency Subcommittee of the Senate Judiciary Committee. Dodd had targeted one of Huggins' previous shows, *Cheyenne*, in the June 1961 hearings into crime and violence on TV. Warner Bros. vice-president William T. Orr defended the show in Washington D.C. against Dodd's arguments that the violence was pre-meditated by executives to boost ratings and advertising revenue. Dodd's efforts to link violent scenes with juvenile delinquency was met with disdain by Orr. "*Cheyenne* reflects the American tradition of not standing still while somebody kicks us around," claimed Orr.[3]

At FCC hearings on January 24–25, 1962, Senator Dodd questioned ABC-TV president Oliver Treyz about "A Lion Walks Among Us" and why he chose to broadcast the episode despite complaints from the code authority of the National Association of Broadcasting and sponsors. Treyz responded by saying it was "a borderline decision": "I wanted to be careful not to use the blue pencil and strike out a program that would discourage creative people. ABC's Continuity Acceptance department had reviewed the program and accepted it," testified Treyz.[4]

One of the main controversies about the episode was the acquittal of Luke Freeman, despite the fact he still met an untimely death at the hands of the adulterous wife in the final scene. Huggins viewed the story as a morality play that demonstrated "the everpresent existence of pure evil in this world." Huggins' revised title for the episode, based on 1 Peter 5:8, hinted at the Biblical implications of the storyline: "Be sober, be watchful: your adversary the devil, as a roaring lion, walketh about, seeking whom he may devour."

Luke Freeman's gospel singing following the murder in the store together with the superimposed text from 1 Peter was a clear indication of the "devil in disguise" plot. Nineteen-year-old Fabian admitted, "I think if it had been one of Hitchcock's TV shows and with no big name in it, nobody would have heard of it."

Huggins was discouraged even further when he learned that Dodd's Committee based their opinions on watching excerpts rather than the entire episode. Plans to film extra scenes featuring Fabian for a theatrical release in Europe were shelved. "I could see it being advertised over there as a wild kind of thing, and I didn't think it would do me any good, so we turned it down," stated Fabian.[5]

Huggins believed the episode touched a nerve because it "attacked the cult of optimism" that flourishes in America. But even before the segment aired, the networks were running scared of governmental regulation and wilting under pressure from the licensees. Huggins was told to effectively censor his show by abandoning adult and controversial content. As a result, three scripts were removed from the schedule and an episode titled "Make My Bed in Hell" referenced from a Psalm of David was seen as offensive and the title changed.[6]

On March 20, 1962, 43-year-old Oliver Treyz was fired. Leonard Goldenson replaced him as ABC-TV president. As vice-president of 20th Century Television, Huggins had control over all elements of production on successful shows such as *Adventures in Paradise* but clashes with his immediate superior Peter Levathes ultimately led to an increasingly frustrated Huggins settling his contract. According to Huggins, "In June of 1961 Levathes was made studio production head, and a few months later he asked for my resignation. I remained at Fox until my contract was settled on terms I was willing to live with. That was the period when the wind-up doll jokes were a national pastime. For several weeks in early 1962 the favorite wind-up-doll joke in Hollywood and New York was the one about the Roy Huggins doll: You wind it up and it goes to the studio and just sits and sits and sits."

Shortly after Huggins was released from his contract, Levathes was fired and Spyros Skouras was elevated to the redundant position of chairman of the board without duties or authority. A disillusioned Huggins decided to complete the remaining year of his Ph.D. in Political Science and quit the film industry to become a teacher in Political Theory.

"For the six months Roy was at Fox, everything he recommended that they do they didn't do and everything he said they shouldn't do they did," said Swerling. "Roy said he realized after six months it was an exercise in futility and he resigned. That's when he went beck to UCLA.

Roy was a frustrated mentor-teacher-professor. It was a role in life he had always wanted to play. His bad experience at Fox triggered that but it didn't come out of the blue. He had considered it prior to that."

But when, in the summer of 1962, Huggins was offered $5,000 a week by Lew Wasserman to rescue a new high profile 90-minute TV Western titled *The Virginian* from first season cancellation, Huggins couldn't refuse.

10

GUILTY UNTIL PROVEN INNOCENT

"To be yourself in a world that is constantly trying to make you something else is the greatest accomplishment."—Ralph Waldo Emerson (1803–1882)

Shortly before joining *The Virginian*, Huggins' concept for *The Fugitive* had been pitched to executives at the Beverly Hills Hotel following the initial rejection by Peter Lavathes while he was vice-president of television production at 20th Century–Fox. The concept was simple. An innocent man, convicted of killing his wife, escapes and is pursued by the police while attempting to locate the real murderer. Jo Swerling, Jr. tells the story of the evolution and selling of the concept.[1]

"When Roy was the fair-haired boy at Warner Bros he became friends with Burt Nodella, the development executive for ABC. Warner Bros. had an exclusive contract with ABC to provide programming. He phoned Roy and said, "Leonard Goldenson is coming to town next week to talk about development. It would really help me look good if you would come and pitch something."

"I'm out of the business and going to school. This isn't something I want to do," replied Roy.

"Please, Roy, as a favor to me for old times sake, come in and toss out an idea or two. I beg you."

So Roy figured to himself, "What the hell, I'll go in there and pitch *The Fugitive*." There were around eight ABC executives in the Beverly Hills Hotel suite, including Goldenson, Everett Erlick, Julius Barnathan, Daniel Melnick, Burt Nodella and a guy who was the head of programming for ABC on the West Coast. He was a character. A guy from Mississippi who complained about *Adventures in Paradise* by saying it had too many niggers in it. Niggers meaning Polynesians.

There was a silence after Roy pitched *The Fugitive*. Normally in those sort of situations, everyone turns to the head guy to see what he is going to say. But in this case they were so sure this was a bad idea they all wanted to get their words in first.

One guy said "Roy, we can't put that show on the air. It's un–American. We have a system of justice that's the best in the world and here you are telling the audience every week that it's flawed and this innocent man is running for his life and the cop is the bad guy."

Julius Barnathan joined in and said, "Yeah. How do we really know that he's innocent?"

"Well, we know that because the narrator says so," replied Roy.

Barnathan replied, "Well, how do we know he's telling the truth?"

"Well, Roy, I gotta go catch a plane," declared Tom Moore.

These are all actual quotes. They all turned to Leonard Goldenson. "You know, Roy, that is the best fucking idea I have heard of for a television series in my life. When do you want to go to work?"

Roy answered, "I can't do it. If I leave the graduate school, they'll never let me back in. I will license it to you and somebody else can produce it."

Quinn Martin was under contract to ABC and quite well thought of after his success producing *The Untouchables*. Roy licensed *The Fugitive* over to them and made a deal with Martin that he would receive creator royalty rights, a percentage of profits, owner book rights, dramatic rights and movie rights. Martin's organization was too small for them to hide the profits the way big studios do, so Roy actually received his contracted share on the back end on that show. That threw off a lot of money for him."

In 1954, osteopath Dr. Sam Sheppard was convicted of the murder of his wife and sentenced to life in prison. Sheppard maintained his innocence, claiming "a bushy-haired intruder" beat his wife to death. Former ABC programming executive Daniel Melnick and Sheppard's defense attorney F. Lee Bailey both claimed this was the inspiration for Huggins' concept.[2] Swerling Jr. disagreed:

> Roy told me his initial idea was to come up with a classic Western hero in a contemporary setting. Part of that process was delineating what are the defining characteristics of the classic Western hero. Using *Shane* as an example, the classic Western hero had a basic sense of right and wrong but was a drifter. He went from job to job getting involved in people's lives and usually helping them out before moving on. He has no family, no significant other, no steady job. The character of Shane was an accurate description of Richard Kimble.
>
> Roy asked himself, "How do I do a series about a classic Western hero in a contemporary setting because the audience will tend to dislike him. They'll ask why he's a drifter and doesn't have a family or a job. The audience wouldn't be able to relate to him." The solution to that problem was to make him an innocent victim of circumstance. Roy then came up with the idea of a guy accused of killing his wife who is being pursued, forcing him to move from place to place using assumed names. He doesn't want people to know he's a doctor but if somebody gets hurt he can't ignore them. They can root for a guy like that.
>
> When Roy licensed the show and turned it over to Quinn Martin, Janssen was Martin's first choice. Roy knew David socially and agreed it was a great idea. He had already used Janssen when he was an unknown in a 1957 episode of *Conflict* called "The Money" (1:12). Roy also used Janssen in *Adventures in Paradise* and as an ex-boxer on *Follow the Sun*."

Huggins' original six-page series format dated September 19, 1960, began with scenes that would later serve as the inspiration for the opening introductory sequence to each episode of the *Fugitive* television series. It is night. A passenger train races toward the camera as the scene fades into the interior of a passenger car and a close-up of a "prematurely gray-haired man in his mid–thirties." He gazes out of the window but his mind is looking inward. A narrator announces the man is "Richard Kimble" as the camera pulls back to reveal two men seated behind him.

The narrator outlines the back story to Kimble's predicament. He is returning from a fourth failed appeal for his conviction of the murder of his wife Helen Kimble. But Kimble knows the real murderer is "a gaunt red-haired man" he saw fleeing from the scene. Kimble has only sixteen days to live before his July 18 execution. As the train continues to speed along the tracks, it suddenly turns onto a spur and crashes. Out of the darkness stumbles Richard Kimble. In shock and confused, he gathers his senses and runs toward freedom.

Huggins' notes read, "In a heightened and imaginative sense Kimble's life as a fugitive will relate to deep and responsive drives, needs and fantasies in the American audience, not the least is Kimble lives with alienation and anxiety.... At the heart of the series is the preoccupation with guilt and salvation which has been called the American Theme."

Huggins' 1960 series format also included references to the character later identified as Lieutenant Philip Gerard and his connection to Javert from Victor Hugo's *Les Miserables*. "One man in the State Attorney's office has been assigned [to apprehend Kimble] and at least in one episode, and probably more than one will deal with the pursuit himself. The story of Jean Valjean and his Javert has not remained a classic for insignificant reasons, and the best will be distilled from those reasons."[3]

Martin acknowledged that the weekly television series would be an updated *Les Miserables* with Kimble (Janssen) substituting for Jean Valjean and Lieutenant Gerard (Barry Morse) replacing Valjean's nemesis police inspector Javert. "Our Jean Valjean," explained Martin, "has to be an educated man, one with social standing. And he had to be the type of person who would win audience sympathy immediately."[4]

Martin hired Stanford Whitmore to write the pilot episode "Fear in a Desert City" (1:01) but after reading the script, Huggins insisted on two revisions. The introduction of a diary that Kimble kept in his pocket and a permanent alias would make it easier for Lt. Gerard to track Kimble. Huggins knew with each weekly episode, Kimble had to start from scratch, leaving no traces on his trail. The diary was omitted and the "permanent" alias of James Lincoln was only used in the pilot episode. Filming began on "Fear in a Desert City" at the bus terminal in Tucson, Arizona, on November 27, 1962. On December 6 the epilogue scene of Kimble walking into the distance with suitcase in hand and the railroad crossing sign prominent in the foreground was filmed at a parking lot off Romaine Street between Formosa and LaBrea in West Hollywood. Kimble running through the stream following the train wreck would be filmed at the Fern Dell section of Griffith Park in Los Angeles one day later (December 7). On the final day of filming on Monday, December 10, the opening title scene of Kimble gazing out of the train window with Lt. Philip Gerard (Morse) by his side was filmed.[5]

One aspect of the script Huggins did agree on was Whitmore's introduction of a "one-armed man" to replace the "red-haired man" from Huggins' 1960 series format. The "red-haired man" was seen as too similar to the "bushy-haired man" described in real life by Dr. Sam Sheppard. Huggins had always denied any influence from the notorious murder. On July 4, 1954, Marilyn Reese Sheppard, the pregnant wife of osteopathic physician Sam Sheppard, was found bludgeoned to death in their Cleveland home. Sheppard claimed to have fought an intruder who escaped the murder scene. His trial received mass media coverage and despite Sheppard's pleas of innocence he was found guilty of murder and sentenced to life in Ohio Penitentiary. His conviction was overturned following a 1966 appeal. Some claimed the popularity of the *Fugitive* television show played a factor.

The consensus of public opinion saw the Sheppard murder case and Hugo's *Les Miserables* as the strongest influences on *The Fugitive* but in February 1965, author and screenwriter David Goodis sued United Artists Television and ABC network for $500,000 for copyright infringement, claiming the premise of *The Fugitive* was based on his novel *Dark Passage*. His novel had been serialized in *The Saturday Evening Post* from July 20 to September 7, 1946, and later adapted into a film starring Humphrey Bogart and Lauren Bacall.

The response was, "After the film was exhibited in theaters and shown on television, Warner Brothers in 1956 assigned contract rights to defendant United Artists and that United Artists produced a television film series. *The Fugitive* was broadcast in weekly installments by defendant American Broadcasting Co."

At a deposition on December 9, 1966, Goodis confirmed that *Dark Passage* had been serialized in *The Saturday Evening Post*. On January 7, 1967, Goodis passed away from a stroke. The case of copyright infringement continued but was dismissed by the Federal District Court on the grounds that *Dark Passage* had fallen into the public domain and that the contract between Goodis and Warner Bros. "clearly conveyed the right to film a film series like *The Fugitive*."

An appeal followed from the Goodis Estate and in November 1972 they received $12,000 in full settlement (the same amount Goodis had received from Curtis Publishing Co. for the rights to serialize his novel in 1946). The attorney admitted the suit had nothing more than nuisance value.[6] Producer and studio head Frank Price experienced many frivolous nuisance lawsuits during his career:

> To me, it's most likely just another nuisance suit. And they irritate me no end. I had to give too many dreary depositions in my career. But it's not unusual for claims to come out of the woodwork whenever there's a success. Sometimes the claims are paid off with a small amount when it's cheaper than lawyer fees. If the claim were legitimate, we would have heard and Roy wouldn't have remained in control of the rights. Suits like this are so frequent probably because courts are lousy places to determine anything that involves creative matters, so lawyers pushing such a claim know they've got a chance.
>
> I am completely positive that Roy did not take his idea for *The Fugitive* from this property *Dark Passage*. But, even if he had, situations and plot lines are not protected by copyright laws. Proof of plagiarism would have required that the characters be the same and have the same names. Identical dialogue must be employed. Any smart thief would make sure that those things are changed. The plaintiff lawyers rely on the fact that juries are unpredictable. You never know how they'll decide, so settle. So they bring action after action, losing some but winning others."[7]

Huggins' recurring name on the credits gave the misleading impression he was creatively involved with the weekly series. But in reality Huggins had distanced himself following the selling of his format and his input into the pilot episode. The main characters and basic premise was the creation of Huggins but the ongoing success of the weekly series was due to executive producer Quinn Martin, producer Alan A. Armer, a talented team of actors headed by David Janssen, writers and directors. Lesser talents could easily have taken Huggins' creation down an uninspired path to early cancellation. Martin turned Huggins' original concept into one of the best-loved series of the 1960s.

But unknown to the general public, *The Fugitive* had been in serious trouble during the first season, as Huggins learned from Leonard Goldenson and Lew Wasserman during lunch at the Universal commissary. Wasserman told Huggins that *The Fugitive* had come very close to cancellation and had been "a terrible public relations problem" but added with a laugh, "Now everyone in town's imitating it."[8]

Janssen had been offered $500,000 to return for a fifth season but turned it down, stating, "I think it was better to leave at the top. I felt, as Quinn did, that we had developed as much as was possible with the show; there was nothing new we could attempt as to character. To do another year would have meant trying to rejuvenate our interest. Why try? None of us was about to go broke. So we ended it."[9]

The end result of Janssen's decision was a two-part episode that aired in August 1967, where Kimble finally tracks the one-armed murderer (William Raisch) to an amusement park. The conclusion to *The Fugitive* was viewed by an unprecedented 72 percent of the television audience, the largest audience share of all time up to that date. Huggins was pleased

Huggins expresses mock shock and horror at the news headline stating that the "Fugitive" has been captured (courtesy John Huggins).

with the final product. "I thought Quinn Martin did a fine job. On the times that I saw it I felt that it was a little different from what I would have done but maybe it was better."[10]

Meanwhile at Universal-Revue studios in early 1962, Charles Marquis Warren had been assigned to *The Virginian* as executive producer based on his success with the early seasons of the TV western *Rawhide*. The original choice for executive producer of *The Virginian*, Richard Irving, wasn't considered a "name" producer and was quickly dropped, thus setting in motion a series of events that would soon lure Huggins back into television.

With Warren's extensive experience writing, producing and directing "B" westerns, he appeared to be a wise choice as executive producer on *The Virginian*. But appearances can be deceiving and it was soon apparent that Warren was taking *The Virginian* in the wrong direction. With *The Virginian* replacing the highly successful *Wagon Train* which had moved from NBC to ABC, first season cancellation wasn't an option. Warren was replaced with Huggins before the first episode aired. The situation was serious enough for MCA Universal president Lew Wasserman to agree to Huggins' demand of $1,000 a day for thirty days work.[11] According to Frank Price,

> The network and the studio were alarmed by the footage that was emerging from the Charles Marquis Warren–produced episodes. That's why, in a panic, they brought in Roy as a consultant. He looked at the episodes, which were in various stages of production, and agreed with the studio and the network. The episodes varied widely in quality. Some making little sense, others showcasing the guest stars to the detriment of the series regulars, plus many other assorted flaws. The continuing cast stars were generally peripheral to the story, so you had no reason to care about them in the telling of the story. That is a severe error in making a series because people watch your show week after week because they like your central characters, and tune in. I was called in by Roy when it came time to try to repair, rewrite, reedit, and fix the episodes." [Price, who wrote the format for *The Virginian*, later succeeded Huggins as executive producer.]
>
> Roy first used me as a writer to write new and additional scenes, often replacing what had previously been shot. We screened most of these segments together, analyzing their flaws and designing solutions. He liked my thoughts and scenes that I wrote as part of the repairs. He then asked me to work with him and I became supervising producer on the series, on those episodes I didn't produce.
>
> We had to do a lot of work very quickly to turn these episodes into acceptable broadcast material. Roy was brilliant and decisive in carrying out the task. Universal and NBC made a fortunate choice when they brought him in. Some producers would have concluded that not much could be done to save it and they would have put Band Aids on the patient. Roy put the patient on the table and proceed to do heart, lung and liver transplants, then followed with a facelift ... while the clock was ticking, as air dates approached.

One of the most important tasks in rescuing the Warren footage was creative editing. Price explained,

> In the year I worked for Roy, I learned how to effectively edit film from him. I learned more from him in that short time than I'd learned in all the years preceding. I asked him where he had learned these techniques and his approach. He said he learned from Bill Orr. I asked where Bill Orr learned. He told me, "Jack Warner, Orr's father-in-law." One of the original moguls.
>
> What I learned from Roy was to approach a rough cut like writing the first draft of a script. View the film before you with a cold dispassion, cutting out anything that doesn't work, no matter how much you loved it in the script or how much it cost to shoot. If it doesn't work, because of performance problems or interpretation problem, lose it. Once you've removed the shit, now start through the film trying to improve the scenes that survive your critical editing process. The editing process becomes like writing a new draft with film. It's amazing how much can be done

to improve a picture if you are subjecting it to the critical test of what works and what fails, and correcting it. I found the skills I learned from Roy invaluable for the rest of my career.

Huggins' long-time friend Richard Bare was handed the task of shooting new scenes to be added to the twelve hours of Warren footage and re-shooting close-ups with new dialogue that was carefully matched so it could be edited into the original footage. Bare recalled, "Roy would have the film editors cut out every scene that didn't meet with his approval. Then he would write new scenes and I would take them down to the stage and shoot them. Some parts of scenes could be salvaged, and in those cases all that was required was to substitute new dialogue by re-shooting the close-ups of the various characters, carefully matching them with the original film, so that viewers would never know the extent of our patch job."[12]

Another major problem with Warren's footage was the timeline. Price had set the time period for *The Virginian* at the end of the West in his original format. He thought the concept of a series occurring at the end of an era might provide interesting storylines. But Price wasn't pleased with Warren's approach that saw the Virginian, Trampas and Steve fighting at San Juan Hill in Cuba in one episode and back at Shiloh Ranch in Wyoming the following week. "The Warren episodes handled my concept poorly," Price declared. "Roy decided, with my concurrence, that it was just a confusing distraction and we established the period just before the Great Blizzard that wiped out the fortunes of all those titled English gentlemen hanging out at the Cattlemens Club in Cheyenne."

Having successfully rescued the Warren episodes, Huggins agreed to take charge of filming new episodes beginning with "The Accomplice" (1:13), although the opening scenes at Trampas' birthday party still showed the 1897–1898 dateline. The episode guest-starred Bette Davis as spinster Delia Miller in a story focused on Trampas (Doug McClure) being arrested and tried for attempted murder and a $60,000 bank robbery that took place one year earlier in Rocky Point. Miller is blackmailing the real robber, posing as reporter Malcolm Brent (Lin McCarthy), for $10,000.

"The episode was filmed before resolving the issue of changing the time period," said Price. "The network wasn't thrilled with the Bette Davis episode but it was acceptable to them. Frankly it was pedestrian melodrama, relieved by the presence of Davis, but we needed to make the air date. Our mission was to have good roles to attract guest stars but make the episodes as much as possible about our continuing leads. Each episode had its own degree of success. Creative endeavors are seldom perfect."

The process from script to screen began with the screenwriter, says Price:

> We used freelance professional screen writers. All of us knew various writers and had good or bad relationships with them. The good ones we would reach out to. Some of them would be busy. Agents would suggest new writers and submit writing samples. So we'd try somebody we hadn't worked with before. Different writers performed well on different shows. If I found that a writer had a good feel for the characters and format of a show, I'd try to repeat them. The advantage of repeating with a writer, even a borderline choice, is that you're aware of that writer's flaws and can compensate to a degree.
>
> The writer might come in with an idea for an episode, which we might like. Or we might suggest an idea of our own. Once we agreed on a premise, then the writer would do an outline. If we liked that, then we'd send him into the script phase, with notes from the outline. Rewrites would start after the first draft was turned in. Sometimes the network was involved in the development process, approving the outline and the final script.
>
> This process could cover two to three months, or longer. Getting a script right could stretch

the process considerably more. Generally it's two to six months to go from conception to production. I've written a script over a weekend and put it into production a week or two later, but that's under crisis conditions. And during the first season of *The Virginian* we were often under crisis conditions.

The hectic schedule and pressure of rescuing *The Virginian* from early cancellation sometimes resulted in frayed nerves. Price continued:

> I once was with Roy in a script conference with Gene Roddenberry on a *Virginian* script during the first season crisis period. Gene had turned in a disappointing first draft. To my amazement, Roy berated Gene for turning in a subpar, unprofessional script. He went through it page and page, outraged that Gene had not done better quality work, accusing him of "kicking it out with his feet." I had never seen a writer treated so roughly. To my amazement, Gene bore it all and agreed to throw away the draft and do a new one. Generally I handle writers with patience and understanding. But I learned from Roy that sometimes you have to use a two-by-four to get someone's understanding and cooperation. I think that, without the rough handling, Gene would have been highly defensive about his work and unwilling to fix it. I think he agreed to the rewrite to bring an end to Roy's intense criticism of his work. Roy was genuinely outraged that, in his opinion, Gene had turned in a carelessly done draft that was not up to proper professional standards. I think Roy chose the times that his display of temper needed to be used but I never saw Roy lose his temper with underlings."

Huggins contributed stories to the first season under his pen names John Francis O'Mara and Thomas Fitzroy, dedicated to his sons John and Thomas and his Irish heritage. Price also contributed ideas to episodes as the producer. Network deadlines and a contract that demanded delivery of 30 75 minute episodes for the first season sometimes forced Huggins and Price to look to existing Universal properties to ease the pressure.

"Duel at Shiloh" (1:15), featuring the story of how Steve Hill (Gary Clarke) came to work at Shiloh Ranch, was an adaptation of Universal-International's *Man Without a Star* (1955) starring Kirk Douglas in the role played by Brian Keith in the *Virginian* episode. "The Judgment" (1:17) was an adaptation of the Universal-International feature *Day of the Badman* (1958) which had been written by Lawrence Roman. Clu Gulager played outlaw Jack Carewe, who threatens the townsfolk of Medicine Bow following the sentencing to death of his brother by Judge Garth (Lee J. Cobb). Price revealed,

> I worked out the ending we used. When the jury, guided by Judge Garth, finds the Carewe brother guilty in spite of the gang's threats, there arises a problem. If the brother is put in jail to await hanging, the gang has time to break him out, thus starting the story over again. To prevent this, I had the hangman waiting and when the death sentence is pronounced, Judge Garth and a few brave townsmen take the brother directly to the scaffold where the sentence is carried out. End of story. Gang is leaderless and fades away. Roy was appalled, but didn't have a better story solution.
>
> The advantage of the immediate hanging is that it gave the gang no time to react and take action. Plus, our ending was highly dramatic and unexpected. Roy would have insisted on changing it if it hadn't worked so well. I had no fixed philosophical or political position on capital punishment, so I only cared whether or not it worked dramatically. My only position now, after many years, is that if you ever have to do it for the most heinous and potentially repeatable crimes, make sure the person being executed is proved guilty beyond any doubt whatsoever. And frankly, the Carewe brothers were despicable characters that I wanted the audience to have the emotional satisfaction or catharsis of seeing one of the brothers get his just deserts. Better ending.

Historical accuracy became an important aspect of *The Virginian* when Huggins and later, Frank Price took control of the show. Price says,

I think careful attention to authenticity and detail makes for a better show that viewers may not consciously be aware of, but on an unconscious or subliminal level they are affected. I remember the response we got when I took the needed time in one episode to make soap in the authentic way at Shiloh Ranch. The audience loved learning about a subject that was totally foreign to them. That wasn't a subliminal reaction of course, but the scene rang true because of its authenticity.

I don't think Roy would have done something obviously historically inaccurate, but he didn't have the same focus on the historical roots that I did. I enjoyed history and I enjoyed journeying back into another era. So I always wanted to know what the facts were in that time. It also concerned me that western writers cannibalized from westerns they'd seen in their past. That made for too many stock situations that were repeated nearly identically in story after story.

I found it useful to learn the facts about why the cattlemen and the sheepmen were in conflict. What was the cause of the conflict between the big ranchers and the small farmers? I found I could makes a drama more interesting if I understood the facts and everyone's authentic motivation. So I researched the Johnson County War and other historical conflicts pretty well. Women in Wyoming had the vote in the Wyoming Constitution. That was a problem when they were admitted to the union. That was resolved by having their votes not count in national elections. As I recall, a couple of women were mayors and judges in Wyoming early on. The draconian divorce laws of Illinois furnished me with a good story of a woman on the run from her ex-husband. Often there weren't extradition laws between states, even counties. So putting a prisoner in prison in another state in that period would be problematic. Can a state hold someone who has not been found guilty of violating its laws? Who pays for keeping the prisoner? Have the two state legislatures passed laws authorizing such? I liked checking the laws because it often added an authenticity to a story that we'd never have thought of otherwise. I felt an audience had a better chance to understand what was at issue if the real facts were presented.

With the first season of *The Virginian* coming to a successful conclusion, Huggins' task was complete but instead of returning to UCLA full-time to complete his Ph.D. in Political Science he accepted the offer of executive producer on Universal's *Kraft Suspense Theatre*. "I think he intended to executive produce *Kraft* and *The Virginian* while I actually did the producing of *The Virginian*. But NBC and Universal decided to make me executive producer of *The Virginian*, so I was not reporting to Roy, and he was free to concentrate on *Kraft Suspense Theatre*," stated Price.

11

Escape from Tomorrow

"How a person masters his fate is more important than what that fate is."—Wilhelm von Humboldt (1767–1835)

"In the early days of television," says Frank Price, "everything on the networks was broadcast live. No film. Except, of course, those live shows were filmed on 16mm film, taken off the TV tube image and the 'kinescopes' were mailed out for broadcast a week later in those parts of the country not connected by the coaxial cable. Continuing character series were hard to do live. Anthologies were the way to go. There were many drama series. *Studio One, Philco Playhouse, Kraft, U.S. Steel Hour, Climax, Playhouse 90*, etc. And a daytime series that I was story editor of, *Matinee Theatre*. We also had half-hour anthologies that were a carryover from radio such as *Suspense, Danger, The Web* and *Lux Video Theatre*.

"When early series on film arrived, they had an immediate impact. *Dragnet*, for instance, came on opposite *Suspense*, and gobbled up most of the audience. Some westerns grew out of *Conflict* and achieved impressive ratings. The anthologies suddenly became an endangered species. One year, practically all were cancelled due to low ratings and 26 new westerns came to dominate television."[1]

Although the anthology was fast disappearing from television, NBC persevered with the format and announced a new anthology drama series in 1963 named *Kraft Suspense Theatre*. Huggins expressed his desire for strong storylines.

"It doesn't matter what we say—we can in fact make a different statement each week. Even contradict ourselves," declared Huggins. "A few years ago in New York there were two stage plays on the same street making contradictory statements and both were hits. One was *A Streetcar Named Desire* with Blanche DuBois saying that if you live by illusions you will be destroyed. The other was *Harvey* saying that if you don't live by illusions you cannot be very happy. The important thing is to make that human statement with validity and to make it dramatically."[2]

Price added, "I think Roy liked the freedom of the anthology format. He had experience with it doing *Conflict*. Also, there was the still existing prestige factor, a carryover from the great days of the anthologies. Roy would have felt complimented that an important sponsor like Kraft wanted to do a show and they wanted him to produce it. There were solid reasons to tackle it. I don't think the risk of failure was high. At worst it might get average ratings. There was important money built into the budget to attract stars. Roy cast some good names on *Kraft*."

Jo Swerling, Jr.'s television career began in 1957 as a coordinator–assistant producer on *Restless Gun* with John Payne followed by *M Squad* (1957) with Lee Marvin, *Markham* with Ray Milland, and *Wagon Train* with Ward Bond and Robert Horton.

In 1960, I was assigned as a coordinator to the weekly anthology, *Thriller*, produced initially by Hubbell Robinson, with Boris Karloff as host. *Thriller* was taken over by producer William Frye after the first few episodes, and I worked with Bill, during which time I also wrote and directed all of the Boris Karloff lead-ins and lead-outs on the show.

After *Thriller*, in 1963, I was assigned as associate producer to producer Frank Telford on *Kraft Suspense Theater*. The opening two-part episode, "The Case Against Paul Ryker," starring Lee Marvin, was released in theaters in 1968 under the title *Sergeant Ryker* after Lee Marvin won the Oscar for his role in *Cat Ballou*. Oddly, *Sergeant Ryker* was Universal's biggest moneymaker in 1968, netting about one million dollars for the company. The reason it was the studio's biggest moneymaker that year was that it was their only moneymaker. All their other theatrical features lost money. Shortly after I was assigned to *Kraft Suspense Theater*, Roy was brought in to take the series over. He promoted me to producer, and the rest, as they say, is history.

Roy Huggins was more of a father figure to me. He was my mentor. Three producers worked under him. Robert Altman, Robert Blees and Frank Telford. I was an associate producer to Frank. He requested me because he had worked on a show with Douglas Benton. Doug was a dear friend of mine and I got to know Frank through Doug. Roy was finding it difficult to control the three producers. Altman, Blees and Telford were a handful for Roy. They were all journeymen. Huggins admired Altman greatly but they disagreed on how to tell a story. He decided that if he wanted the show done to his satisfaction without endless discussions and arguments, he would be better off producing it himself and building a staff.

"The End of the World Baby" (1:03) was a *Kraft Suspense Theatre* starring Katherine Crawford and Peter Lorre. Roy used to tell me, "The least important person on a movie set is the director. Without a writer you've got nothing, without a cameraman you've got nothing, without actors you've got nothing, but you could do without a director. If all the rest of the people are good, they can direct themselves. Someday I'm going to have the chance to prove this."

He wasn't saying a good director isn't important. There used to be a mystique about "New York directors." These were the guys doing the shows that were produced in New York such as *The Defenders*. These shows were considered to be of higher quality than those shows that were shot in Hollywood. Irvin Kershner was hired. He was a respected director who had worked on *Naked City*. After three days of shooting he was two days behind the six-day schedule to complete the episode. The executives in the Black Tower were furious and wanted him replaced. Roy was liking the footage and reluctant to replace him. There was nothing wrong with his work, he was just killing us financially.

After three days the executives told Roy to replace him. Roy removed Kershner but did not replace him. Roy instead told the actors to rehearse scenes and block them with a cameraman. The first assistant director, who had never directed anything, would say "Action" or "Cut." The actors would collectively decide if they needed another take. Roy said, "When you've rehearsed and are ready to shoot the scene, call me and I'll come down to the set. I'll watch the rehearsal and if there are any notes or comments I'll tell you and then go shoot it."

The rest of the show was shot on schedule and you could not tell where Kershner's work left off and the collective, combined efforts of everyone else started. Kershner's agent called and said, "Irvin wants to see a screening of the episode. The purpose of which is to determine if we wants to take his name off of it or not." He saw the picture and elected to keep his name on it.[3]

Huggins' daughter Katherine Crawford initially entered the acting profession with some reluctance:

Daddy is the one who persuaded me to go into acting. I had always been in the drama productions in school but at 15 I was already one of the top three junior photographic fashion models in Los Angeles (*Seventeen* magazine, etc.) and it was something I felt strong in. One day Daddy said to me that I really "didn't want to be a model." I was surprised. It seemed to me he didn't understand the success I was having and could have with it. I planned on going, after graduation, to New York and Europe and having a very good life until I wanted to get married at around 28. That was my plan. For a long time he kept trying and I kept resisting. I did some acting in TV shows and commercials that came to me through my the modeling, and still held my position. Finally I worked with a director who created such a great experience of the process of acting in film that it changed my mind completely. So I completely flipped my position and tried out for the Royal Academy of Dramatic Art in London and was accepted. A week later Screen Gems offered me a contract with them (they were a very important company then) and I turned them down in favor of RADA.

After graduation from RADA I had been working for a while as a guest star and had reached a level of success and reputation in the industry. At that point, Daddy said to me that he wanted to break the rule we had agreed to at the beginning about never working together (in order to avoid a nepotism charge), since it was turning out to mean that everyone else could hire me, except him. He said he had a role I was perfect for and he wanted me to do it. I agreed. He had to resist the pressure to put Tuesday Weld in the role instead of me, as she was fighting for it. Nevertheless my reputation was good, and he held his ground.

This particular story was somewhat risqué and European, with an edgy "style" to it. It would star Peter Lorre, Gig Young, Nina Foch, and me. A very "big" cast for television. The cast members were all very warm and friendly with me, but as usual, because of my shyness, I didn't have very much interaction with them. Working on scenes is not usually a time to socialize other than short comments and questions about the work at hand.

I noticed from the beginning that there were problems with Peter. He was very pleasant and kind but he was suffering from age-related issues and was not well. He had caretakers who helped him to walk to and from the set very slowly, over long distances, he needed pills at specific times which was apparently very difficult for him and took more long periods to complete, so in general the entire production was being held up for long periods nearly constantly. In television you don't have that time. It's not like in motion pictures where most of the actor's time is spent waiting for the lights to be set. In TV there is often no rehearsing other than for blocking. So these time delays were a big problem.

The director, Irvin Kershner, seemed to me to be very unhappy in general. In fairness, being badly behind schedule can do that to a director (and who knows, maybe *he* wanted Tuesday Weld too!). He rarely related to me. We just worked. He was not warm with anyone that I saw, and with the continuous time delays he had reason to be upset, so I never took it personally. But I never felt comfortable with him. My scenes went fine as far as I knew. He never corrected me, and I was fast, so if you ignored his tone and body language, everything was all right. He never commented on my performance or asked for changes. My performance was my own.

On the fifth day we were more than two days behind. On a seven-day shoot that's disaster. So the director was fired. That was big. It never happens in television. And instead of hiring a new director, my father took over. Oh! All right ... I heard about it from the assistant director, as everyone else did. I hardly noticed when he came on set because he remained remote. He and I never talked while I was working normally, or even talked about my performances, and I wasn't sure how it would feel having him behind the camera. I had a couple of the most pivotal scenes still left to do. In one, I was to seduce Gig Young and finally toss him off the parapet of the castle balcony to his death on the cliffs far below. I think we both were uncomfortable with the situation!

For my scenes, Daddy went to the back of the stage and watched on the monitor, sending the AD forward to direct. During the seduction part of the scene, the AD was called back to talk to my father and when he returned, he came forward to me as I stood feeling pretty naked on the top edge of the "castle wall" in a skimpy leotard. He looked up at me and beckoned me to lean forward so he could whisper in my ear, and said, "Roy says be sex*ier*." I had to ask him to repeat it to be sure that's what he said. Oh dear! I turned pale. I had sort of thought I *was* being sexy. I hadn't the foggiest notion how to be sex*ier*. I was shy and 19. What did I know? But whatever I did next, they printed the next shot, so it obviously *was* sex*ier*. Okay! Hard to do in front of your father.

After completion of filming, I did hear that "Hollywood" was talking about the show. The European style and subject matter, the firing, Roy taking over, the delays, Tuesday Weld being jilted in favor of me. It had become the subject of the month and most in Hollywood couldn't wait to witness the car wreck when it finally came on TV.

I had, in the meantime, moved on to work on other shows, as usual. The morning after the show ran, I got a call around 8:30 in the morning from my agent. People in Hollywood, other than actors and directors, aren't even up at that hour so this was odd. My agent told me that Universal's phones were ringing off the hook to find out who the "new girl" was. And even Ross Hunter, the famous producer of Sandra Dee and Doris Day films, had already called Monique James (the MCA casting head) to say that I was a star and to get me the right roles. But most importantly, Frank Price had already called at that early hour to cast me in *both* of his current shows.

The show was a huge hit. It was fabulous and everyone in Hollywood saw it. Daddy was vindicated. Though for me personally that wasn't the most meaningful thing that happened as a result of that show. One of the people who tuned in to watch the disaster was Frank Price. His watching it changed both our lives. The following morning I went in to thank him ... but that's another story.[4]

All anthology shows depended on "name" actors to boost ratings. *Kraft Suspense Theatre* included Tippi Hedren, Jeffrey Hunter, Mickey Rooney, Lee Marvin, Richard Crenna, Jack Klugman and Gena Rowlands.

"'A Cruel and Unusual Night' (1:28) starred Ronald Reagan," recalled Swerling. "He played a judge who had put a guy on Death Row. The guy escapes, kidnaps the judge and places him in a cage in an abandoned warehouse. He threatens to kill him within a week. He wants to put the judge through the same agony that he was put through."

Huggins commented,

> Its intention was to dramatize the sheer horror of waiting to be executed. On the final day of shooting I was notified from the set that Ronnie was refusing to read one of his lines, on the grounds that he was "damned if he was going to be a mouthpiece for Roy Huggins' propaganda against capital punishment!"
>
> I was somewhat surprised because the line was in the script when Mr. Reagan accepted the part, but I checked the scene, decided the line was not vital, and sent down word to strike it and get on with the production. Six months later I ran into Mr. Reagan at dinner at the home of a mutual friend, and I started to joke with him about the incident.
>
> I suddenly found myself hearing Mr. Reagan saying that he hadn't decided exactly how he felt about capital punishment, that it was a sensitive and complex subject.... And that was how I learned that Ronald Reagan was running for something or other."[5]

"After *Kraft Suspense Theatre* completed its run and everyone went their separate ways I stayed with Roy. Altman's assistant Bob Eggenweiler followed Altman, leaving just Joel Rogosin and myself," stated Swerling Jr. Price says, "The anthologies tried to hold on a bit, *Kraft Suspense* being an example. Kraft liked having a show with its brand name up front. There was a prestige factor involved. *GE Theatre* lasted well into the 1960s. Ultimately the cost of shows became too great for any single sponsor to bear the load, so the form disappeared. And the ratings of the anthologies were too undependable."

Huggins saw changing attitudes of the audience as a big factor in the disappearance of the anthology format. "The audience is the most important factor in television entertainment. The mass audience resists the new, the innovative, the provocative, the disturbing, the controversial, the subtle. That audience has demonstrated that it wants continuing characters, preferably ones that are lovable. Hence anthology shows, which could offer a variety of characters, locales and situations each week, became difficult to sell."[6]

Swerling Jr. continued,

Following his departure from *Kraft Suspense Theatre*, Huggins was offered the position of vice-president of Universal Television. After a short time in the job, Huggins realized his future lay in producing and writing and in 1964 he formed his own independent company, Public Arts Inc. A contractual deal with Universal provided payment for his services as a producer and gave him an interest in the net profits of any series he created.

It was a corporate name for Roy Huggins. There was no staff or employees. Just Roy Huggins who was the owner. Once he formed Public Arts, he eschewed credit from that point on. So he adopted pseudonyms. Depending on what was the level of activity under his Public Arts banner, he would delegate work on various projects. He would view all the episodes but he wouldn't be sitting in the cutting room on a day-to-day basis working on the editing. If the final product was acceptable, he would trust the people working on it. If he felt it was going south, he would step in and make changes.

At the request of Jennings Lang, Huggins created and produced a follow-up show to the internationally successful *The Fugitive*. Jennings was the first to say he was ripping off *The Fugitive* but he said to Roy, "If you're involved, it's okay to rip yourself off."

Run for Your Life was a "man-on-the-run" concept with a twist. Paul Bryan was running from his own fate, having been told by his doctor he had only two years left to live. Ben Gazzara played Bryan. I wrote the format for *Run for Your Life* based on an original idea by Jennings Lang. Jennings presented his idea to Roy. A successful guy who's fairly young finds out he only has two years to live. The audience discovers through the narrator that it's a mistake. The medical reports were mixed up and it's a case of mistaken identity. The guy doesn't really have two years to live but he thinks he does.

Roy and I went back to the office laughing. "That's the worst idea I ever heard," declared Roy. He suggested we make it for real that the guy has only has two years left to live. Roy then asked me to write a format because we had to hire a writer for the pilot. This was 1965. We decided the guy would be a lawyer and I handed my completed format to Luther Davies. He wrote the pilot and didn't receive any separation of rights. Once we had the format, Roy was stuck for a story for the pilot episode. This was rare for him but he was having difficulty. I had read an article in *Vogue* magazine about a type of woman in Europe. Affluent, beautiful, young and smarter than men. Chicerinos. I brought the article to Roy and said, "What if our hero Paul Bryan travels to the South of France and meets this girl who can do everything better than him. It drives him crazy."

That's all I had. It was just an idea. Roy liked that idea. He then wrote the story called "The Rapture at 240." He added the characters and the plot. As a gift to me he gave me, story credit on the show. I personally will not take credit for his work. I had a character and an idea that he developed into a story. He was grateful enough to me for giving him the idea to act as a catalyst. Luther Davies then put Roy's story in screenplay form. It debuted on *Kraft Suspense Theatre*.

Katherine Crawford recalled filming the pilot episode with Ben Gazzara:

I always liked Ben. He was a very gracious man. Gentle. With me, that mattered. There were underwater shots and I was an experienced diver so had no problem. Ben had no experience, but went ahead with great bravado. But when I came in the next morning, I was told an alarming story of Ben being in the hospital and they were waiting to find out when he would return. He did return later that day, seeming fit as a fiddle and saying only that he was fine. His vulnerability showed through despite his strong exterior though, so I felt badly for him, but I don't think we spoke of it after his return for more than a second.

At that point there was no problem with Daddy casting me. I was considered a new "find" and up-and-coming in the industry, and it was old news about my being his daughter. So it was a fun and interesting show to do. I was still shy, so I still stayed on my own most of the time, but Ben was good to work with. We really didn't spend time together, outside of the work on set, except to be generally nice to each other.

In television, directors really never try to coach you, so there's never any discussion of your character or performance. I always wished they would and treasure the few TV directors who did work with actors. Billy Graham directed the pilot. He was the quietest director I knew. We worked together a lot. Sometimes he even read the newspaper during a shot ... or so it seemed to me. Only once during all our shows together did he make a comment to me ... and it wasn't a good one. I laugh now. But he turned in good shows. It's a technique. Let the actors go as they wish and print when they finally do it right. He did a fine job though, obviously. But really the actors come in and hand in the performance and that's it. The underwater dancing was the only part that stands out. I was choreographed one morning in a room at the studio by a dance choreographer. It was quick and not perfected, but that was that. It was shot against a green screen. It was a bit uncomfortable for me. But you move on.

When I watched the show again a few years ago, I remember thinking that the dialogue was asking for a different, more flippant performance for the girl. But that's how I was back then. Very serious myself, so I didn't even see that other side of her. So it was played in that serious way which was more me than the role ... but it worked, I think. And as I said, no one tried to change it. Daddy never would visit me on set. That would not be comfortable. So it was a pleasant fairly uneventful shoot."

Before *Run for Your Life* debuted as a weekly series, Huggins found himself involved in agency politics as Swerling Jr. recalled:

There was no love lost between Meta Rosenberg and Roy in either direction. It all started on *Run for Your Life*. The Rosenberg-Coryell Agency represented Ben Gazzara and Vince Edwards. *Ben Casey* was a Rosenberg-Coryell package. When they found out NBC were planning *Run for Your Life* against *Ben Casey*, they immediately began to rile Ben Gazzara. They told him he had made a horrible mistake and the scripts were bad and his career was over. All of which didn't sit very well with Roy. Ben was very difficult during those months. The show went on the air and got good ratings and Ben fired his agents. We got along famously with Ben from then on. We worked together very well.

Run for Your Life premiered on NBC at 10 p.m. ET Monday, September 23, 1965. Huggins described the inspiration for the show:

I read widely into the classic literature concerning people who were going to die and what they did with their lives. Two broad answers came out. One was more or less Faustian, in Goethe's sense. Faust had built something for others. Good deeds had become his companion and God stepped in and invalidated his bargain with Mephistopheles.

But there was another direction—this might be called either the Promethean or possibly Rabelaisian concept. Promethean in the sense that he fought the gods. Rabelaisian in the sense that life should be experienced to the fullest. Paul Bryan clearly follows the latter course."[7]

The hedonistic lifestyle of Paul Bryan wouldn't be based on ego but on a form of utilitarianism where the pursuit of pleasure has consequences and must be measured against the greater good. Bryan wouldn't be a mere thrill seeker but an ethical man with a sense of responsibility. He would be forced to end relationships not out of selfishness but out of a desire to protect the loved one from future pain because of his terminal condition. This role would be reversed in two memorable episodes starring Claudine Longet. Swerling said,

Roy was a close personal friend of Andy Williams and Claudine. It was because of this relationship that he went out of his way to find a good role for her in the show. "The Sadness of a Happy Time" (1:30) was the perfect answer ... with just the right twist ... this time the girl making the decision, more for Paul Bryan than for herself ... to say goodbye. Roy was also familiar with Claudine's singing ability and it was his idea for her to sing in the episode. Roy was a fan of the group "Brazil 65" which was up-and-coming at the time and led by Sergio

Mendez. We also included them in an episode. One of Mendez's hits was the Antonio Carlos Jobim song "Meditation." It was decided that Claudine would serenade Paul with her unique interpretation of "Meditation" using French instead of Portuguese lyrics. The sequence came out so well that when Herb Alpert saw the show on the air, he put Claudine under a recording contract, and she had several hit albums as a result.

This experience was so rewarding for all of us that we not only came up with a sequel on *Run for Your Life*, "The Word Would Be Goodbye" (2:30), but went on to work with Claudine many more times. In an episode of *The Bold Ones, Lawyers* called "The Rockford Riddle" (in which Claudine played a murderess), in an episode of *Alias Smith and Jones*, and in a pilot with Peter Duel called *How to Steal an Airplane*. Personally, I had a huge crush (alas, unrequited) on Claudine, despite the fact that I was happily married with two children at the time. I'm sure in those days I would have gladly jumped off the Golden Gate Bridge if she were to suggest it. She was, without a doubt, the most attractive and charming human being I had ever met."

Associated Press syndicated writer Cynthia Lowry provided her own take on *Run for Your Life* (November 1, 1966):

> One week we encounter the hero, Paul Bryan, in a dinner jacket at a chic penthouse party and the next he is crawling through a tropical jungle. Most of the time he is saving a pretty girl. The principal action comes from new characters encountered each week.
>
> Some programs are better than others which is true of all series which have many contributing scriptwriters.... Ben Gazzara plays the hero with a quiet irony which is often highly effective.... Week in and week out, however, it is one of television's superior offerings.

The early success of *Run for Your Life* was tempered with the death of Huggins' mother on November 9, 1965, at the age of 84. Belle Huggins had never remarried following the tragic premature death of her husband Edward almost fifty years earlier and remained in Portland for the majority of her life. Katherine Crawford recalled, "Her last words were 'Ed? Is that you, Ed?' Daddy's eyes teared up whenever he told me that."

Run for Your Life encountered controversy and negative publicity for the first season episode "Hoodlums on Wheels" (1:21). Paul Bryan and a mother (Marsha Hunt) and daughter (Karen Jensen) are taken hostage by an outlaw biker gang known as The Saints, led by Goebels (John Drew Barrymore). In a speech delivered November 14, 1966, to the Ministers' Symposium in Long Beach, California, Huggins commented,

> Last season the show that brought the most dramatic response from the audience was called "Hoodlums on Wheels." It began the day I read about a group of motorcycle delinquents. A self-confessed outlaw gang, who broke through a police line in Northern California and clubbed down a group of citizens marching in protest against the war in Vietnam. I was struck by the fact that these delinquents who were intelligent enough to intellectualize their being outlaws, conscious dissenters from a peaceful society, were yet fiercely patriotic.
>
> I felt there was an apparent kinship here with para-military groups such as the Minute Men. We did a story dramatizing the viciousness of the pride they took in "busting up them peace marchers." I had predicted the mail response would be large and polarized, with unfavorable mail coming from the organized groups and accusing us of obscenity and Communism. I was wrong in one respect. The unfavorable mail far outweighed the favorable. But it was organizationally inspired.

The controversy surrounding the episode and the extreme right-wing backlash which threatened the withdrawal of sponsors didn't transfer to television critics. It was nominated for the Golden Gate Award for Entertainment at the 10th Annual San Francisco International Film Festival.

The two-part episode "Flight from Tirana" and "A Rage for Justice" (2:16–17) featured Ossie Davis as a black soldier accused of desertion, black marketeering and aiding the enemy. Prosecutor Major Joe Rankin (Sam Wanamaker) is convinced of his guilt while his defense attorney Paul Bryan believes he defected to Albania to help his drug-addicted wife. Huggins explained his reasoning behind writing and producing the episodes before the Ministers' Symposium: "Several months ago it began to be apparent that the so-called White Backlash was real and was growing. I put a story into work—it's in production at the moment—that tries to define backlash, to focus on the heart of the problem: That people are allowing a reaction to the actions of a few Negroes to carry over and color their attitudes toward all Negroes and to legitimate demands of Negroes."

The reaction to the episode once again resulted in controversy with some Southern stations refusing to broadcast it, resulting in a drop in the ratings.

In "Hang Your Head and Laugh" (2:12) Kim Darby played a 15-year-old girl running away from her grandparents in New Jersey in order to live with her father in New Mexico. The episode explored the relationship between Paul Bryan and Darby's character, Tina Baker. Both have secrets and are running from their past. Baker's extrovert personality hides her own failings. Bryan and Baker see reflections of themselves in each other's hidden, secret fears. Swerling Jr. commented,

> Kim was brilliant in that episode. She was always a terrific professional and so talented. We considered her a lucky charm and tried to put her in any show where she came within a country mile of being right for the part. Every show she did for us came out as one of our best. Her shy quality was very charming and came across in a lot of the characters she played.
>
> For the second year we had to decide which episode to send in to the Blue Ribbon panel as our Emmy contender. I thought that we should send in our best episode, "Hang Down Your Head and Laugh." Roy disagreed and opted for a two-part Michael Ritchie episode, "Cry Hard, Cry Fast," in which Paul Bryan causes an automobile accident on the freeway that kills and badly injures people as a result of his failure to get enough sleep the night before. The episode dealt with how this affected his life. It had won an award from the National Safety Council and was placed in the category of a public service by the Federal Highway Administration. Roy had received a letter from Ed Nelson, a supervisor for the Safety Council, stating, "We find it especially exciting because we have, for a long time, sought to present the multiplicity of traffic accident causes and the difficulty of identifying specific causes of any particular accident as the framework for a situation of potentially great drama. We've also felt that a dramatic presentation of this kind would serve the public interest well, in that it would help to make clear the simplistic "solutions" to traffic accident problems are of little validity. We thank you."
>
> Roy felt because of its public interest content it would be more beguiling to the Blue Ribbon jury. A friend on the jury told me he voted for the episode but the others didn't because they couldn't sit through it for two-hours. Later, they banned two hour shows. *I Spy* won for a second year in a row. I am convinced to this day if we had sent "Hang Down Your Head and Laugh," we would have won the Emmy. It was that good a show, written by Carol Eastman, who went on to write the screenplay for *Five Easy Pieces*. We made a big mistake sending the other episode in.

Run for Your Life was officially canceled at the end of season two but suddenly renewed four days later. Says Swerling, "*Run for Your Life* was still getting very strong ratings but there was guy at NBC who was fixated on the fact the show had gone three years when Bryan only had two years to live. If it went another year the audience would completely reject it. Roy said you had to look at it like *Little Orphan Annie*. She had been the same age for 30 years. The guy at NBC didn't go for that argument. They believed that since we tell the audience each week that Paul Bryan has two years at the most to live, the audience would

At a mock funeral to celebrate the third season (1967) renewal for *Run for Your Life* are (left to right) Paul Freeman, Robert Foster, Steve Heilpern, Ben Gazzara, Richard Benedict, Philip DeGuere and Jo Swerling, Jr (courtesy John Huggins).

reject the show after two years. The ratings and reviews were very good at the end of the second season, and the show was nominated for a couple of Emmys, so that might have been pointed out to them by Roy and could have influenced a change of strategy."

The controversial subject matter of many episodes continued to create problems for NBC. Huggins said, "We have attacked capital punishment, the coldness of the Cold War, the ease with which firearms can be obtained and freely carried about, and the failure of our prison systems to rehabilitate prisoners. And we have dramatized a dozen other controversial issues. In the privacy of our unit we refer to ourselves as makers of soap-box opera."[8]

"The Committee for the 25th" (2:04) was one of the episodes that caused a stir. The Las Vegas mayor, the Las Vegas Chamber of Commerce, casino owners and various governors all expressed outrage at the storyline that saw Paul Bryan suggesting a 25th Amendment to the Constitution to ban gambling. "Roy did not like Vegas," said Price. "He did win money in Las Vegas early in his career, but later he was banned by the casino operators from playing. He was too good. Roy was an expert on poker. "The Committee for the 25th" was very critical of Vegas."

The episode centered on former San Francisco mayor Dwight Sinclair (Wendell Corey) and his estranged daughter Sarah (Brooke Bundy), a go-go dancer. Las Vegas club owner and Mafia boss Carl Cappi (Edward Asner) has her hooked on heroin to keep her dependent on him. Huggins and co-writer Luther Davis were accused by the Chamber of Commerce of "a prize piece of fiction done in the grand style of *Batman*." Huggins noted, "The mail response rose into hundreds of letters, not a single one unfavorable except those postmarked from Nevada. My friends keep asking me if I'm not frightened and I keep answering that I am absolutely fearless—but I've hired someone to start my car for me."[9]

Season Three continued to feature controversial storylines as Swerling Jr. recalled. "One of our best episodes, 'Down with Willie Hatch' (3:08), guest-starring Don Rickles, had a downbeat ending wherein Paul Bryan gives Hatch what he believes to be the right advice, but which backfires and causes Hatch to suffer a mental breakdown. The episode ends with a contrite and saddened Bryan watching his friend being taken to the hospital in an ambulance, illustrating the old saying that the road to Hell is paved with good intentions. It was a very non–Hollywood ending and intellectually honest. Nevertheless, the ratings on the following week took a terrible dump, which we believed was blowback from our audience, punishing us for making our series hero look like an ordinary, flawed human being."

A third season episode directed by Ben Gazzara, "The Killing Scene" (3:19), starred Robert Duvall and Tom Skerritt. In Europe, Bryan reads in a paper than a client he unsuccessfully defended in a murder trial is about to be executed. Bryan gets pangs of remorse and comes out of retirement to see if there is any way he can save this man from going to the chair. He finds businessman Richard Fletcher (Robert Duvall) running a small gas station in a little community. Fletcher is married with kids and heading an exemplary life but Bryan discovers he is guilty of murder. Bryan begs him to come clean and give himself up. Fletcher doesn't want to sacrifice his family and small business but finally gives in to pressure from Bryan and agrees to turn himself in. But they arrive at the police station thirty seconds too late. Says Swerling, "It was a very powerful anti–capital punishment statement. Roy or myself wouldn't make that movie today if our lives depended on it because we both changed our position on capital punishment. At the time we were very against it."

Gazzara directed Kim Darby's second *Run for Your Life* episode, "Carol" (3:24). Darby, who was pregnant in real life, played pregnant Carol Sherman, who makes the choice to have an abortion to win back her boyfriend (Ron Russell). Abortion, which was illegal at the time of broadcast, was another example of *Run for Your Life* tackling controversial subjects. Gazzara said, "In some respects, doing a TV series is like factory work. Keeping your enthusiasm high is not easy. The weeks, months of playing the same character, with predictable reactions to mainly predictable situations was getting me down.... Things turned around for me when I started to direct some of the episodes. My mind and my imagination became engaged. My sadness started to lift and I began to feel useful. As an actor I was responsible only for part of the whole but now the entire presentation would depend on me. Each of those small movies would stand or fall on my vision."[10]

""Carol' was one of our best shows. Ben did a terrific job directing and Kim Darby was great in it," recalled Swerling Jr.

Bryan's travels finally came to end when *Run for Your Life* was canceled after three seasons. There was no final episode offering a resolution to Bryan's medical condition. Huggins hoped the show would have been renewed for a fourth season given its respectable 27.8 share:

"I felt we could have continued one more year. Our numbers were still good. The reviews were still good." But once again the timeline proved to be the stumbling block and going into a fourth year for a show with a two-years-to-live premise wasn't seen as viable for NBC head of programming Mort Werner. "To the network, a season equaled a year. In their thinking, he'd already lived a year too long," stated Huggins. Had the show gone to a fourth season, Huggins never intended a final episode where Bryan would be cured. "I thought such a resolution would be terribly contrived, and against the grain of what the show was about. I felt the audience would see right through that. And I really didn't want to do it anyway."[11]

Run for Your Life never equaled the success of *The Fugitive* but provided a showcase for promising young directors such as Michael Ritchie and trusted veterans including Leslie H. Martinson, Richard Benedict, Stuart Rosenberg, Leo Penn, William Hale, Nicholas Colasanto and Alexander Singer. The memorable theme music was provided by Pete Rugolo, the man also responsible for the classic title and incidental music on *The Fugitive*. Born in San Piero Patti, Sicily, Italy, on Christmas Day 1915, Rugolo emigrated with his family to America at the age of five and later studied music at Mills College, Oakland, under French avant-garde composer Darius Milhaud. In 1945 Rugolo joined the Stan Kenton band as their musical arranger, creating "progressive jazz" in the process. Four years later he was music director of Capitol Records in New York. This was followed by arranging and composing work for MGM and working as West Coast musical director of Mercury Records where he recorded a series of albums.

His jazz music background influenced his television work on *The Thin Man* (1957), *Richard Diamond, Private Detective* (1957), *The Fugitive* and *Run for Your Life*. Huggins would use him extensively in the years ahead. "Pete Rugolo and Roy were extremely close personal friends," declared Swerling Jr. "Pete and his wife Edy would be invited to dinner parties. Roy kept using Pete because he delivered really good scores for the shows, but I have a hunch if Pete had a really bad week that Roy would have kept using him out of loyalty."

Huggins recalled working with Rugolo:

> I was a great fan of his. I was a fan of Stan Kenton, and I realized the Stan Kenton sound was really Pete Rugolo. I began using Pete just about the time that Quinn began using him on *The Fugitive*. I think it was around 1964. I had been at Warners where the whole music was controlled. I didn't have freedom on these choices until I made my joint venture with Universal. Then I had freedom of choice, and my first choice was Pete. If Pete was available, he did it. He had this great drive. It was marvelous.
> The thing that I loved about his sound was that it was very close to Schoenberg. Close to atonal. I'm not a musician, but I fell in love with atonal music almost at the moment it came out. Pete used it beautifully, in his own way. And I wanted that sound.
> [*Run for Your Life*] was really an anthology. Pete had a lot to do. And he wasn't allowed under the rules at Universal to conduct his music. The conducting was done by Stanley Wilson. It would have been better if Pete had been able to conduct. Pete's a great conductor.[12]

Rugolo loved his time on *Run for Your Life*, explaining, "It was a different country every week. It was a challenging thing and [Huggins] loved my music. He loved the jazz feeling. I tried to write a fast theme, a moving theme at the beginning. And I could write jazz chases. There was a lot of racing-car stuff in it too, and it just felt good with jazz. There were a lot of shows where Gazzara would go to Spain, and I would write a concerto with a guitar. I had to write German music, Italian music, Japanese, Chinese, because he always traveled to a different country."[13]

In *Run for Your Life*, Huggins helped create a quality series and was actively involved with the show for its entire 85-episode run (with 29 episodes credited as writer John Thomas James). Huggins concluded, "*Run for Your Life* dealt many times with the gap between things as they are and things as society insists that they are. The scripts often concerned the conflict between social conventions and real moral dilemmas. We generally took the position that the rule was not as important as the specific human circumstance, and that the heavies in our world are not 'bad guys,' but victims of circumstance, of institutions, of a way of life. In this we were exploring, perhaps even preaching, a kind of situation ethics. And *Run for Your Life* managed to stay on NBC for three seasons."[14]

12

ONE STEP AHEAD

"Every creator painfully experiences the chasm between his inner vision and its ultimate expression."—Isaac Basheris Singer (1904–1991)

Although Roy Huggins earned his living in the entertainment industry, he viewed his work with the mind of an intellectual and gave regular speeches on various aspects of television and its place in society including the job of the producer. In one, he explained,

> The degree of control over his work exercised by a producer varies in every case, depending on the producer's standing in the industry. His knowledge of his craft, the success of his show, the degree of independence he demands and the degree of control the network programming department attempts to exercise. And the producer function itself may sometimes be fragmented, a show being produced by a committee within a studio.

But successful shows are almost always the responsibility of one man, and he will usually influence the character and quality of that show as strongly as he possibly can. His job is sometimes made easier and more rewarding because of help from a star, a key associate, a skillful writer or two and a few sensitive directors. More often it is made difficult because good writers, good directors, good actors, are as rare as excellence is in any field.

One more subdivision remains: The separation of the producer whose only goal is a high rating from the producer who feels a responsibility to the audience, or perhaps to something beyond the audience, which compels him to try for more than mere entertainment. I believe there are far more producers in the second category than in the first, and the separation is a sharp one. Those in the first category are belligerent in their

Huggins, Katherine Crawford and Frank Price at Universal Studios in January 1967 (courtesy Katherine Crawford).

distaste for writers with something to say. "If I want to deliver a message I'll call Western Union" still echoes off the commissary walls. And the work of the producers who say it usually reflects that kind of inventiveness.

The attitude baffles me. Each week I have the privilege of addressing myself for one hour to over 30 million of my fellow countrymen. Very few men in history have had that opportunity. Now and then I fill that hour with something that is neither meaningful nor particularly entertaining and I squirm with guilt and pure discomfort until a show comes along that I can find some value in. I don't believe I have the right to waste—literally to steal—one hour from 30 million people. If an occasional show says absolutely nothing, but was truly and freshly entertaining, I have no quarrel with myself. The first obligation is to entertain, because possession of that priceless hour per week must be won by attracting and holding an audience week after week.

Being truly entertaining while saying nothing is not easy. A story is a statement. If you have no point to make, you have no story to tell, so there is no conflict in my dual intention of entertaining the audience while trying to move or reform or provoke them.[1]

A recurring subject in Huggins' speeches was violence and censorship. His experience on *Bus Stop* had made him wary of government intervention and control. Huggins preferred to push back boundaries that restricted creativity and the voice of the individual. But he admitted that self-imposed boundaries sometimes had their place. In a speech he gave to the congregation at the Westminster Presbyterian Church, Pasadena, California, in April 1967, on the subject of "Film and the Pornography of Violence," he said,

I have always deplored, and publicly criticized, uninformed, sweeping and unqualified criticisms of violence. Violence is not only a legitimate ingredient in drama, it is an equally vital ingredient in comedy. Without violence there would be no dramatic art....

But when violence is used explicitly and literally for its own sake unrelated to character or premise, it serves a different and dangerous theme. And when violence is used not only literally and for its own sake but in a manner which assumes that the audience will accept it without any sense of shock, without empathy, without a sense of common humanity, it leaps the bounds of tolerance and becomes pornography. As a filmmaker I need not tell you censorship is anathema to me. However, the producers of pornography of the sado-masochistic variety are not entitled to cry "censorship" when a civilized society reacts against their kind of pandering. But the shocking fact is that our society is not reacting against it...

Motion pictures cannot create cultural attitudes out of nothing. Films are made up of expertly transmuted, commonly held daydreams; but the common daydreams of a society are only part of the products of popular art forms. Those art forms in turn draw upon the society's common fantasies as sources. Only in a society which is producing audiences already disposed to such obscenities can a popular art form successfully provide them.

Audiences for sado-masochistic pornography of this kind are lacking in what psychologists call affect, the capacity for empathy, for entering the feelings of others. This condition must, in part, be a product of our current cultural condition—perhaps predicament is the proper word... This is a condition that does not augur well for our culture. Perhaps the enemies of the American dream are not, after all, seventy-five hundred miles away.

Violence was one of many subjects that concerned Huggins in the mid–1960s. Despite his success in television, he found that the medium had serious limitations compared to movies made for the theater. Budget, screen size and format, audio and the access to the top talent in the industry couldn't be matched by television, but Huggins soon discovered the major significant difference was lack of live audience participation. As a writer for Columbia and RKO, Huggins had experienced the feedback of a live theater audience:

Sitting in the darkness of a theater watching something you have written or directed or produced surrounded by men and women unknown to you, and to whom you are equally unknown, is a harrowing experience. You look, but what you see is alien to you.... A scene you almost deleted takes on a new meaning because a line, or just a look in an actor's eye, has produced an audience reaction you didn't expect.... What you are doing is seeing your film through the eyes of the audience, cued by their restlessness or laughter, or sweetest of all, their breathless silence.[2]

Apart from sitcoms taped before a live audience, the filmed television drama has no audience apart from the actors and crew. The *Maverick* episode "Gun-Shy" was the catalyst that secured his belief in the importance of a live audience:

> The show was on footage and my colleague felt strongly that it was ready for delivery. I felt just as strongly it was not.... If "Gun-Shy" had not been made for TV, my friend and I would not be quarrelling, we would have taken the film to a theater and let an audience tell us what we needed to know.
>
> But the producers of television film have no such quick and easy way of evaluating their product. It is possible for many shows within any given series to be dull, or even actively annoying to audiences with no measurable evidence of this being registered. The rating on a show the audience actually disliked can be quite high for a variety of reasons: First and most significant, it's free, so turning on the television set is not a significant act; second, there may be nothing else that looks attractive during that time period; third, it may be a habit to stay tuned to that show or that station; fourth, there may be a favored show following this one or preceding it.
>
> I could list a half dozen additional reasons why any given show on any given night, or even any given series of shows, may get a high rating and yet be the kind of "entertainment" that you sat through in wonder. But to the networks and the makers of that show, the high rating means quality, and I have yet to meet a man who could prove a show was bad if its rating was high.
>
> So, without the unarguable answer of the box office, the failures are not immediately or specifically exposed and the vital lessons that lead to ever-improving quality are not learned. This is television's great problem, and in relation to motion pictures, its greatest weakness.[3]

Huggins thought he could solve his problem by gathering an audience who hated *Maverick*. After edits to the episode, an audience who loved *Maverick* was assembled. But ultimately Huggins considered the audiences too small and too professional to represent the average viewer. Despite his reservations, "Gun-Shy" received a high Nielsen rating. Huggins stored the experience for future reference. That day came in the mid–1960s on the Universal backlot: "One day I looked up and saw a busload of happy tourists passing by. I recognized them immediately: There were our unseen, unheard audience, the very people I had so desperately needed when I previewed 'Gun-Shy.' I wasted no time in asking the executive in charge of the tours if I could steer some of those people into a large projection room to show them a television-show-in-progress. The answer was a fast and happy yes."

Over the coming weeks Huggins gathered audiences of one hundred or more to watch *World Premiere* TV movies or one-hour series episodes. Huggins sat with the audience, noting laughter where no laughter was intended and no laughter where laughter was expected. After watching the rough cuts, the audience was asked to complete a questionnaire similar to a movie preview card. The results brought to Huggins' attention errors, confused plots and oversights in the most popular episodes or TV movies.

"Was this putting too much faith in a group of amateurs? Of course not, that's what the audience is. The results of the experiment were more stimulating, more helpful and more edifying than we had dared to expect," declared Huggins.[4]

After a few weeks, Huggins' experiment was brought to an abrupt and permanent end when union problems became apparent. Around the same time the Audience Studies Institute

(ASI) based in Hollywood created a screening process that in itself was far from perfect. According to Frank Price,

> It was customary to test pilots for new series before a recruited audience. There was a theater on Sunset that was dedicated to this purpose. The company operated under the name ASI. Professional researchers staffed the company. The audience used dials to register their level of interest in each scene they watched. Afterwards they filed out questionnaires, which were closely analyzed. A small group was selected to be a "focus group" and they would become a verbal discussion critic panel led by a trained moderator. Regular series episodes were never tested. Too expensive.
>
> I had reservations about the process. It could help you with editing the picture, highlighting slow or exciting scenes. But my reservations would be illustrated by what happened when different versions of *All in the Family* were tested. Two pilots for different networks tested poorly. Finally one made for CBS got barely acceptable results, but luckily got ordered. Testing could not judge radically different premises. Familiar material got better reactions. Therefore, the testing eliminated the worst pilots, but also eliminated the potentially best. Audiences had to be more prepared for something so unlike their regular shows. So my judgment was that the testing reinforced mediocrity.[5]

Huggins' only pilot of the year proved to be successful. *The Outsider* (1967), directed by Michael Ritchie from a Huggins teleplay, starred Darren McGavin as David Ross. Abandoned by his family as a five-year-old in Seattle and a runaway from schools in search of his identity and sense of worth in society, Ross is a former convict pardoned after serving six years for killing a man in self-defense. Ross is a hardened outsider with an insider's knowledge of surviving in the state penitentiary. Eking out a living as a Los Angeles–based private eye, he lives on the edges of society and has the quirky habit of keeping his gun in his refrigerator. Ross is hired by businessman Marvin Bishop (Edmond O'Brien) to investigate Carol Dorfman (Anna Hagan), who is accused of embezzling company funds. He becomes involved in a murder case after finding her dead from a shotgun wound. And when Ross discovers Bishop was having an affair with Carol, his investigations take him into the seedy world of nightclubs and LSD. Reviews were mixed with Cynthia Lowry of the Associated Press (November 1967) stating: "The program, pretty routine whodunnit stuff[,] wandered up some curious side streets. The camera and sound were deliberately distorted ... to indicate how one of the heavies was making out during an LSD trip. No action show these days, of course, is complete without some reference to drugs and hippies. With all the action and violence.... *The Outsider* undoubtedly will be a series next season." The film critic for *The Robesonian* (N.C.) (November 21, 1967) was more generous with the praise: "It's a taut, slickly produced, Bogart-type private eye yarn which benefits from Darren McGavin's tight-lipped playing of the lead character."

The *NBC World Premiere* pilot gained Ritchie a nomination from the Directors Guild of America for "Outstanding Directorial Achievement in Television" and resulted in a weekly series that ran for one 26-episode season in 1968–69. Huggins had no input into the series following complaints from the network about the pilot's violent content. Production duties were passed on to veteran writer-producer Gene Levitt.

The year 1968, a busy one for Huggins, produced mixed results. The first project to air was a pilot for a series that failed to sell. *The Lonely Profession* (1968), adapted by Douglas Heyes from his novel "The Twelfth of Never," starred Harry Guardino as private eye Lee Gordon, who investigates the murder of the mistress of a multi-millionaire.

With *The Sound of Anger* (1968) Huggins changed direction from the private eye to the corporate world of lawyers. The central characters were brothers Brad and Neil Darrell (Guy Stockwell and James Farentino), partners in a law firm who came into conflict with rival senior attorney Walter Nichols (Burl Ives). The *World Premiere* drama involved the lawyers defending two teenage lovers accused of murdering the girl's father. "When NBC viewed the original pilot they didn't like Guy Stockwell one of the Darrell brothers, and also thought it would be a stronger theme to have Burl Ives as a partner in the firm who also acted as a father figure and mentor," recalled Jo Swerling, Jr. "James Farentino and Stockwell didn't look like brothers so they replaced Stockwell with Joseph Campanella, who looked more Italian."[6]

In his syndicated column "A Closer Look at Television," Ernie Kreiling (December 31, 1968) questioned the validity of the two-hour "made-for-television" movie. He found "The Sound of Anger"

> [n]either spectacularly good or depressingly bad. This tale by Roy Huggins was a pleasant and entertaining story to a point.... As with most such films, the stories simply do not deserve the two-hour—actually, 100 minutes treatment. The tension inherent in a good whodunnit was considerably diluted at times with pretty pictures that meant little and with dialogue that failed to move the plot along. In this instance the characters were well drawn and reflected a little greater depth than usually seen in these television efforts.

Huggins and Senator Edward Kennedy attending a function for Senator Robert Kennedy shortly before his assassination in 1968 (courtesy John Huggins).

The Whole World Is Watching (1969) aired five months later (March 3, 1969), featuring the new cast and revised format. Richard Levinson and William Link provided the teleplay centering on a campus revolt and the alleged murder of a policeman by a student. "The second pilot became the actual pilot with the first pilot airing as a *Movie of the Week. The Lawyers* was a lot of fun to produce," stated Swerling Jr. He continued,

> We had a good time with that show. Personally, it was fun for me because it enabled me to take time to go to downtown LA and audit a bunch of trials, including the trial of Bobby Beausoleil, one of Charles Manson's followers, for research purposes, which was both interesting and entertaining. Also, Burl Ives and Joe Campanella were two of the best and most cordial actors I ever worked with. Farentino was a pretty good guy and a good actor, but, of the three, he had the most Prima Donna DNA. One of the best things about making the show was that it was on the air every third week, which made air-date delivery pressure (chronic in most weekly shows of that era) virtually disappear.

The Lawyers came under the umbrella title *The Bold Ones* (1969) which featured three different shows broadcast on alternate weeks. The "wheel" format harked back to Huggins' experience on *Warner Bros. Presents*. The recent success of *The Name of the Game* (1968) had encouraged Universal to expand the format to new shows but the reasoning behind the format wasn't purely creative. Price explained, "Sometimes the wheel was used to persuade a network to buy a series when they didn't like any of its component parts enough to commit to a full series. So, if you're not totally convinced that *The Lawyers* is a series that will succeed, you get two other chances with *The Doctors*, etc. The format allowed network executives to avoid making a choice and hide their indecision behind the screen of a 'fresh' format."

The *Movie of the Week* concept was conceived by a hungover Huggins on a beach in January 1968. His idea was greeted with rejection, first in late January by Universal vice-president in charge of television Sidney Sheinberg who told Huggins his idea was uninspired, unworkable and unsalable. Grant Tinker, Universal vice-president handling liaison with ABC, thought the concept economically unfeasible. Next in line was Herb Schlosser at NBC. Huggins conceded it "was a perverse thing to do, like selling a fox to a chicken farmer." NBC had its own successful two-hour TV movie with *World Premiere*. It didn't need Huggins' 90-minute concept.

Meanwhile Dave Kaufman of *Variety* contacted Huggins. He had heard through the grapevine about Huggins' meetings and wanted to confirm his inside information. On March 21, 1968, Kaufman announced the *Movie of the Week* proposal to readers: "Public Arts Inc., Roy Huggins' production company, is undergoing a shift in emphasis from theatrical and two-hour idioms for TV to a new concept, a weekly series of 90-minute pictures to be aired first-run on TV under the tag 'Movie of the Week' ... Huggins, prexy of Public Arts, is planning on a minimum budget of $500,000 for his shows."

Following the public announcement, Huggins' next stop was a meeting with "over a dozen dour executives" at the CBS programming department on March 27. After Huggins presenting his idea, Mike Dann responded, "That's probably the worst idea I ever heard."

With NBC and CBS both rejecting Huggins' concept, his final stop was the offices of ABC and Leonard Goldberg, vice-president in charge of network programming. Barry Lowen, Barry Diller and two other ABC executives were also present at the 55-minute meeting in room 1905 of the Century Plaza Hotel. Huggins dictated a record of the meeting when he returned to his office:

Two of those present were skeptical about the viability or legitimacy of calling a show whose actual length would be only 76 minutes a "movie".... Barry Lowen wondered if there wasn't a better title than "Movie of the Week." I said it was the only possible title, that every aspect of the series must evoke the image of a movie, and anything that might suggest a TV series—a host, or anything else that might make it look like an anthology series could be fatal.

Barry Diller made a strong impression on me. He did more listening than talking, and toward the end of the meeting asked the only really tough question: "What makes you so confident this idea will work?" ... He wanted to know why ABC should buy an idea that had flatly been rejected by the other two networks.

Huggins referred to the *World Premiere* two-hour TV movies as proof there was a market for his idea. The audience "would make no distinction between a 90-minute movie and a two-hour one." When asked about the content of the *Movie of the Week*, Huggins stressed action, suspense, mystery, the occasional Western and pilot. Comedy and soap operas were off limits. Universal would produce the shows at a minimum of $500,000.

The budget Huggins proposed met with instant disapproval from everyone present but Huggins felt still felt confident. There was an anxious waiting period, and then Huggins decided to contact his lawyer after being told of meetings between Lew Wasserman, Sid Sheinberg and Grant Tinker. Tinker told Huggins that Wasserman and ABC were in talks but Huggins' fee was too high. Producer Jerry Adler was mentioned as a replacement for Huggins.

On May 28, 1968 Dave Kaufman of *Variety* announced:

> Television's most ambitious vidpic project, new ABC-TV series for 1969–70 called "Movie of the Week" will involve an estimated $14,000,000 to $15,000,000 for production. Leonard Goldberg, ABC-TV network veepee, yesterday termed the project a new programming concept and said it entails a series of 90-minute feature films to be aired, beginning September 26.... "Project will probably be done by a number of companies," said Goldberg, who explained, "We have talked with all the majors as well as the indies in Hollywood, and we will decide this week or next which will produce it.

Huggins immediately set about filing a suit against ABC. The corporation responded by saying the idea for *Movie of the Week* was born within the American Broadcasting Company. This was followed by a claim from Universal's parent company MCA that they originated the idea within its executive offices. Individual credit wasn't mentioned.

Huggins decided he needed a break and vacationed with his family in Spain in July and August. On his return he received a letter from Harry R. Olsson, Jr., the general attorney for ABC: "Sometime prior to the meeting with Mr. Huggins that you referred to, our people had been discussing with Universal and other companies a 'Movie of the Week' series. There was nothing unique, novel, or original in what Mr. Huggins and our people discussed. Feature motion pictures made for television, and weekly broadcasts of those movies on TV are certainly 'old hat.'"

Although credit for creation of the concept had been taken from Huggins, he was still offered the opportunity to produce "six or seven shows per season" by Goldberg. Huggins declined, knowing it would involve dropping the suit. But after further advice from his lawyer Louis C. Blau, Huggins finally dropped the suit. The weakness of Huggins' argument lay in the fact that *Movie of the Week* was an original concept with no original characters or plot as was the case with *The Fugitive* which was also sold as a concept on paper only. When *Movie of the Week* premiered, Barry Diller was given credit for the series. Dwight Whitney, writing for *TV Guide* (July 20, 1974), credited Leonard Goldberg along with Diller. A mention of Roy Huggins was noticeably absent.

Although Huggins was in charge of all Public Arts productions, he sometimes preferred to maintain a low profile. "From time to time, for no specific reason I was aware of, Roy would be the de facto executive producer on a film but would take no credit. If the Public Arts card appeared in the end credits, you can be sure Roy was the man in charge, with or without an executive producer credit in the opening," commented Swerling. *Any Second Now* (1969) was one of those films. Stewart Granger, making his TV movie debut, starred as photographer Paul Dennison, who attempts to kill his cheating wife (Lois Nettleton) in an automobile accident. When she survives and loses her memory, he lives in fear that it may return.

Like all producers, Huggins was sometimes involved in mediocre material that was placed on the shelf for future broadcast. Chuck Connors played Buddy Bates, a man running for mayor who has just served seven years in jail for manslaughter in the TV movie *Set This Town on Fire*. Although filmed in 1969 it was held back for broadcast until 1973. Swerling recalled,

> The director, David Lowell Rich, was a good director but very arrogant. In his own mind he had no flaws and was perfect. We went to the dailies on the first day. Lynda Day played Molly Thornburgh, the girl next door. She was wearing a highly styled beehive hairdo. Something you'd expect from a model or a tough-minded businesswoman or executive. The girl next door should have been wearing a pony tail. It was disconcerting because it was so out of character for this part. I had the privilege of going down to the set to discuss this problem with the director.
> The scene was shot on the first day but appeared in the middle of the film. Roy avoided reshooting like the plague. He preferred to fix things in post-production. We decided this wasn't a fatal error as her early scenes could be shot with her wearing a pony tail. I told David, "We love the dailies. One little problem. We feel the girl's hair is out of character. Any other scenes we need a simple hairstyle for her."
> David Lowell Rich is nodding as I speak, appearing to be thinking about my comments. When I concluded, he said, "You know, Jo, you couldn't be more wrong." It was a well-crafted reading so that when he said "wrong," it would come as a surprise.
> "I don't think so. Everybody in the projection room reacted in the same way. It's got to be changed. There's no argument about it. Drop this hairdo. You really chose this and thought that it was appropriate?" He replied, "Jo, if I didn't think it was perfect I wouldn't have said print it." I thought in my mind, if I ever have any say, this guy will not direct another picture I'm connected with. I wrote him off completely with that arrogant statement and never did use him again."

The Challengers (1970) was a TV movie that was preempted because of the death of former President Dwight D. Eisenhower on March 28, 1969. The Grand Prix racing drama starring Darren McGavin, Sal Mineo, Anne Baxter, Susan Clark and Juliet Mills finally aired almost one year later, on February 20, 1970, and earned Pete Rugolo an Emmy for Outstanding Achievement in Music Composition—for a Special Program. "The music was one of the best things about that pilot," commented Huggins.[7] The plot resembled a motor racing soap opera: Cody Scanlon (Sean Garrison) and Paco (Nico Minardos) compete for the affections of thrill-seeking heiress Catherine Burroughs (Susan Clark). Other strands of the plot included Nealy (Farley Granger) and Ritchie (Richard Conte), underworld gamblers; Stephanie York (Anne Baxter) coming to terms with her husband's dangerous profession; and Jim McCabe (Darren McGavin) and his wife Mary (Juliet Mills) involved in their own problems. In Europe, *The Challengers* was released in theaters with the promotional blurb, "They Race for Glory When They Race Against Death."

Reviews for the pilot were mixed. Kevin Thomas of the *Los Angeles Times* (February 20, 1970) stated, "Although there's a reliance on the backlot for many exteriors *The Challengers* is actually a fairly lavish effort.... Director Leslie Martinson tends to jump from one camera to another within one scene to a dizzying degree, yet this technique admittedly does keep a very intricate tale moving fast." The *Variety* (February 25, 1970) critic was scathing in his criticism: "Producer Roy Huggins has better taste than this incredibly cliched soup-bone.... This was so predictable a potboiler on and off the track ... that no amount of hysterical editing and direction could bail it out...."

Huggins looked to his past for his next project and returned to directing for the first time since *Hangman's Knot* back in 1952. In *The Young Country* (1970), Stephen Foster Moody (Roger Davis), a drifter and gambler, searches for the rightful heirs to $38,000 found on a dead man. Moody contends with suspicious Sheriff Nat Fenley (Walter Brennan), Honest John Smith (Pete Duel) and Clementine Hale (Joan Hackett) as he seeks to resolve the issue. Swerling said,

> With *The Young Country*, Roy was trying to bring back a western with the flavor of *Maverick*. He felt Roger Davis had the comedic sense that could make it work. He was a fan of his acting. It was filmed as a pilot but went down the trail of unsold pilots. When Roy was looking at the dailies, Roy noticed that Roger had a good side and a bad side to his face. His bad side made him look unsympathetic and didn't reflect the charm the character needed. Once he pointed it out to me, I could see it. We took several scenes that had been shot favoring his bad side and redid parts of them. Particularly his close-up.
>
> A poker game scene had been shot with the camera favoring his bad side. We had the original scene on a Moviola on the set. He had Roger reverse his eye line and shoot on the other side of his face and flop the film over. Roy got no argument from Roger. He had a lot of respect and admiration for Roy so it wasn't a problem for him.

Frank Price commented on Huggins' mixed success with feature-length pilots: "Roy's technique of storytelling, which was rooted in the classic brick-by-brick plotting of the pulp fiction detective story (his roots), worked better in the one-hour format of a series than it did in a two-hour movie. I don't think his movies for television were particularly successful, certainly not in comparison to his series."

The Hollywood Reporter (1970) reviewer was unimpressed: "It is a light-hearted Western cut in from the old *Maverick* mold and therein lies its trouble, since a Maverick by any other name is not necessarily a Maverick.... *Young Country* seems to be bits and pieces of its progenitor, simply tied together to make a feature film with attractive trappings in the guise of Vilis Lapenieks' photography."

Huggins' experience on *The Young Country* was almost a dry run for his next job, a comedy TV Western loosely based on the recent (1969) hit move *Butch Cassidy and the Sundance Kid*. With Huggins in control of the series, the lead character Hannibal Heyes became a Bret Maverick type, with certain stories based on his earlier series. According to Frank Price,

> When I moved away from producing, I took on the assignment of handling sales of our Universal shows to ABC. I had an excellent relationship with the guys at ABC that stemmed from when I produced *It Takes a Thief* [1968] for them. Glen Larson came to me with the idea of *Alias Smith and Jones* [1971]. It was a mid-season order and under the gun from the beginning.

Huggins (right) directs Roger Davis (sitting on sidewalk) in *The Young Country* **(1970) (courtesy John Huggins).**

I supervised him as he wrote the script. Then I was executive producer of the pilot. Remember, I did the pilot, as executive producer, with a young and inexperienced Glen Larson, who was secretly getting writing help from Doug Heyes as I gave him the notes and directions that were needed to get the script ready. I had been the one insisting on Peter Duel and Ben Murphy. I got Roy's opinion on casting and he thought Steve Forrest was the right choice, someone mature enough to play romances. Generally, since I often spoke for both the studio and the network, Roy accepted my views unless he had a basic strong creative reason to disagree. And if he had that, I could be persuaded.

I took our 90-minute *Movie of the Week* pilot through production and post-production, put a temporary score on it, got a great result in a test screening, then flew to New York City and screened it for the ABC executives, who loved it, and I got the series order.

I got a series order from ABC so I wanted a good executive producer to run the series. Glen was too inexperienced to do that job. So I got Roy involved. I also thought Glen would learn to be a better producer by working for Roy. Glen did learn a lot from Roy and became a star producer-writer. The pilot aired as an installment of *Movie of the Week* shortly before the hour series debut. The series therefore was in production long before the pilot aired. The pilot's rating played no role.

Jo Swerling, Jr. added, "There was no question Glen Larson ripped off *Butch Cassidy and the Sundance Kid*. One of Glen's great talents, aside from the fact he was a pretty good writer of light humor, was his knack for knowing just how much he could change a ripped-off movie so he could avoid a lawsuit. But he got sued all the time. Universal was sued by Fox regarding *Alias Smith and Jones* and *Butch Cassidy and the Sundance Kid*. But Fox didn't prevail." Price adds,

> While Larson was inspired by current hit movies, he came up with creative thoughts and approaches that gave his conceptions an independent life. *Battlestar Galactica* lives on today with a huge fan base. It's not just a *Star Wars* ripoff. Which is why Lucas couldn't win a suit. *Alias Smith and Jones* was not the movie *Butch Cassidy and the Sundance Kid*. Putting the outlaws to work for the government was a very creative idea which made the series fresh and, again, not plagiarism. Butch and Sundance were real people in the West. Bill Goldman didn't create them.
>
> Glen did not have the standards that Roy did, but he had a facile creative mind. He came up with the concept of *Quincy* when I discussed with him the fact that no one had ever created a good coroner show. I explained it was too grim an arena. He came back with the idea of how to infuse the subject with humor, which of course made all the difference. It was like inventing the paper clip. Seems obvious, but no one had done it before.

With Huggins in control of the weekly series, the character of Hannibal Heyes as played by Pete Duel was transformed from a lovable but not too bright outlaw into a quick-witted Bret Maverick–style charmer. Larson wasn't entirely happy with the revised format and his new boss, and said: "The effort was to present a contemporary Western. Television is often following on the heels of what is playing in the big theaters. It's like audience research. Roy and I had a lot of differences over that issue. He was made my boss and I didn't have the last word. But it made a lot of sense for Frank to bring in a guy who'd had the most successful lighthearted Western in the history of television. At that point you can see the differences in fingerprints in where I thought the show should be and where Roy thought the show should be."[8]

Time limitations imposed on a mid–season show forced Huggins to reach into his previous work for material that could be readied up and shot immediately. "The Girl in Boxcar #3" (1:05) was a recycling of a first season episode of *The Virginian*, "Run Away Home" (1:29). Hannibal Heyes and Kid Curry replaced the Virginian in the boxcar, accompanied by $50,000 and a inquisitive young woman. "Return to Devil's Hole" (1:07) was another story adapted from *The Virginian*. Duel played James Drury's equivalent role, escorting the outlaw's "wife" (Diana Hyland substituting for Nina Foch) to their hiding place in Devil's

Hole territory (the Badlands). Fernando Lamas took the role originally played by Michael Rennie in "Vengeance Is the Spur" (1:22). "Strangers at Sundown" (1:27) was recycled as "Stagecoach Seven" (1:09), and "The Exiles" (1:16) as "Which Way to the OK Corral?" (2:20).

Roy also recycled six old scripts from *Maverick* because of time limitations," recalled Swerling Jr. "Exit from Wickenberg" [1:03] was a reworking of "Two Tickets to Ten Strike" [2:24]. "Journey from San Juan" [1:13] was based on "Escape to Tampico" [2:06], "Dreadful Sorry Clementine" [2:10] was based on the classic *Maverick* episode "Shady Deal at Sunny Acres" [2:10], "Everything Else You Can Steal" [2:13] reworked "Point Blank" [1:02], "McGuffin" [3:10] borrowed from "The Savage Hills" [1:20] and "Don't Get Mad, Get Even" [2:21] was based on "Game of Chance" [1:15]."

Familiar stud poker devices were also recycled by Huggins including the Maverick Solitaire a.k.a. the Five Pat Hands Trick, the Hoyle Rule, and cutting the Ace of Spades on the first attempt trick with a knife through the deck only to find the Ace palmed from the deck by Bret Maverick and Hannibal Heyes before the cut.[9] Despite the references to previous work imposed by network deadlines, Huggins was a prolific writer of original scripts. According to Jo Swerling, Jr.,

> Roy was remarkable. He would go out in his car with a tape recorder. There was something about driving that would set his mind loose. He would dictate into the tape recorder. Sometimes he would drive up north or south into New Mexico and stay in motels. He would come back with a complete treatment with dialogue. He had a story secretary whose principal job was to transcribe his treatments. He would then hand the treatments to a writer. They would have a meeting and make changes. The secretary would transcribe the entire story meeting and get rid of all the false starts and include only what they concluded. The writer would take that material and write a script. It was practically a script he was handed. Roy would come back with two or three complete stories. I used to say, "I don't think that a human being is capable of that. What I found out was that Roy was actually a hired assassin for the CIA. They would send him out to some remote part of the world to assassinate somebody and in the meantime they had fifty writers in a basement making up these stories so that he'd have that cover when he came back from his secret mission."

John Huggins also witnessed his father's long car journeys. "I saw Father do this forty or fifty times. He would take off with no particular destination in mind. He was a miserable driver by then and we always seemed to be a little worried imagining him talking into his tape recorder and just wandering aimlessly. He would come back in three or four days with as many episodes. He would come up with an entire episode in a day."[10]

Roy Huggins said that he discovered his writing technique "quite by accident while driving to deliver a lecture at Stanford and I needed a story for the show. Occupied by the driving, I found that I could do this kind of work better than sitting on a beach or in my study at home."

Swerling Jr. continued, "Roy would dictate his stories in scene form, like a treatment, and put in sample dialogue. Dorothy Bailey was his assistant and secretary. Another person transcribed his stories and attended story meetings. Roy's would come into the office at 11 a.m. and stay until 8 p.m. He'd go home for dinner and then go to his pool room out by the swimming pool and work on his scripts or reworking other scripts until 5 a.m. In his later years he would come into his office at 3 a.m. I had the role of making any and all decisions in the morning and attending meetings. I wasn't to disturb him unless it was an emergency."

John Huggins added,

> My father's hours of operation were quite strange. He would wake up between 1 and 1:30 in the afternoon and go into the studio and have story meetings. Then he would hit the editing rooms until 9, 10 p.m. have dinner with some writer or director and come home, get into bed and write until 5, 6 a.m. He liked the quiet. No phone ringing or kids running around. This was his schedule. I would see him during the week as I was getting up for school and he was going to bed. He'd be in the kitchen and he was at the end of his day as we ate breakfast. He always wrote on a yellow legal pad with a red felt pen in cursive that was incredibly difficult to read. One of the prerequisites for his assistants who would transcribe these stories and type them out was to learn his writing. He had very few assistants but they stuck with him."

Thanks in part to Pete Duel and Ben Murphy, *Alias Smith and Jones* was attracting a young female audience on both sides of the Atlantic and the stars were being featured in teen magazines. *The Daily Variety* (January 27, 1971) reviewed the premiere episode "The McCreedy Bust" (1:01), from a story by Huggins (as John Thomas James), where Heyes and Curry are hired by "Big Mac" McCreedy (Burl Ives) to retrieve a stolen bust of Caesar from Mexican ranch owner Armendariz (Cesar Romero):

> [T]he series has a nice mixture of wit and action going for it with only a modicum of violence.... The two key characters ... looked good in this ... playing their parts in a loose style that fits their whimsical fictive characters.... The future of the series rides with the character development of the pair and their relationship, and from this point of view shows promise.

The premise of two outlaws being granted amnesty if they stay out of trouble for one year presented a problem Huggins previously encountered on *Run for Your Life*: Going into a second season, why were Heyes and Curry still seeking amnesty? Once again it was a matter of real-life time versus "Little Orphan Annie" time. When *Alias Smith and Jones* was renewed, hopes were high for another successful season despite tough opposition from NBC's *The Flip Wilson Show* (1970). Huggins remained heavily involved as executive producer and writer. However, *The Daily Variety* review of the 90-minute premiere episode of season two, "The Day They Hanged Kid Curry" (2:01), was not encouraging: "Opening show has the pair ... trying to save a guy jailed for murder, because he claims to be Kid Curry, who happens to be one of them. Develops the guy wants all the attention he will get from this, even though a rope waits him. All this is about as easy to swallow as acid.... Duel and Murphy are okay but need good material more than amnesty."

Duel was still having trouble relating to Heyes' character as the second season got underway:

> I still haven't found my way around playing Hannibal Heyes. I know what Heyes should be, at least I did in the pilot. He favors sweet talking, card-playing and safecracking and needs situations to display those attributes. But when you put a series together in a hurry, it's hard to get scrappy dialogue for such occasions. That's difficult to do even with plenty of time. I make it a point never to criticize writers—they have the hardest job going—so I often work around the situation and dialogue, trying to have fun."[11]

Early into the second season Roger Davis, who provided the voice-over narration for the title sequence, was reunited with his *Young Country* co-star Pete Duel in "Smiler with a Gun" (2:04). Once again Huggins provided the story of double-cross involving a gold mine. When old prospector Seth (Will Geer) invites Heyes, Curry and smiling fast-shooter Danny Bilson (Davis) to help him dig for gold, they agree to their share of $5,000 apiece if they hit a rich vein. When they reach their target and celebrate by getting drunk on corn whiskey, Bilson steals their horses, canteens and food and makes off with the $20,000 in gold dust.

During filming on location, Duel collapsed with a bad virus during a heat wave and was sent home for a few days to recover. Unknown to Davis or Duel at the time, it would mark their final work together and take on added meaning when troubled actor Duel committed suicide by gunshot to the head in the early morning hours of December 31, 1971. Earlier that month, Duel appeared depressed as he expressed discontent with what he saw as the daily grind of acting on a weekly television show: "Any series is a big fat drag to an actor who has interest in his work. It's the ultimate trap. You slowly lose any artistic thing you may have. It's utterly destructive. It isn't the work that tires you, it's that it's all such a dreadful bore that makes you weary. I've enjoyed the odd show here. We get good people. It's not the show. It's the system. Finish a show one night, start another the next morning. If we had a few days between to study, to prepare."[12]

Duel wasn't the first actor to complain about feeling trapped in a television series. A decade earlier, Clint Walker expressed similar views about working on *Cheyenne*, comparing himself to a "caged animal." His words sounded similar to those of Duel: "The TV series is a dead end street. You work the same set, with the same actors, and with the same limited budgets. Pretty soon you don't know which picture you're in and you don't care."[13] But their reactions to the drudgery of work were very different. Walker stayed with the show until its conclusion, while Duel ended his own life, although Duel's boredom with work was compounded with occasional epileptic seizures resulting from an automobile accident as a teenager, depression and heavy drinking resulting in his driver's license being suspended in June 1971 for a DUI incident on October 24, 1970. In December 1971 a depressed and tired Duel told his sister Pamela that he intended to commit suicide.[14] Huggins recalled,

> I guess it was the day before he shot himself. "I went in to see the dailies on that day. Peter was so much better than he had ever been before—and he was always good. But on this day, there was nothing he could do that wasn't funny. He had an energy that was incredible, and yet all of it worked. In other words, it didn't seem to be out of character, or over the top. And then he shot himself. I saved those dailies. I still have them, because this was a performance—a day's work—that was extraordinary. And I came to the conclusion that Peter might have been what used to be called a "manic depressive." We have another word for it now (that's more politically correct). And I think he was at the very peak of his manic cycle on that day before he died. He was producing *art* in this flimsy medium of television. And then he came down off that peak, and blew his brains out.
>
> I was required to replace him. I had no choice, really. I closed down production. Within twelve hours, I got the word from ABC to replace him and go back into production "right now"—which I thought was rather cold and unfeeling. But they're a corporation, and corporations don't have souls. And so I grabbed a guy that I thought was kind of charming, and light. But he was not the right choice. He certainly was not a good choice to replace a dark, intense actor like Peter Duel. But I went out and I grabbed Roger.[15]

Jo Swerling, Jr. recalled the events after Duel's unexpected death:

> Roy's reaction was shock and sadness. Roy had a good working relationship with Peter and admired his talent. Ironically, Pete's dailies (about three days' worth) on the affected episode, were the best we could remember. His immediate decision was to send the company home, which we did, and let the series end. This decision was immediately overruled by ABC, which threatened to sue Universal if we failed to continue delivering shows as per the contract. In order to make air dates, we had to stay in continuous production. Pete's death took place very early on

Friday morning (New Year's Eve). By Friday noon we had the approval to replace Peter with Roger Davis. We located Roger in Aspen, got him on a plane, and I met him for a wardrobe session at Western Costume at 6 p.m.

The company was reassembled and was shooting scenes not involving Pete's character by 1 p.m. with all hands showing up except the director of photography Bill Cronjager, whom we replaced. He was so upset by Peter's death he preferred not to complete the episode. By Monday, we were re-shooting scenes with Roger playing the role. Later, we were accused by some Hollywood columnists of being ghoulish, but we all felt Peter would not want to be the cause of a couple of hundred of his friends to be thrown out of work. I had to cancel a New Year's weekend trip to San Francisco because of the tragedy ... for which my wife would never forgive me.

The four remaining Duel episodes, broadcast after his death, received the highest ratings to date for *Alias Smith and Jones*. Season three saw *Alias Smith and Jones* continue to maintain a respectable thirty share in the ratings and the storylines keep to a high standard. Spectacular location work in Moab, Utah, added to the new look. Swerling, recalled, "It was part of an all-out effort to pump new life into the series after the tragic loss of Pete Duel. I don't know if it actually worked for the audience as intended but it did make the nervous executives at ABC calm down a little. After all, the Monument Valley look worked well for John Ford."

Television critic Harold Schindler of the *Salt Lake Tribune* (September 26, 1972) was impressed:

> The weeks spent last August filming on location in Moab, Utah, with Ben Murphy and Roger Davis were clearly a plus for the series and the state. Roy Huggins, executive producer, and Jo Swerling, Jr., producer, picked a superior location for the cinematography and the camera crew obviously enjoyed its work (shades of John Ford!). The more Roger Davis appears in these productions the more comfortable he seems in the role. Roy Huggins' old Maverick touch radiates in these increasingly entertaining segments.

The initial order of only twelve episodes for season three revealed a lack of confidence in the series by ABC vice-president of program development Barry Diller. Sharing the Saturday evening prime-time slot with the new martial arts western *Kung Fu* (1973) every fourth week didn't help. But the greatest threat came from placing *Alias Smith and Jones* opposite the popular *All in the Family* at CBS. It was almost inevitable that *Alias Smith and Jones* wouldn't get a mid–season renewal. Cancellation and the halt to production came in early November with the final episode broadcast on January 4, 1973. Heyes and Curry still awaited their amnesty. *Alias Smith and Jones* had proven so popular in the United Kingdom where it was broadcast on BBC2 that the BBC offered to pick up the show but production costs were too high to make it feasible. Because of Ben Murphy's wage demands, his income rose from $450 per episode in the first two seasons to $5,000 per episode for the final season. In total, one episode cost on average $190,000 to produce. A major factor behind the early cancellation was Pete Duel. Had he lived, *Alias Smith and Jones* may have survived a third season. His tragic death made it difficult for many fans to find humor in the episodes and accept Davis as his replacement. Frank Price said,

> I think I placed a higher value on Peter Duel's value to the show than Roy did. Roy took Duel's death somewhat in stride. He liked Roger Davis and immediately brought him up as a replacement, if the network could be persuaded to continue with the show, which we did persuade them to do. Roy, you'll recall, used various actors on *Maverick* so he was accustomed to interchangeable parts. To some extent he viewed actors as fungible. I think Roy liked Roger Davis personally, probably preferred him to Peter, and certainly found him easier to work with. Roy was most optimistic that Roger's presence would fill the hole left by Peter's suicide.

Roy had an interesting view of actors and directors. They were people of limited ability. Top writers were the people of real talent. I had put a lot of creative energy, time and enthusiasm into the creation and selling of this series. Peter's suicide was devastating to me. All my work down the drain. Good, successful series are hard to come by. Plus I really liked him and enjoyed his talent. I hoped Roy was right that Roger would make it work, but I didn't believe it. Maybe he could have, had not the death cast such a shadow over the series.

According to Swerling, "I think Barry Diller lost interest in the show after the death of Pete Duel, and basically scuttled it, even though it was getting very respectable ratings. I do recall the replacement sitcoms, *Here We Go Again* starring Larry Hagman and Diane Baker and *A Touch of Grace,* a remake of the British show *For the Love of Ada,* didn't do as well as *Alias Smith and Jones* was doing when it was dropped."

13

Fallow Ground

Break up your fallow ground and sow not among thorns.—Jeremiah (4:3)

Adele Mara gradually retreated from acting following the birth of her children. John Huggins explained,

> Mother didn't miss acting. She'd had enough. Being placed on the blacklist took the wind out of her to some extent but more importantly she had three sons to raise. Although she had the means to have somebody else cook, Mother loved to do it herself. She told us, "You can't rely on some woman to cook for you so you had better learn to do it yourselves." To this day Thomas, James and me are the cooks in our families.
>
> As a kid raised in Dearborn, Michigan, she learned to slaughter chickens and thought nothing of gutting fresh fish. Later in life she would prepare the Spanish dishes handed down from her grandmother, make her own pate and hang her own prosciutto and prepare Japanese dishes such as Peking duck and shabu-shabu. When she was on location with Father, she would often discover her own cooking class.
>
> She would put on fabulous parties and was incredibly stylish. Mother loved to laugh and swore like a truck driver. Sometimes after a glass of wine she would put on her castanets and dance and make those castanets sing.[1]

Katherine Crawford added, "Adele swore with style, not with anger, that I saw. She was fun. Blunt. I like that. I think Daddy enjoyed her directness."[2]

Roy Huggins' knowledge of beekeeping at his extensive apiary on his Mandeville Canyon estate was put to use one day at Universal, says Swerling:

> We were in the office on the Universal lot, and Roy got a call from the gate guard at the north gate. He said there was a swarm of bees in a nearby tree, and they knew about his interest in bees, so he wondered if Roy wanted to capture the swarm. If not, they were going to call the exterminator. Roy said he'd be right there, and asked me to come and help him. I told him I was scared of bees, but he said not to worry. All we needed was a burlap bag, which he could hold under the swarm, then shake the limb, and the swarm would drop right into the bag. "Piece of cake."
>
> So, we went to the prop department and got a small stepladder and a burlap bag, then on to the tree. I was wearing my standard wardrobe of the era ... sport coat and tie. We placed the stepladder at the base of the tree, but the ground was not smooth because of the tree's root system, so I had to kneel down and hold the ladder to steady it ... right in the line of fire. I didn't want Roy to lose his footing and fall, so I held onto the ladder while Roy climbed up the three steps and performed his extraction.
>
> It worked exactly as he said ... except that not the whole swarm went into the sack. About

three-quarters of it did (including the queen). But the other quarter dropped like a bag full of jelly beans on to my back. In a panic, I let go of the ladder and started to run, simultaneously peeling the sport coat off my back and letting it drop to the ground, where the quarter-swarm of very pissed-off bees continued to attack it.

Fortunately, Roy didn't fall when I abandoned the ladder, but he did get stung a few times. Miraculously, I didn't get stung at all. Fast forward to almost exactly a year later, when it was my birthday. Roy came in and presented me with a large jar of honey, which had come from that very swarm, which was still thriving and being very productive.[3]

Meanwhile, work on *Alias Smith and Jones* was mixed with other, less successful projects. Pete Duel (as Peter Deuel) had filmed *Only One Day Left Until Tomorrow* in 1968 as a pilot for a series to be entitled *The Scavengers*. The story centered on two adventurers reclaiming a stolen jet from the son of a dictator. The pilot was shelved until Duel's success in *Alias Smith and Jones* prompted the network to release it under its revised title, *How to Steal an Airplane*, in October 1971. Swerling recalled,

> One of the incidents which took place during the filming was unforgettable, The Lear Jet we had chartered for the title airplane belonged to the owner of a large fast food restaurant chain and came equipped with its own excellent pilot, but one not trained in doing airplane stunts. The owner insisted that we use his pilot. The plane performed heroically, taking off through a wall of flames from a burning truck and doing various other maneuvers. All that was left to do was to land, refuel and take off for home. It's important to note that this was a small, private dirt strip in the desert near Joshua Tree, California, that we had to pave with tarmac so that it would be approved for this type of jet aircraft. The strip was barely long enough for take-offs and landings, so it was necessary, when landing, to touch down at the very beginning of the tarmac.
>
> The pilot was coming in properly, but just before touchdown, he hit a slight downdraft which made the plane lose altitude abruptly, making it hit a joshua tree with its landing gear. The gear was sheared completely off the plane. The pilot made a split-second and correct decision to veer off the runway and pancake the plane in the desert sand rather than on the hard runway, to minimize the friction and possibility of a fire. Neither the pilot nor the co-pilot were injured, but the plane was a total loss. My understanding was that the insurance settlement was around 750K, which was just about equal to the budget of the entire project.[4]

Sam Hill: Who Killed The Mysterious Mr. Foster? (1971), yet another attempt at a western series, failed to sell. The pilot saw alcoholic Sam Hill (Ernest Borgnine) become sheriff of a small town. In order to keep his job, he must find out who killed a visiting preacher and stole the $10,000 intended to build a new church. "*Sam Hill* was reminiscent of the old Wallace Beery move *The Champ*. Ernest Borgnine was the old sheriff who had this urchin attach himself to him. It was actually a pretty good show but it didn't get picked up for whatever reason. It would have been a standalone show and not part of a 'wheel.' They were looking to bring the western back."[5]

The TV Movie format often provided a showcase for pilots but the standalone *Movie of the Week* still had its place in the schedules. *Do You Take This Stranger?* (1971) starred Gene Barry, Diane Baker, Lloyd Bridges and Joseph Cotten in a tale about stealing the identity of a dying man in order to inherit his million dollar fortune. Swerling says, "The major difference between making a pilot and a *Movie of the Week* was in the casting process. It was faster and easier to get *Movie of the Week* guest stars approved by the network than pilot running characters. Also, there was a meaningful difference in the pay scales for writers, directors, and actors ... a premium being paid for pilots ... so budgets for pilots were higher. Other than that, the process was pretty much the same."

In 1972, Frank Price approached Huggins with the concept for a *Movie of the Week* based on Martin Caidin's novel *Cyborg*, about an astronaut who has to be "rebuilt" following a near-fatal plane crash during a training mission. Price recalls,

> When I pitched the concept of *The Six Million Dollar Man* to him, he tried to patiently explain to me why not only he wouldn't be involved with it, but that I shouldn't either. He thought I'd lost my mind and he was concerned I'd hurt my career. We later had some laughs over that. I should have known better than to approach Roy with the concept. I think to him the superhero concept was childish. I had grown up with *Superman* and *Batman* comic books as new concepts in entertainment. So I understood them. Roy didn't.
>
> The whole genre of superhero comic books emerged, as I recall, around 1938 when Roy was probably in college. I doubt that Roy read the Edgar Rice Burroughs books *Tarzan* or *John Carter on Mars*, which I devoured avidly. Roy was widely read in non-fiction as an intellectual, but his popular fiction taste and preferences seemed more narrowly channeled. His formative background was hard-boiled pulp detective stories, a darkish version of reality. Which, of course, is how he concentrated his writing efforts. Roy was somewhat astounded when *The Six Million Dollar Man* became a popular hit. I'm sure he still thought it was an awful idea. Different people are right for different shows.[6]

Cool Million (1972), an *NBC Wednesday Mystery Movie* created by Larry Cohen, starred James Farentino, rotated in a "wheel" format with *Banacek* starring George Peppard and *Madigan* featuring Richard Widmark. Huggins was enthusiastic about the show: "It's about as close as I can get to pure escapist entertainment. But I try to keep it on solid ground. I want the audience to enjoy it and they can't enjoy it if they don't believe it."[7]

Farentino described the concept of the show to Hollywood correspondent Vernon Scott:

> He only works for very rich individuals or big corporations who can afford a million dollars. They hire the character I play—Jeff Keyes—to save themselves millions of dollars. He's the last resort when all other channels of investigation have failed. Jeff is no charmer or James Bond. If he doesn't get the job done, he loses the million bucks. My character owns his own jet plane which helps explain why his fees are so high. I think the series will give entertainment value to viewers who really crave something feasible. This isn't like *Mission Impossible* which is a fairy tale.

Producer Swerling didn't share the enthusiasm of Huggins or Farentino:

> I thought the concept wasn't a good idea, but I didn't express this view at the time and tried to be supportive of Roy. The *Mystery Movie* format, like a number of our projects, was originated by Jennings Lang and it was a way of getting stars who were reluctant to do a regular series to do television in an important way. So Rock Hudson, Dennis Weaver, Peter Falk, etc., were persuaded to do a limited number of episodes. This allowed them to maintain the quality of their efforts better and to have less grueling production schedules. The format was one that NBC bought into, but the other networks didn't really buy this approach.
>
> The gimmick of the show was this former CIA guy turned private investigator named Jefferson Keyes who could solve your problems for one million dollars plus expenses. This was the sales pitch for the show, which worked. My fear was, if you give a guy unlimited resources, he doesn't have to use his wits that people expect to see in a detective show. All this guy had to do was to throw money, at it. If you give a guy enough money he can do anything.
>
> The stories just weren't very ingenious. Jim Farentino was a nice enough guy but he wasn't the brightest star in the galaxy. Writers would stay up all night to take a line that's going to come out of this guy's mouth and bend it a little but so that it isn't delivered in the first cliché that jumps into your mind. Invariably when we watched the dailies, Jim would use that first cliché. Jim was

uncomfortable with dialogue that had any style to it. Maybe he had trouble memorizing his lines and he just expressed the thought in the way that was the most comfortable to him. Which was the ordinary, humdrum, everyday manner. That used to drive Roy crazy. Maybe unconsciously Farentino would remove all the style from the dialogue and it would come out flat and uninteresting. That contributed to the problem.

While *Cool Million* employed exotic locales and had a sense of style enhanced by the excellent music of Pete Rugolo, the viewers didn't watch in sufficient numbers to merit a second season.

Huggins' reputation for rescuing struggling series was once again put to the test when he was brought in to produce two segments of *Jigsaw* (1973). The show was part of yet another "wheel" format with the unusual factor of the three shows being that they were produced by different studios. *The Men* (1972) consisted of *Jigsaw* (Universal), *The Delphi Bureau* (Warner Bros.) and *Assignment Vienna* (Metro-Goldwyn-Mayer). *Jigsaw* featured James Wainwright as the rebellious Lt. Frank Dain, working as an investigator for the Bureau of Missing Persons. His character was partly based on the real-life Detective Sgt. John "Jigsaw" St. John. With six segments completed, the show was in trouble. Huggins revamped the format, removing Wainwright's character from his police department affiliation and turning him into a private investigator incorporating aspects of Raymond Chandler and Dashiell Hammett by mixing various personality traits of Sam Spade and Philip Marlowe.

Huggins decided to shake the show to life by introducing the subject of lesbianism in a violent story revolving around a house of ill repute. Huggins was pleased with the loss of strict censorship on network television despite the fact the ABC Department of Standards and Practices asked for the word "gay" to be changed to "she's not straight."

"Television content has taken an awesome step forward this last year. Once theatrical releases such as *Love Story* and *Patton* were put on the tube with most of their dialogue intact, it suddenly seemed hypocritical for made-for-TV productions not to be able to keep up with the same sort of sophistication," explained Huggins.[8]

James Wainwright praised Huggins for his efforts. "What a difference it made having Roy there. We knew that the show was off-target.... Huggins came in and immediately hit on what was wrong. He understood the need for my character of Frank Dain to be freed from being a robot. We gave him humor and cynicism and a gentleness."[9] Swerling recalled,

> My most vivid memory of *Jigsaw* was the procurement of the first script we shot. James Wainwright had a falling-out with his producer, Stan Kallis, and Frank Price asked Roy to take over the show, which they agreed should be about a regular private eye, rather than one specializing in missing persons. Roy read all the material that had been prepared, and he hated it all, so we had to start from scratch.
>
> We had two episodes to shoot, rounding out the initial order. It was a Wednesday, and we had to be on the stage the following Wednesday, shooting, in order to make our air date ... so we had one week to get a script written, prepped, and ready to shoot. Roy and I discussed the writers we knew who were both good and fast. None of them was available. Roy agreed to do the second script, but he needed someone for the first one.
>
> While we were wracking our brains, one of our associates, Herb Wright, walked in. We told him our problem, and, without hesitating, he said, "Why don't you use Steve Cannell?" Both Roy and I said, "Steve who?" Herb explained that Steve was the story editor on *Adam-12*. Since *Adam-12* was in production, we assumed he wouldn't be available. Herb told us that didn't matter, that Steve could write a script for us over the weekend. We called Steve and met with him that day. He said he'd always wanted to work for Roy, and agreed to do it. Roy suggested they

meet the next day (Thursday) and come up with a story, then Steve could start writing on Friday and get us a script on Monday. Steve said he couldn't meet on Thursday because he had an *Adam–12* script to finish, but he could get together with Roy on Friday. Roy wasn't sure that would work, and told Steve he'd get back to him.

After Steve left, Roy asked me what I thought we should do. I simply answered, "Who else do we have?" Roy and Steve met on Friday, came up with a story, and, bright and early Monday morning, there was a script on Roy's desk which we shot without changing a word. Cliché of the day: The rest is history. It was the beginning of a very long and fruitful relationship between Roy, Steve, and myself which was very rewarding to us all."[10]

Despite Huggins' creative changes, he couldn't save *Jigsaw* from cancellation. He made another attempt to revive the comedy Western in 1974 with the pilot *That Is The West That Was* (1973). Originally titled *Hickok*, the television movie re-united Huggins with Ben Murphy who swapped Kid Curry for Wild Bill Hickok, teaming him with Kim Darby as Calamity Jane and Matt Clark as Buffalo Bill Cody. Calamity Jane turns press agent for Hickok in the mistaken belief he killed ten victims in a family feud. Meanwhile Buffalo Bill, who has a crush on Calamity Jane, sees Hickok as a rival for his affections and is bewildered by Calamity Jane's hero worship of his rival. Once again Huggins' attempts to restore the comedy Western to prime-time resulted in apathy from a public tired of the genre. Swerling Jr. recalled,

> *This Is the West that Was* was an interesting challenge. It was an attempt to spoof, and thereby expose, some of the legends of the old west, particularly those of Wild Bill Hickok, Buffalo Bill Cody, and Calamity Jane, as myths which blundered their way into history, becoming wildly distorted along the way. The script, by an excellent writer of westerns, Sam Rolfe, was awful and was extensively re-written by me (uncredited). It was directed by a distinguished television director, Fielder Cook, who, the previous year, had done a wonderful job for us on the Ernest Borgnine pilot *Sam Hill*. Fielder did a wonderful job getting great performances from an outstanding group of actors but somehow, when it was all strung together, it didn't make much sense. Ben Murphy was cast as Hickok, partly due to relationship and partly because we thought he was as suitable for the role as any other available actor at the time. I thought Kim Darby was spectacular in the role of Calamity. We always looked upon Kim as our lucky charm. She never disappointed us, only made us look good. Roy did one of his most magical editing jobs on the film, creating a whole new opening prologue out of stock footage from famous western features, and then tied everything together with a wry, witty narration, delivered by Roger Davis.
>
> When the editing was completed, I was the lucky one who got to accompany the final, un-dubbed cut to NBC for their contractual viewing. It was one of the most humiliating experiences of my life. To a man, they absolutely hated it. They wanted to cut the character of Cody, which was an outstanding comic performance by Matt Clarke, out of the whole film. Finally, they decided to just bite the bullet and slip it into their schedule during the summer when viewing audiences were at their nadir. It was released that summer to mixed reviews and the highest rating of any of their *Movie of the Week*s that year. Go figure.
>
> I do think that the kind of light comedy best exemplified in *Maverick* and *The Rockford Files* represented Roy's favorite approach to filmed entertainment ... you might call it cliché-busting. That's why he continued trying to come up with variations on that theme. The problem was that in order to reach the audience, you had to first reach a roomful of uptight corporate executives who had the power to say no, but not necessarily the taste to back it up. Or, maybe they just got up that morning and had a fight with their wives before coming to the office. Or, maybe they were right and did have their fingers on the pulse of the American audience. We'll never know."[11]

Drive Hard, Drive Fast was a drama filmed in 1969 but held back for broadcast until 1973. Race car driver Mark Driscoll (Brian Kelly) agrees to drive the attractive Carole Bradley (Joan Collins) from Mexico City to her home in New Orleans in the car belonging to her husband (Joseph Campanella). A bugged car, romantic triangle and pursuing psychopath (Henry Silva) add to the dramatic mix. Swerling recalled,

> I believe Roy Huggins appeared on camera as a newscaster, and I reprised a role that writer-director Doug Heyes created for me the first episode of *The Bold Ones: The Lawyers* which he also wrote and directed ... that of the "Fat Blonde Reporter." In that episode I was throwing questions at a police lieutenant about a recent crime. When I went to the dailies, I hated the way I looked, and I was in such shock that I didn't notice the editor had replaced my voice with the voice of Helen Alexander, my secretary. The projection room crowd got a big laugh out of that!
>
> In *Drive Hard, Drive Fast* I was an on-camera bit where I was in a group of reporters holding recorders and mikes, shooting questions at someone, in this case, the race driver played by Brian Kelly. Doug wrote me into three different scripts playing the same role.

After the third one, I told him, in no uncertain terms, that the Fat Blonde Reporter had retired for good."[12]

Although Frank Price was married to Huggins' daughter, their respective careers kept them busy within their own social groups.

> Outside of work we rarely socialized, but when we did it was always pleasant. Roy had his group that he had been part of for many years and I had my own group and there was almost no overlapping. Remember, his job was focused on turning out series episodes and occasional pilots. Mine was on running the biggest studio in the business, so Roy was one of many producers under contract. He was a "star" producer, but so were Jack Webb, David Victor, Bill Sackheim and Leonard Stein, so part of my job was to keep these producers as happy as possible. My socializing tended to be with network executives or our staff executives. The occasional dinners that Katherine and I would have with Roy and Adele were basically father-daughter dinners. Additionally, Adele and I got along well so the evenings were always enjoyable, particularly since I had great respect for Roy's talents.
>
> Roy was proud of his membership in Phi Beta Kappa, and as I recall wore his key on his key chain. He and Herb Schlosser had that in common and mutually admired their Phi Beta Kappa keys. They belonged to a very exclusive club, elitist by all means with difficult membership requirements. Roy had great respect for intellectuality and did not suffer fools lightly.

14

REVOLVING DOORS

"Not knowing when the dawn will come I open every door."—Emily Dickinson (1930–1886)

The creation of *Toma* (1973), *The Rockford Files* (1974) and *Baretta* (1975) are intrinsically linked in a convoluted journey from concept to television screen. Frank Price recalled the evolution of each series beginning with *Toma*:

> We had developed the pilot script for *Toma* and planned to do it as a "back door" pilot by making it as one of our *Movie of the Week* or *Movie of the Weekend* commitments for ABC. Tony Musante seemed to be perfect casting but he didn't want to do a television series. With no other exciting casting on the horizon, I spent a lot of time with Tony, persuading him finally to do the series. My meetings with Musante in New York City were always friendly and involved long, long discussions about "art" and "commerce" and "integrity." They could be very frustrating because he generally was dogged in his opinion. I signed him to do the pilot but couldn't get him to fully commit to the seasons beyond the first. The most I could get from him was that he would do half the episodes of subsequent seasons. Our conversation had started with him not wanting to do a series. The fact I talked him into doing the series at all led me to believe I could talk him into much more once he'd experienced success on the air. I ran out of time because, if we didn't shoot the pilot, we would miss out on the season opportunity. I decided to go with the most I could get from him."[1]

Prior to *Toma*, Musante had made an impact as street punk Joe Ferrone, who along with Pfc. Felix Teflinger (Beau Bridges) terrorizes a group of New York subway train passengers in *The Incident* (1967). Price continued,

> My reasoning was that I would have a year in which to change his mind and the problem with the second season would only come up if we had a hit series. As it turned out, we did have a successful season. But I got defeated in my renewal strategies. First strategy was to change Musante's mind. I tried everything, including great opportunities in motion pictures, actual commitments. He refused to change his mind. I also, working with Roy, had developed an alternate strategy that envisioned *Toma* as part of a wheel, like *NBC Mystery Movie* or *The Bold Ones*.
>
> The scripts of *The Rockford Files* and *Baretta* were both developed as potential candidates to be sister shows to *Toma*. The wheel could consist of two shows or three shows. However, ABC, whose programming head was now Barry Diller (never a fan of Universal), was uninterested in a wheel type of show and they specifically were not interested in the *Rockford Files* script. The real motivation was that we needed a sister series to sell the wheel in case Musante wouldn't change his mind about a second season. There could also have been efforts to do something with the Rockford character on *Toma* during the *Toma* season, since making Air dates was very difficult.

I vaguely recall Roy and Cannell failing to persuade ABC to let them devote one of the *Toma* episodes to a Rockford story (which would have given us a pilot of sorts—naturally that would have been without Garner). There were many schemes afoot, both to help alleviate the difficult production schedule and to prepare for the lack of Tony Musante in half the episodes of the next year. Since I couldn't deliver Musante for all the episodes of a second year, Diller canceled the show.

During the same pilot season, Diller (suffering from failing ratings of most of his new shows) was offered a deal to go to Paramount so he left ABC. Michael Eisner, reporting to Fred Pierce, took over the job of programming head. I went immediately to Eisner, showed him the successful ratings history of *Toma* and asked him to try to bring it back. He agreed. I got a commitment for *Toma*, if I could deliver Musante. I tried again. Still no dice with the stubborn Musante. I had hoped, with the success of the series and the experience of working with Roy whose work was turning him into something he'd never been (a star), that he'd see the light. I offered more money. That didn't work. I flew him out for a meeting with me and Lew Wasserman where we offered him committed roles in motion pictures if he would commit to *Toma*. He turned everything down. He had an image of himself as a dedicated artist.

So I then explored something that everyone considered insane. I met with Robert Blake, a highly respected actor who surely wouldn't do a television series let alone come in as a replacement choice. My lunch meeting with Blake was successful. To everyone's amazement he agreed to replace Musante if I could get the order from ABC and Eisner. I had an excellent relationship with his agent-manager that helped facilitate this and Blake and I hit it off beautifully. Roy, needless to say, had been consulted at every step of the way on all this.

With the Blake commitment in hand, I went back to Eisner, told him I couldn't get Musante, but that I could deliver somebody even better: Robert Blake. I told him to view *Electra Glide in Blue* [1973], where Blake played a highway patrolman with humor. Over the weekend, ABC executives watched that movie. Everybody liked Blake, so I got an order for *Toma* starring Robert Blake. That's what Roy and Cannell set out to deliver. But, as the creative process simmered and boiled, the project started looking less and less like *Toma* and more like the script on *Baretta*. I was developing a strong case of anxiety. I had sold *Toma*, but it was becoming clear that Robert Blake and Roy Huggins and the creative team would only produce *Baretta* and that's what it should be and it should be titled that too.

That meant I had to take a very difficult meeting with Eisner. I had to explain why I couldn't deliver what I sold them. I also, as a good salesman, had to make the case that this series was the same thing, only much better. Fortunately Eisner went along with the pitch. We then went full force into doing *Baretta* with Robert Blake, a show which retained some elements of *Toma* but was mostly new. Getting this show on the air was one of the most difficult, nail-biting sales tasks I ever faced. But it got done and we had a sudden new hit in *Baretta*, stronger in the ratings than *Toma*. And everyone at ABC thought I was a genius.

Naturally I am telling this story from my viewpoint. The story of the three blind men, who have never seen an elephant, but are trying to describe one by their sense of touch, comes to mind. One touching the ear of the elephant described an elephant as a leafy-like creature. The second, grasping the elephant's leg, felt it to be a tree-like creature. The last, touching the trunk, described it as a snake-like being. Since most of the people actually doing the show never participated in my meetings, they didn't know what was going on at the top levels of the network and the studio. And I wasn't in the production meetings with the producers and writers, nor the meetings with the lower level network executives.

> Swerling recalled his viewpoint of the creation and evolution of *Toma*:

Edward Hume originally wrote *Toma* for NBC. They didn't pick it up and we took it to ABC who ordered it as a *Movie of the Week*. It was a back door pilot. A back door pilot is a term for a one-shot TV movie that turns out to be a pilot. They didn't have to underwrite the script. That had been paid for. ABC-Universal had to make a deal with Tony Musante in the event that if it sold as a series he would participate.

It was an idea that was brought to Roy by Lew Wasserman, who had read an article in *Time* magazine about a detective in Newark, New Jersey, who wore different disguises when he worked undercover on the streets. He had a tremendous arrest and conviction record using these odd methods. Wasserman thought it would make a great series. Roy agreed with Wasserman.

The real-life detective David Toma was moved to Los Angeles and placed in a hotel. He was technical advisor an the show and was involved on a day-to-day basis. He even made some guest appearances. When it morphed into *Baretta*, he ceased to have any day-to-day involvement but he was still well compensated. He received a fixed royalty per episode during its three year run.

David Toma tried to talk Musante out of leaving. Musante later admitted that, creatively, *Toma* was the most rewarding year of his career. Tony said, "I'm not interested in playing the same guy each week. That's not the actor I want to be. I want do plays, the occasional feature and other television. I just don't want to be stuck in the role of one character." This was his philosophy going into the job. It was unique.

It was engraved in stone that MCA would secure a seven-year contract when a person signed on to a series. There were no exceptions to that. Roy persuaded them to make an exception. His argument was, "If the show is not successful, it doesn't matter. If the show is successful, no actor in his right mind would walk away from it knowing he's got bargaining power. But Tony Musante stuck to his word. Years later Musante admitted he wished he hadn't left the series.[2]

Huggins pitched a story to Stephen J. Cannell who was working on *Adam–12* at the time. Cannell completed the script in two days and was offered a producer position on *Toma*. Although Cannell wrote the opening episode after it had sold, he hadn't been involved in the pilot. Huggins took Swerling's credit away and gave it to Cannell because only one producer credit was allowed.

Huggins' next project reunited him with James Garner. Huggins' original story was turned into a pilot teleplay by Cannell. *The Rockford Files* introduced viewers to private eye Jim Rockford, who attempts to find the murderer of a young girl's (Lindsay Wagner) widowed father. Associated Press television critic Jay Sharbutt reviewed the pilot (March 28, 1974):

> A *Maverick* it ain't, but it may work, even though it was the sort of whodunnit that raised initial hopes with a brisk strangling, then seemed to take forever before the traditional Great Chase got under way.... Despite this plot, the show was liberally sprinkled with funny, offbeat little things that often gave it the sly *Maverick* touch. If the show becomes a series and the impression persists Messrs. Garner and Huggins could find themselves with another winner on their hands.

Although the show would prove to be a major success, Huggins was only actively connected with *The Rockford Files* for the first season. Price said,

> Having been closely involved as head of the studio, I recall Roy came up with the character and series concept. The Western may have grown weary, but Garner as a private detective bore a lot of resemblance to Bret Maverick. I was a strong believer in Robert Blake and I wanted him in a series. Blake, as a prospect for Jim Rockford, was only topped by James Garner. Garner in this kind of role and working with Roy was a known quantity. Robert Blake was a roll of the dice.
>
> We were having some difficulty getting scripts available for *Toma*. Roy came up with his idea to create another show that could alternate with *Toma* and give us more time to develop scripts. A writers' strike led to the shortage of scripts at the time. The original concept for *The Rockford Files* was Rockford only worked on closed cases. This was to be his specialty as a private eye. This got abandoned very early. It was more of a hook for selling the show. Roy picked up the MCA-Universal Studio phone book and found the name of a top agent at MCA who worked for Wasserman called Mickey Rockford. Roy said, "Hey that's a good name."
>
> I was aware of all this before Steve Cannell was involved. It's possible that he and Steve Cannell thought of producing a back door pilot utilizing *Toma's* production commitment, but that came after Roy's creation. Roy wrote the story treatment in his usual fashion. His normal

treatments were quite detailed, with each move of the story carefully detailed. Remember, Roy learned to write detective novels by studying Raymond Chandler, even copying in long hand one of his books so that he could get used to the thinking and style. So Roy constructed a story brick by brick.

If Roy followed his normal practice, he gave this treatment to Steve Cannell to write the screenplay. Steve had the rare gift of being able to write action stories with a good edge of humor. So Roy and Steve were a perfect combination. I'm sure Cannell would not have agreed to do the screenplay unless he was credited as co-creator. And that certainly would have been justified since he was bringing it all to life in the screenplay, making a dramatic vehicle out of Roy's prose outline.

I'm sure Cannell added his own character touches to Rockford. But Rockford is essentially one of Roy's characters. The alienated loner. That's a characteristic of much of Roy's other work. But not of Cannell's. So the real creation was Roy's. The execution was Cannell's. The final editorial work and film editing was Roy's. I wasn't in on the meetings between Roy and Steve Cannell. So it's always possible that I'm wrong in some detail here. I doubt it, however. I knew Roy and Steve both very well. But there is no question that the creation of Rockford was a joint effort and I'm just detailing the probable steps in how that took place. Roy and Steve Cannell, in a deal between themselves, created *The Rockford Files* and of course the character since that is what *The Rockford Files* is about. How they wished to share credit and royalties was their business.

Swerling recalled,

James Garner was among the nicest, most professional, least temperamental guys I've personally worked with but Roy and Garner had their ups and downs. Stephen Cannell thought he walked on water. James Garner always respected the scripts. He ran the set and the crew was his family. But if anybody wasn't pulling their weight they'd be gone. *The Rockford Files* was the smoothest running show you could possibly imagine because of how professional and cooperative and un-temperamental James Garner was. Garner wanted Cannell as writer-producer and Meta Rosenberg as executive on the show. He didn't want Huggins in an executive position because he knew there would be "terrible conflicts" if he did. Huggins being the source of conflict. Rosenberg insisted to Huggins on having Stephen Cannell as producer on *The Rockford Files* or she wouldn't do it. Huggins had the supervising producer role at this time. Huggins and Meta didn't get along.

Price added,

Meta Rosenberg was an agent. Whatever title she carried, she was still an agent. Jim Garner was her client and her mission was to do what he wanted. Together they were responsible for Jim's flop *Nichols*, on which Meta got the title of executive producer. She had firm opinions but no producing skills. *Nichols* was just a bad, ill-conceived show. The idea of using the turn of the century as a Western theme was certainly not new. There were terrible fights between the NBC executives and Meta in the course of producing the series. And Jim always backed up Meta. Jim was playing a guy who was the butt of the jokes, likable but too much of a patsy. The series failed and there were bitter recriminations all around.

When we were casting the pilot, NBC executives adamantly were against Garner and Meta because of their unpleasant experience working with them on *Nichols* but they gambled on *The Rockford Files* because Roy was involved. I rather liked Meta. She was interesting to me. When I got to know her better, she told me of her life as a very young woman, married to an older top talent agent who represented writers. She had affairs with a number of the name writers, including Scott Fitzgerald. I found her stories of an earlier Hollywood, long before TV Hollywood, fascinating. She was a good photographer and addicted to photography. But she was a tough lady, schooled in the tough world of bare-knuckled Hollywood competition.

Roy knew how to write the right character for Jim even though he had said he would not work again with Garner. When Roy came to me and said he'd changed his mind and that he thought he actually could work with Jim and Meta, he was probably not being completely honest with me. Roy had met with Meta who was aware of the *Rockford Files* script, liked it and wanted to do it. I questioned him very closely about this, but he was firm in his conviction that it would work. I told him I would have to overcome NBC's aversion to the team. Roy insisted on a deal that guaranteed him his producing fee and ownership, even if he was forced off the show. I agreed to the deal because I felt he'd be entitled to his deal if Meta and Jim conspired to get rid of him. I also felt that would help prevent their forcing him out since it would be so expensive.

I had to work hard to soften the network stance against using Jim. I sent the script to John McMahon, head of NBC West Coast, and told him that I had Garner committed to it. We wanted an immediate pilot commitment from them. I indicated it would next be sent to CBS and ABC, neglecting to mention ABC had already passed—no matter who starred in it. I told him that we, Universal and Roy Huggins, were capable of controlling Meta and Jim, and that we would not have the bad experience that they had suffered. To my gratification, NBC, overcoming agonizing doubts, gave us a commitment for a movie of the week–length pilot based on our script. The pilot was a great success and the network gave us a series commitment.

Roy functioned on *The Rockford Files* for all of the first season. In order to maintain control of the series, Roy had to have a contract that prevented Jim from getting rid of him. Roy was convinced Garner was hostile to him because of the failure of *Nichols* and would want to have him fired. I agreed with Roy and made the deal. I didn't want Meta and Jim getting rid of Roy. That would leave me holding the bag.

Roy decided not to take credit as executive producer and allowed Garner to credit Rosenberg. As the show progressed, he dealt more and more with Jim and Meta through Steve Cannell and Jo Swerling. Roy wrote seventeen story original treatments out of twenty-four first season episodes. He was concerned with two factors, script and post-production.

The first season was a success, but Garner threw temper tantrums about Roy, probably prompted by Meta. Jim felt the series could be done by Meta along with Steve Cannell and Juanita Bartlett. What I didn't anticipate is that Meta and Jim's desire to get rid of Jim was so strong that they were prepared to see him paid for each episode but render no services. When the show was renewed, Meta and Jim took the position that Jim couldn't work with Roy, but would be happy to work with Cannell. Garner wanted success without Roy's input. The network, faced with demands from the star of their latest hit, folded, as usual. I was left holding the bag. I had to take time from my responsibilities to deal with problems that came from the network executives, now exposed directly to dealing with Meta through Steve Cannell.

The reason for Jim's dislike of Roy? Well, it could be fueled by someone else with an axe to grind. Like Meta, Roy was highly intelligent, an intellectual, a writer protective of his creative ideas. Garner was an actor, charged generally by his emotions. And there's no IQ test necessary for that field of employment. Jim sounded terribly intelligent with Roy's words in his mouth. In real life, he had to make up his own dialogue.

Roy left behind a show that was well staffed, with people who were well trained. The second season started off on the wrong foot with Garner playing the butt of the jokes rather than the sophisticated guy who makes others the butt of the jokes. The network complained to me and I complained to Meta and Cannell. That led to a meeting and confrontation between me and Garner, where he got physically threatening in demanding I stop the criticism. I told him we didn't want the show turned into another *Nichols*. He said *Nichols* was his favorite show, the best thing he'd ever done. I said he could have whatever opinion he wanted, but the audience thought it was crap. That's when he smashed a cocktail table against the wall of his motor home. I took the opportunity to ease out the door of his motor home and felt relief at not being trapped between him and the door.

Regardless of the dispute, they stayed away from the buffoonish approach for the rest of the season. So Cannell managed to keep it reasonably on track for the rest of the series' life. Meta's duties were primarily budget and casting, and she was totally dependent on Cannell.

The first season of *The Rockford Files* featured fifteen episodes credited to John Thomas James. "The Kirkoff Case" (1:01) was originally intended to be an episode of *Toma* ("How to Get Away with Murder") but never went into production. Huggins adapted the story for the opening episode of *The Rockford Files*. The episode opens with Jim Rockford (Garner) chasing Travis Buckman (Roger Davis) onto a beach. Losing his trail, Rockford encounters Tawnia Baker (Julie Sommars), who invites him back to her apartment where she spikes his drink. So begins a convoluted story. Baker was involved in an affair with Charles Kirkoff, and Buckman with Mrs. Kirkoff. Both were found murdered with their son Larry (James Woods) inheriting $20 million. Larry hires Rockford to find the murderers while under suspicion himself for their deaths.

The appeal of Garner's portrayal of Rockford was evident in the first episode. He is everyman and not some impossible tough guy figure removed from the experience of the viewer. He loses teeth in fights, can't afford fancy restaurants, asks his father (Noah Beery, Jr.) for aspirin and often doesn't get paid for his efforts. He struggles to get along.

Juanita Bartlett had progressed from being Meta Rosenberg's secretary on *Nichols* to a story editor on the first season of *The Rockford Files*. She recalled,

> I lived at home with my parents. My father had been ill and wasn't able to work and Mom had to take care of him. Becoming a writer was a matter of survival. I had to take care of my family and my secretarial position didn't pay enough. I heard producer Frank Pearson was interested in submissions for a new Western called *Nichols*. I don't know where I got the courage but I was desperate. I asked Frank, "May I submit this? You don't have to worry about my ego but I'd like the opportunity to at least submit." He asked Meta if she had any objections and she said she hadn't. Her only demand was that Frank deal with me as he would any other writer.
>
> I worked long and hard completing the script before I turned it in. When I hadn't heard from Frank for a few days, I was thinking he hated it and didn't know how to tell me. But he told me he hadn't read it yet. The following week at work he approached me and led me to the end of the hall where he opened the door to a tiny office. "This is your office. You're going to be on the writing staff." I cried for the next two weeks. I would be sitting at my desk before my typewriter and burst into tears. It was so nerve-wracking but it was also a wonderful chance. I could fall flat on my face, but I was fortunate that Meta kept my secretarial job open should I fail. But I had the support of Frank and the other writers on the show.
>
> When *Nichols* was cancelled after one season, I went freelance working on shows such as *Alias Smith and Jones* until *The Rockford Files* came along. I was writing once again for Jim Garner. He's a decent, wonderful man and that comes through on the television screen. Steve Cannell was one of the nicest human beings I've ever known. I loved him dearly and got along with him beautifully. He was so helpful and a sweet, dear man. His death was heartbreaking but at least he hit the top.
>
> I liked Roy Huggins. He was a nice man and very talented. He used me a lot. It didn't scare him that I was a woman. Prejudice against female writers existed at that time but it didn't exist for Roy, so I benefited. He gave me a chance when other people wouldn't. It changed my life. At the beginning of my writing career, I didn't have a bank account and had to refinance my car to survive. The success of *The Rockford Files* meant I could relax. I was very fortunate and was surrounded by people I really cared about.[3]

Juanita Bartlett provided five teleplays based on stories by Huggins. "The Dark and Bloody Ground" (1:02) introduced the recurring character of attorney Beth Davenport (Gretchen Corbett). She persuades Rockford to help a woman accused of the murder of her husband. Soon Rockford becomes the target of those wishing to put a halt to his investigations. Once again Rockford's promised $200 a day plus expenses ends in empty pockets.

In "Exit Prentiss Car" (1:04) Janet Carr (Corinne Michaels) hires Rockford to check on her husband in Bay City. Rockford finds him dead from a bullet to the stomach with the gun yards away under drapes. The police call it a suicide and tell Rockford to stay out of Bay City but Rockford persists and uncovers a case of blackmail tied to an insurance scam.

"Find Me If You Can" (1:08) has the intriguing premise of Rockford investigating the woman (Joan Van Ark) who hires him.

> Woman: Do you look for missing persons?
> Rockford: Who do you want me to find?
> Woman: Me! I want to know if I can be found. I don't want your job to be difficult, I want it to be impossible.

"Caledonia—It's Worth a Fortune" (1:11) begins with dying convict Gerald Hyland (Don Eitner) telling his wife Jolene (Shelley Fabares) about a fortune in Caledonia, California. She hires Rockford to find it ($746,000 in rare stamps). Hyland's former business partner Leonard Blair (Richard Schaal) wants half for himself and only he has the directions to where the stamps are buried. But only Jolene and Rockford know the name of the town.

In "Say Goodbye to Jennifer" (1:18) Rockford is hired by an old friend, fashion photographer John Micelli (Hector Elizondo), to track down model Jennifer Ryburn (Pamela Hensley).

Given the quality of Huggins' scripts in the first season, Garner's criticism of his work seemed unjustified. According to Garner, the discontent peaked when Huggins sent an unsatisfactory script through without consulting Garner first. This resulted in Garner effectively firing Huggins as a writer on the show. Garner stated Huggins "went ballistic."[4] That would be an understandable reaction to Garner's successful ousting of Huggins from any future involvement in *The Rockford Files*, although Huggins stated he only intended to stay with the show for one season anyway. His "creator" contract that ensured he would continued to be paid a salary as long as the show was on the air was another source of aggravation for Garner, who disliked the fact Huggins received over a million dollars "just for conceiving the character."[5] Swerling recalled,

> I would say that in spite of my admiration for Garner, I think he and Meta were off-base in this instance. Of course Roy wasn't pleased by what happened, but his reaction was anything but "going ballistic." As far as Roy's standing firm on the requirements of his contract, there's absolutely nothing wrong with that. The detonator of the whole rift was the result of an interview Roy had with a *Daily Variety* columnist named Dave Kaufman. This guy would take you to lunch and pry information out of you, taking notes on a soggy cocktail napkin while inhaling multiple martinis. It's no surprise he was a chronic misquoter, and he even fucked up my relationship with Robert Blake on *Baretta* by misquoting me.
>
> In the case of Rockford, Dave called Roy and asked him for any comment about the state of TV in Hollywood. Roy responded by telling him that the level of production at Universal and the whole town was so high that it was almost impossible to assemble a top-notch crew ... that we had trouble doing so on *Rockford*. The part that didn't make it into Kaufman's article was what came next.... Roy said that with Garner's help and relationships, we had been able to assemble a first-rate crew. That was the little omission that caused an irreparable rift between Roy and Jim and Meta.
>
> I vividly remember a phone call from Meta, early in the morning on a day when Roy had left for New York. She was in a rage and asked me if I had read the Kaufman interview. I said I had not. She ranted that she and Jim were livid that Roy had dissed our crew. I told her that I couldn't imagine him doing such a thing, and that she and Jim should at least give Roy the

benefit of the doubt, because I was sure that he had probably been misquoted, which, of course, turned out to be true. I implored her to not jump to any conclusions until she could talk to Roy, who was on a plane and couldn't be contacted and therefore wasn't able to defend himself.

She wouldn't hear any of it, said it was just like Roy to say something like that, however, oddly, she said she respected me for standing up for him. Of course she and Jim were dead wrong, but the incident destroyed the relationship. It was all downhill from there. I absolutely agree with Roy's holding the studio to their contractual obligations. What Jim and Meta did in this case was irrational and wrong.

In 1975 Huggins worked on *Baretta*. It would run for four seasons. Price recalled, "Roy Huggins came up with the name Baretta. An anti-hero, loner cop who plays by his own rules and bends the law. Roy and Jo created the gritty style of the show. Blake was critical of the pilot script, ad-libbed lines and was not easy to work with. Cannell preferred working on *The Rockford Files*.

Former child star Robert Blake was born on September 18, 1933, to Italian-American parents in Nutley, New Jersey. Christened Michael James Vincenzo Gubitosi, he made his acting debut in 1939, becoming well known in a series of *Our Gang* and comedies and as Indian sidekick Little Beaver in thirty-two *Red Ryder* westerns. As an adult, Blake caught the attention of audiences as brutal real-life killer Perry Smith in the Richard Brooks–directed *In Cold Blood* (1967). He followed this with notable performances as Native American "Willie Boy" in *Tell Them Willie Boy Is Here* (1969) and as Arizona motorcycle cop John Wintergreen in *Electra Glide in Blue* (1973).

"Blake won an Emmy for Outstanding Actor in a Drama Series in 1975," said Swerling. "Blake always thought he had sold out and wasn't comfortable making the series. He felt *In Cold Blood* should have propelled him into movie stardom. Roy and Blake ended up throwing scripts at each other at times. Not everyone would put up with being criticized without retaliating. However, when the show and the day-to-day relationship ended, Roy and myself admitted we were kind of fond of the guy. In spite of his bad behavior we always did it to make the product better."

Price recalled, "Everybody's relationship with Robert was difficult, including Roy's. A lot of humor was generated through use of his short stature. The first year of *Baretta* was best because Blake accepted Roy's authority over scripts and production. Once success occurred, he used the power that an actor has who is the sole star of a hit series. He used up creative people like Kleenex. The quality steadily deteriorated as Roy was pushed aside and Blake took over. Blake was short but in muscularly good shape. He had an explosive temper and used physical intimidation. He had humor and could be charming, but there was a touch of insanity just below the surface. Roy collected his episode payments and let others handle the unhandle-able."

The first season featured six episodes credited to John Thomas James. "Woman in the Harbor" (1:03) opens with a dead body of a young woman floating in the harbor. Tests confirm it to be Virginia Marriott (Anne Colman), a former junkie and hooker recently under the supervision of parole officer John Shockley (Brock Peters). When Tony Baretta (Blake) meets his friend Shockley at the airport, he tells Baretta he last saw Marriott in Mexico where she was still alive. The positive ID is phony. Baretta re-opens the case after Shockley is run over and killed as he leaves the airport.

In "If You Can't Pay the Price" (1:04), Baretta places aging mobster Louis Durone

(John Marley) under surveillance in an attempt to intercept an $8 million shipment of amphetamines from Mexico. The episode provided an interesting character study of a strained "friendship" developing between Baretta and Durone as they both use their experience to gain the upper hand.

"The Half Million Dollar Baby" (1:05) featured Ann Prentiss playing Annie, the possessive, neurotic photographer girlfriend of Baretta in a story that relied on the familiar Huggins plot device of unclaimed stolen money. Unknown to Baretta, his girlfriend decides to keep a suitcase containing $500,000 for herself following a car chase involving the criminals. Baretta becomes the target of the gang, who demand the money and give him twelve hours to find it. When Annie tells Baretta she's leaving him, his suspicions are raised and he confronts her at the Greyhound bus station.

"Ragtime Billy Peaches" (1:06) once again saw Huggins freely borrowing his own material from *The Double Take* in a case of identity theft in a murder mystery about the death of a young woman whose past can't be traced. Richard Dysart played the lawyer with political ambitions whose young dead wife isn't who she appears to be.

In "The Coppelli Oath" (1:07), young Niki Coppelli (John Friedrich) promises his dying brother he'll kill Baretta. Feeling remorse over Coppelli's death, Baretta makes his own promise to bring to justice those responsible for turning young kids into drug dealers on the street—and to stop Niki from following in the footsteps of his dead brother by becoming a drug pusher working for Sal Bodine (George DiCenzo).

In "The Secret of Terry Lake" (1:11), Baretta discovers that attractive Terry Lake (Margot Kidder) is involved in a setup to frame Marcos (Joe Santos) for the murder of a mobster. But Lake is only a pawn in a mobster power play with her blind son being promised $50,000 for an operation to restore his sight in return for her testifying at the trial of Marcos.

The fact that *Baretta* was a mid-season replacement resulted in Huggins looting his own plots for two episodes but under his influence the first season of *Baretta* resulted in a mixture of gritty realism and hard-boiled fiction influences offset by the humor of Blake and warmth of his relationship and interaction with Billy Truman (Tom Ewell) and his pet cockatoo Fred. In real-life Fred was Lala, a Chinese-speaking cockatoo born in Hong Kong; his was taught key English words such as "Freeze" by respected films and television animal trainer Ray Berwick. His fame earned him a weekly $1,000 salary with a showbiz temperament to match and his own stunt double named Weird Harold. *Baretta* went on to reach #8 in the Nielsen ratings in the 1976–77 season before cancellation in June 1978 after four seasons.[6]

The Story of Pretty Boy Floyd (1974), a 90-minute *Saturday Night Mystery Movie*, was a well-received account of Depression-era outlaw Charles Arthur Floyd, who escaped poverty by turning to crime. Written and directed by Clyde Ware, it starred Martin Sheen as "Pretty Boy" Floyd. "It turned out really well and was one of the projects we were most proud of," commented Swerling. "It also starred Sheen's real-life brother Joseph Estevez, and our favorite good luck charm, Kim Darby. Pretty Boy's son, Jack Floyd, served as technical advisor on the film. An interesting bit of history: After Pretty Boy Floyd was gunned down by Melvin Purvis and other FBI agents at an Ohio farm, he was given one of the biggest funerals in the history of Oklahoma, second only to that of Will Rogers. It seems Floyd was looked upon as a sort of Robin Hood in that part of the country, and literally thousands of people turned out to pay their respects."

The year 1975 began with the broadcast of *Target Risk* (1975) starring Bo Svenson as bonded courier Lee Driscoll, who must fake the theft of $2,000,000 in diamonds entrusted to him in order to ransom his kidnapped girlfriend. Huggins was upbeat about the project. "I was beginning to think there were only four jobs held by television heroes—doctor, lawyer, cop and cowboy. Then one day I received a novel by Giles Tippette based on the adventures of a bonded courier. Now here was a fascinating character. The courier is a man of mystery who delivers anything. He is a one-of-a-kind man in a new and different line of work which has never been mined by television or films. I felt it was a fresh, new idea with great potential."[7] Huggins had to hold his enthusiasm in check when the pilot failed to gather enough interest for translation into a weekly series.

For his next project Huggins turned the gangster era of the 1930s. *City of Angels* (1976), co-created by Huggins and Stephen J. Cannell, featured Wayne Rogers as jaded private detective Jake Axminster, working out of Los Angeles in the mid–1930s. In his outer office, receptionist Marsha Finch (Elaine Joyce) shares the switchboard with a call girl service across the hall from the offices of attorney and friend Michael Brimm (Philip Sterling). The corrupt Lt. Murray Quint (Clifton James) is a cop with an intense hatred of Axminster. The 1976 pilot *The November Plan* was released theatrically in Europe but split into three 50-minute opening episodes for the series debut in February 1976.

According to Roy the style and fashion of the 1930s was foreign to the audience. There was a great exception to Roy's rule—Quinn Martin's *The Untouchables* (1959). I asked him about this and Roy replied, 'The reason *The Untouchables* worked is because it was extremely violent. The audience's love of violence overcome the fact it was a period piece.' Roy's theory didn't apply to feature films, just to television. *City of Angels* was not a big success and was a one-season wonder, although I thought it had a great look." Jo Swerling, Jr. stated:

"Wayne Rogers wasn't a major problem. He showed up on time, hit his marks, said his lines, and was pretty good in his role ... but he was a relatively constant pain in the bootie. What we had to deal with was an operatically inflated ego at work, expending excess with the first episode going through numerous rewrites. "I'm not sure the public is going to like this character. Invariably people make a comparison between Sam Spade, Lew Archer and Harper, which is unfortunate. This character is a little different. He has no emotional attachments, no plants, no animals."[8]

Rogers' comments proved to be correct with Jake Axminster failing to connect with enough viewers to stop cancellation after only 13 episodes. Huggins contributed stories to seven episodes. "The success of *Chinatown* in 1974 may have been one of the factors that sparked Roy to do the '30s detective show *City of Angels*," said Swerling. "He violated one of his own principles. Roy had a theory that there were only two periods in the world of television series. One was contemporary and the other was the Western.

Other periods of history would be rejected by audiences because people watch today's television to see what is current and in fashion. You had to stay hip with modern trends. The energy calling attention to itself. Wayne is a very smart guy, particularly in finance and business administration, which has been the basis of a successful career since his luster in the world of TV faded away."[9]

Huggins once again turned to the world of lawyers for the CBS sixty-minute pilot *Hazard's People* (1976). Criminal attorney John Hazard (John Houseman) and his associates Michael Chandler (John Elerick), Trish Cornell (Jesse Welles) and Ernest Clay (Roger Hill) seek to help noted surgeon Dr. Carl DeLacy (Michael Tolan) after he is arrested on the charge of murdering his mistress.

"Working with John Houseman was a delight. What a nice, super-bright, charming professional he was," recalled Swerling Jr. "The writer of the pilot, Heywood 'Woody' Gould, was a quirky, eccentric guy. The film turned out fine, but didn't test particularly well and got lost in the vast wasteland of unsold pilots, which was a disappointment because I was looking forward to working with Houseman."[10]

The Invasion of Johnson County (1976) was yet another pilot that attempted to revive the ailing Western genre. Bill Bixby starred as educated Bostonian Sam Lowell, who teams up with cowboy George Dunning (Bo Hopkins) to protect a group of humble ranchers from a cartel of Wyoming cattle barons who have raised a private army to steal their land and property. "It was based on an actual historical event and turned out well, but didn't sell. Bixby was a good pro and a gentleman," commented Swerling Jr.

15

BEST SELLERS

You cannot write anything that will convince unless you are yourself convinced.—Somerset Maugham (1874–1965)

Universal TV president Frank Price was looking for new projects to capitalize on his recent success with the mini-series *Rich Man, Poor Man* (1976). Price recalled, "I sold NBC on a project called *Best Sellers*. We searched for suitable properties that we could acquire. *Captains and the Kings* was one. I asked Roy if he'd be interested in producing it. He liked *Captains and the Kings* and got Doug Heyes involved. Since he and I both had Irish ancestors, *Captains and the Kings* had a special appeal."[1]

Based on the hit novel by Taylor Caldwell, the six-part mini-series chronicled the adventures of Irish Catholic immigrant Joseph Armagh (Richard Jordan) through the years 1857 to 1911. As Armagh makes a new life for himself in America, his encounters with racial and religious prejudice and corruption among those in power results in the idealism of his youth being replaced with a quest for personal power and the desire for his son Rory (Perry King) to become America's first Irish Catholic president. "It covers sixty years of the hero's life, from age fourteen on," described Huggins. "It also deals with the attitude toward the Irish in those days. People were absolutely fierce in their prejudice. They were considered to be one step below black slaves."[2]

Obvious parallels with the Kennedy family struck a chord with the viewers and the mini-series was a major ratings success with Patty Duke Astin winning an Emmy as Armagh's emotionally fragile wife Bernadette. Producer Swerling recalled,

> We were casting the first episode and somebody felt we should do an in-depth survey of the acting pool in New York. We wanted fresh faces in the younger parts. We didn't want to use the same people who had done a lot of work in Los Angeles so I was sent to New York to interview New York actors. Eleanor Kilgallen was the head of casting out of the New York office of MCA. The very successful Kilgallen-James acting agency had been bought out by MCA. Her partner Monique James became head of the contract talent department.
>
> I met many new actors in New York including Christopher Reeve. Of all the people that I read, I felt we had actors in L.A. who were as good and we wouldn't have to fly out and put them up in a hotel. Except for one. This girl who came in to read for the wife of the lead. Joseph only marries this girl to further his political career. Her father is a big oilman and he sees a chance to make lots of money. This girl is a plain Jane type. In walks this actress who had done no film and had only performed on stage. She was wearing a dress that looked like it came from the Salvation Army, with no makeup. She had been nominated for a Tony for her role in the Broadway play

Trelawney of the Wells. She looked very plain and read a couple of scenes for me. I was knocked out and called Roy and said, "This girl is spectacular. Her name is Meryl Streep. She's perfect for the part."

Roy replied, "But this is the part Patty Duke is interested in playing."

I couldn't argue the point. Patty Duke was an Academy Award–winning actress who had name recognition. She ended up being our only Emmy-winning actor on the show. I could have given Meryl Streep her first film role. Not longer after that, she did the mini-series *Holocaust* which launched her career and now is arguably the best actress in the world. One of the reasons I thought Meryl Streep would have been better for the part is the fact Patty Duke is very short and seeing Patty standing next to Richard Jordan was a little distorting and grotesque."[3]

Huggins followed his *Captains and the Kings* success with two more mini-series under the *NBC Best Sellers* banner. *Aspen* (1977), based on the novel by Burt Hirschfeld, was a three-parter shot on location in Aspen, Colorado. Sam Elliott starred as attorney Tom Keating, attempting to clear the name of a man (Perry King) sentenced to die for the rape and murder of a teenage girl. Swerling recalled,

> We traveled to Aspen to shoot establishing shots and to photograph the interior of the Pitkin County Courthouse, which we duplicated on a sound stage at Universal. We took our backlot Western Street, filled it in with snow, some synthetic and some actually made up with granulated ice, and it made a very convincing paraphrase of downtown Aspen. It was expensive, but effective.
>
> Roy would always forcefully let us know when we screwed up and it happened during the shooting of *Aspen*. Doug Heyes staged a very spectacular establishing shot of our Aspen street set, with a high boom shot of the entire area which settles on a Jeep sedan coming down the street, then booming down to a close shot of the driver's side window. This shot was followed by cutting inside the Jeep to reveal Sam Elliott driving ... our intro of the character. We all watched it being shot and thought it was absolutely beautiful ... until Roy saw it in dailies. He had Doug, me, and Dorothy Bailey, who was Roy's assistant and associate producer of the show, on the carpet. We were astounded at first, till he pointed out that the driver's side window on the Jeep was so fogged up, you couldn't see that it was our star who was driving it. He pointed out, quite accurately, that it could just as well have been a stock shot if we had to cut to an interior angle to reveal our star. He was absolutely right, and none of us had thought of it. Another lesson learned from our mentor ... and never forgotten.

Arthur Hailey's Wheels (1978), a lavish production set in the Detroit automotive industry, featured Rock Hudson as Adam Trenton, project development executive for National Motors. The five-part mini-series included the familiar mix of boardroom intrigue, extramarital affairs, drugs, blackmail and a bad guy in the form of crooked car dealer Smokey Stevenson (Anthony Franciosa) out to destroy National Motors. Gary Winter joined Huggins to work on *Wheels* after beginning his career at Universal in 1968. Winter revealed:

> After a couple of years in film editorial I made producer with Glen Larson. Larson, Swerling and Joel Rogosin were all equals underneath Roy Huggins at one point. When Larson broke away from Roy and joined Fox to create *Fall Guy*, it left me stranded without a show or an executive producer. I had a good reputation at Universal and Jo Swerling and I were friends on opposite sides of the camp. I had worked for Larson and Swerling was right hand man to Huggins.
>
> At the time, Huggins was in charge of two mini-series simultaneously, *Wheels* and *Captains and the Kings*. Roy was a very intelligent man with a sense of humor but when I was officially introduced to him he said, "You're Glen's boy, aren't you?"
>
> There was this Glen Larson connection and he was going to play with me like I was the ball of string and he was the cat. I was hired to work on *Wheels*. Roy would come to the studio at five o'clock in the afternoon to view the previous day's notes and check on the editors. He would "peel the onion" and continue to make changes. Some of it was tightening but a lot was artistic

choices such as where to put the beat. As Roy was giving his notes, I was talking into my tape machine.

Roy noticed and told me, "I want you to take all the notes and transcribe them to give to the editors so I know they're accurate."

I saw that as a compliment. We had five editors working simultaneously. Roy would hold court in the pecking order of how long you were with him and how high up your title was. I was one of the last. He was trying to teach me. He would critique my notes for spelling and grammar.

"Roy, I didn't talk as if I was writing a book. I talked in editor language."

"Well, it has to be correct, Gary."

Every night for a month he'd check my notes. *Wheels* was based in Detroit and we were getting stock footage of the 1968 riots. The editors cut it in as Roy had requested. There was a shot that panned from the street up to the Detroit bank. Roy said, "Let's reverse print that shot." He would just talk out into the projection room and notes would be taken.

I said, "Roy we can't do that. It won't work."

Roy shouted, "Stop the projector! Stop the projector! Turn the lights on. What does Glen boy want to tell me now?"

We were smiling at each other. He was never disrespectful and he never chewed me up.

"Roy, we can't do it because there's a man walking across the screen."

Roy was very quick on the uptake and he would get offended if he thought you were talking down to him.

"Yes, I see him Gary."

"Well, if we reverse print the shot, the man will be walking backwards."

"You know, another of Glen's boys years ago told me that I couldn't reverse a shot. I want you to redo the shot."

My producer Bob O'Neill and Jo Swerling both strongly advised that Roy didn't see the shot. On the night I was due to show it to him, Roy chewed up Mark Malis who was the head of casting at the time. I heard him on the phone while I was sitting in his office.

"Mark, it's Roy. Yes, Adele and I had a wonderful time last night. I want to congratulate you."

On the other side of the phone Mark is saying, "For what?"

"Well, obviously you've been made the executive producer of *Captains and the Kings* and *Wheels* because you think you're in charge of casting."

He never cursed but just diced up Mark and made it known Roy was executive producer and Mark was not to do anything without running it through him. This conversation went on for fifteen to twenty minutes and I'm thinking maybe I shouldn't put the film in the screening room.

Roy looked at me and said, "Are we ready to go to the screening room, Gary?"

We always walked like a *Bonanza* group. Roy would be in the middle with Jo and Bob to one side, then Dorothy Bailey and me on the outside. We walked wide to Room 7. The room was slowly filling with executives.

Roy said, "Gary, you've got something to show me?"

I replied, "I don't think so, Roy."

"I've heard you have something to show me."

So we rolled the footage and Don Sipes and Charlie Engel started laughing. Roy was absolutely stone faced. "Turn the lights on." He turned to me and said, "I told you that wouldn't work."

"Roy, I've got you on tape. I take the notes."

"Play it."

The entire room went silent as we listened to Roy. He looked at me and said, "That's not my voice. Don't you think I'd know my own voice? That's not my voice and obviously that shot doesn't work, does it Gary?"

"No, Roy, it doesn't."

We finished the screening and I was bemused and frustrated and a little mouthy. Swerling, O'Neill and Sipes then told me, "You know, he really likes you Gary. He wouldn't play with you like that unless he really liked you."

Roy made his own pleasures. I believe he was playing with me because I was one of Glen's boys and after *Wheels* was going to Fox to join Larson on *The Fall Guy*."

Lee Remick was nominated for an Emmy for her performance as Trenton's ignored wife Erica, who finds solace in drugs, alcohol and sex outside of marriage. The repeat broadcast, minus the final two episodes, was understandably a ratings failure. Price said, "I think the quality level of our novels for television was pretty good but my hopes and dreams for the novel form were being dashed by the fact that it was becoming clear that in reruns they performed poorly. Way below expectations. That seemed the death knell of a form I had pushed for so hard. Also, I had not liked the fact that *Best Sellers* had been programmed on Thursday night, since Monday night seemed the ideal night to draw the female viewers who were the core of the novel for television audience. We would have had more impressive ratings on Mondays, the night *Rich Man, Poor Man* aired to huge ratings. But the low repeat numbers were discouraging and I saw no way of correcting that problem."

Price's final project for Universal was James Michener's *Centennial* (1978). He said,

Centennial was mammoth since it was, as I recall, 26 hours long and filled with stars, a huge commitment for NBC and the studio. I had John Wilder in mind from the beginning. I wanted the creative benefit of having the screenplay written primarily by one writer, an approach that worked on *Rich Man, Poor Man* where I had Dean Reisner write it all. I didn't want the material broken into sections and distorted by different writing styles or approaches.

I also used the project to attract John Wilder to Universal so he would be a part of my "star" producer-writer stable. Selling series was greatly aided if you were able to offer a big name talent to run the show. John was in that category. Also, he had some prior relationship with Michener that warmed into a helpful friendship as the project progressed. I don't think Roy Huggins would have been a good choice to pair with a star novelist like Michener. Disagreements would have erupted. I knew Wilder was a diplomatic talent handler and I wanted Michener to be supportive of the result, which novelists sometimes aren't. Running a studio required Machievelian thinking sometimes."

Price left in June 1978 because Fred Silverman was about to take over at NBC, "a development I didn't like." He continued,

I was fighting to get out of my contract at Universal and go to Columbia. I had decided after producing *Ironside* and *It Takes a Thief* during the same year—a successful but somewhat grueling year—that I did not want to be a lifelong TV producer, like Aaron Spelling or Roy. That seemed like well-paid drudgery. Motion pictures seemed to me the right place to be.

I wanted to make pictures that people paid to see rather than turn out product that was sandwiched between the commercials, which seemed demeaning. Television was an advertising medium. The reason the networks existed was to sell advertising. The entertainment we produced for them was bait to pull in the eyeballs to watch commercials. I aspired to do movies that weren't interrupted by artificial breaks for pitch men. Movies that people actually paid money to see, not something they got free. One values something that you pay for. I think Roy had a disdain for commercials and basically ignored them. They didn't really exist in his world.

Earlier I stopped doing Westerns because I noticed I was being called a Western "expert" in newspaper articles and that worried me. Unemployment in the future loomed in my imagination, when the inevitable day would come that Westerns would disappear. That's why I got off *The Virginian* before the fourth year and produced the well-regarded but ratings-challenged *Convoy*. That helped erase the troublesome "western expert" label. David Dortort and Charles Marquis Warren had that label. They were in their sixties. At least. I was 35.

Ironside and *It Takes a Thief* cemented my credentials as an all-around versatile producer. But movies drew me because of the chance to have the time and the money to do the best work possible. When I became an executive in TV at Universal, I hoped to become head of Universal TV and use the experience to move to motion pictures as a studio head. Long shot thinking, but it came to pass."

Between *Best Sellers* assignments, Huggins completed a pilot whose theme was reminiscent of *Target: Risk*. Both pilots involved couriers. In *The 3,000 Mile Chase* (1977), Cliff DeYoung played bonded courier Matthew Considine, traveling cross-country to a New York murder trial with government witness Paul Dvorak (Glenn Ford). Assuming false identities, they are pursued by professional gunmen. Swerling commented, "*The 3,000 Mile Chase* was not one of our most auspicious pilots. The series was to be called *The Courier* and, obviously was about a courier who totes sensitive and/or valuable items around the world which others would like to get their hands on. Glenn Ford was the consummate pro and a very gracious gentleman."

Huggins' final *Best Sellers* mini-series for Universal was *The Last Convertible* (1979), based on the novel by Anton Myrer. Swerling made his directorial debut on episode two. He said,

> The story was about a group of Harvard roommates (and their girlfriends) and was broken up into three time frames: Their freshman year, which culminates with the attack on Pearl Harbor, was episode one. The war years was episode two. The twentieth reunion of the class was episode three. Episode two, the war years, was heavily based on stock footage, which I had collected over a period of several months, looking at virtually every World War II picture ever made. Rather than prep a director with all the stock footage and the specific material the writer wrote based on that footage, Plan A was to have me direct the scenes involving stock integration and have another director do the straight dramatic scenes. At the time, the Directors Guild of America had a rule precluding using two directors, simultaneously, on a film. So, we thought it would be simpler for me just to go ahead and direct the whole episode. Therefore, the DGA, in all its wisdom, gained a new member and lost a job for an established one.
>
> Although I had directed second units and pick-up shots many times in the past, this turned out to be the only complete episode I ever directed. As a film director, I was definitely a one-trick pony. It was a lot of fun, though. The cast was so great, they didn't need much, if any, direction, so I could spend my time worrying about the action stuff and only concern myself with not jumping the proscenium, or breaking any of Roy's "Rules for Directors," and keeping the atmosphere on the set comfortable for the actors so they could do their best work."[4]

Huggins left Universal in 1980, and his long-time associate Swerling left in 1981. Their penultimate project for Universal was *The Jordan Chance* (1978) starring Raymond Burr as attorney Frank Jordan, who was imprisoned for seven years for a crime he didn't commit. His main goal in life is to defend those wrongly accused and convicted. Swerling said,

> Raymond Burr was a very hard-working guy and a gentleman, who owned an island in the South Pacific and felt responsible for the well-being of the people in his village. He spent lots of money and time on his island. The only wrinkle I would have about Raymond is he was a time vampire. He would drop in on your office when you were buried in work and chat with you. But you couldn't refuse him."

Despite having the proven star power of Burr, the pilot failed to interest networks enough to commission a series. Swerling recalled working on his final project with Huggins at Universal in 1980:

> *The Secret War of Jackie's Girls* was the project I would most like to forget. It was brought to Universal by a producing team, Florence Small and Alan Surgal, under the umbrella of their

company, Penthouse Productions. Florence Small was the sister of a one-time head of CBS News and, as such, had some clout with the networks. Universal executives thought they were too inexperienced to be in charge of a production of this magnitude, so they asked Roy to supervise it.

I believe it was Charlie Engel who approached Roy with the proposition. Roy gave me and others the script Ms. Small had prepared, and I was horrified. Not only was it terrible in every way, but the premise was totally false. Originally, it was based on a true background, which dealt with female pilots, like Jackie Cochran, who ferried aircraft from the U.S. to bases overseas. One of the geniuses at NBC rightly concluded that ferrying aircraft was intrinsically boring, and that the concept should be changed to a small band of female pilots who performed secret missions behind enemy lines, using a new type of aircraft ... helicopters!

This idea was so utterly fictive ... there were no female combat pilots in World War II, nor were there any helicopters, at least not until the very end of the war, when there were a few experimental ones. This was the form the script was in when we first read it. Dorothy (who was Roy's assistant, but who had received associate producer credit before) was as negative on the script as I was. Of course, Roy hated it, too, but, much to our surprise and amazement, he accepted the assignment. He immediately started to revise the script. Small and Surgal, who turned out to be a married couple (we didn't know this at first), immediately were at odds with Roy and fought him all the way.

Their son, Jon Surgal, was first introduced to us as their driver. Then, as if by magic, he became their son. Then, they insisted he be given credit as executive producer. The studio caved in to Florence's demand. At that point, I took my name off the picture. Anyway, the whole project was a disaster and a nightmare of confrontation and unpleasantness. The only fun I had was supervising the modification of three two-seater Bell helicopters, making them look primitive enough to be believable as early designs. Also, working with the aerial second unit, gaffed by the great chopper stunt pilot Jim Gavin, was a hoot. We all hated the project so much, we renamed it (for our use only): *Chopper Pussies*."

Swerling continued at Universal without the guidance of Huggins. "I was not panicked but felt a definite sense of loss. I would call Roy my rabbi even though he was a Catholic who came into the office on Ash Wednesday with a cross of ashes on his forehead. He insulated me from the executives in the Black Tower. He watched my back and I watched his. Within a year I left Universal for Stephen Cannell."

John Huggins recalled the story behind the Ash Wednesday tradition:

Mother wasn't a churchgoing Catholic but she did her Rosary every night, would take us to church on the high holidays and we never ate meat on Friday. Father Jose Maria was a Jesuit priest and a well-respected figure in Spain who would visit and stay at our house. We observed certain holy days and on Ash Wednesday, Mother would appear out of nowhere and before I could say anything she would put an ash cross on my forehead. I would say, "Mother you can't do that, you aren't an ordained priest."

She would reply, "There ashes have been blessed by Father Jose Maria. So they're perfectly fine to use." Mother kept her own private stash of blessed ashes and would place the ash cross on our father as well.[5]

In 1978 Meta Rosenberg produced an updated version of *Maverick* called *The New Maverick*. The CBS-TV movie saw Garner and Jack Kelly reprise their roles as Bret and Bart Maverick and introduced Ben Maverick (Charles Frank). The result was the short-lived spin-off series *Young Maverick* (1979) starring Frank as Ben Maverick, the Harvard-educated son of British-born cousin Beau, and Susan Blanchard as his love interest Nell McGarrahan. The show lasted eight episodes. Reviews were understandably harsh. Peter J. Boyer of the Associated Press (November 1979) wrote: "Ben Maverick ... has inherited, the CBS promotions tell us, the Maverick 'good looks and charm, great skill with cards and a healthy respect for cowardice.' Unfortunately, he has not inherited Roy Huggins, who made the original *Maverick* with a special touch, or the exquisite charm of James Garner's Bret—things that cannot be written into the script."

In 1981 ABC revived *Maverick* yet again in *Bret Maverick*. Bret was now owner of a ranch and part-owner of the Red Ox Saloon in Sweetwater, Arizona. But once again the series floundered despite the weekly presence of James Garner. Rosenberg and Garner parted company after seven episodes. Garner then approached Huggins through his agent but Huggins wasn't impressed with the new format. *Maverick* was now located in one town, Bret's wandering days behind him. *Maverick* wasn't true to Huggins' original concept and the show was cancelled before Huggins could tell Garner he wasn't interested. In the final episode, Jack Kelly briefly reprised his role as Bart Maverick in a brief cameo scene that brought the series to a premature end.

Frank Price concluded, "It's interesting how Meta and Jim tried twice to return to *Maverick*. The only thing they lacked for success was Roy. It was a source of considerable annoyance to Roy that Warner Brothers was the 'author' of all those series. So any further variations on *Maverick* would not have generated any payments to Roy. It's hard to do a living author out of his creations but Warner Brothers did."

On February 2, 1979, Jack Whittier Huggins passed away from a heart attack at his home in Tucson, Arizona. He was sixty-seven years of age and left behind a son and four daughters. After graduating from the University of Oregon with a Bachelor of Arts degree in English in May 1936 he earned a masters degree from UCLA in 1939. Marriage to Roann Elizabeth Thornburg on January 20, 1941, was followed four years later by a change of location as he joined the teaching staff at the University of Arizona where he specialized in Irish literature. He also initiated the Southwest Studies department with his class on Literature of the Southwest United States. He was a popular teacher who in 1966 was named Outstanding Teacher at the University of Arizona and his course was famous for debunking many myths of the Old West. The paths of Roy and Jack Huggins diverged later in life but the younger brother always looked to Jack as a figure of high intellect who he continued to aspire to. His passing cut the links to Roy Huggins' childhood and youth.

Huggins and Adele Mara at the Pioneer of the Year Award dinner for Frank Price in 1982 (courtesy Katherine Crawford).

Huggins left Universal in 1980 and effectively went into semi-retirement. Frank Price, then head of Columbia Pictures, had a role in luring Huggins back to television as executive producer on

Blue Thunder in 1984. The feature film starring Roy Scheider had been a hit for Columbia and a spin-off series seemed a good option. But Huggins soon encountered friction. "The people at ABC wanted to produce the show. I wasn't being allowed to produce the show, so I quit. I had the same argument 35 years ago when I started television. These people weren't even born then," stated Huggins.[6]

Although in a position to employ Huggins on film projects at Columbia, Price reasoned, "It would have taken a special kind of project for Roy to have transitioned to features." He continued,

> The writer-producer is king in television. Roy was one of the first. They still rule television. Writers are the people that are able to guarantee that there will be a script written each week and therefore the show will air each week. A producer who can't write lives in total fear of the fact that if one writer does not turn in a script, the screen will go dark. A writer-producer can always write the script himself if an outside writer fails.
>
> The director, sometimes writer-director, is king in features. Roy felt the role of director was an artificial creation of the motion picture business and that French critics had created a false aura about directors that permeated the business. He pointed out that drama had existed for over two thousand years and during all that time plays were directed either by the writer or, more often, by the lead actor. The lead actor often formed a company and chose the plays and directed them. It wasn't until motion pictures that the cult of the director was born.
>
> I'm sure Roy was influenced in his dismissive attitude toward directors by the fact that he was a writer. Writers in Hollywood motion pictures are certainly on the low end of the totem pole. The normal role of feature producer would have been a poor fit for Roy and a waste of his talents. Although we nearly got together on a *Texas Ranger* project with Chuck Norris, but it didn't happen.

16

Rejuvenation

"Leadership and learning are indispensable to each other."—John F. Kennedy (1917–1963)

Stephen J. Cannell admitted his television show *Hunter* was in serious trouble during its first season. Fred Dryer, 42-year-old former New York Giants and Los Angeles Rams defensive end, had been cast in the lead as homicide detective Hunter. Critics were not kind about the acting or scripts. The television audience shared their lack of enthusiasm, relegating *Hunter* to the 65th prime-time show. NBC cut *Hunter* from its schedule after three months of weak ratings and found a home for it on Saturday evenings a few months later. Ratings improved but it was only Cannell's good relationship with NBC that granted the show a "mercy pickup" for a second season.

Cannell decided to give Huggins a call to take over the reins while he and fellow production partner Frank Lupo worked on other projects. Cannell looked to Huggins as his mentor. "My first impression of Roy Huggins was seeing him walking across the Universal lot in 1971. I was twenty-eight and standing alone watching him trailing assistants like planetary moons, gesturing as he walked. He was heading toward the editing building where, I later came to learn, he was the maestro extraordinaire."[1]

Huggins agreed to come out of retirement to help his good friend Cannell and immediately set about charging the approach to the stories. "My approach has always been to make it a movie. You've only got 50 minutes, but make it as close to a movie as you can. By that I mean put the emphasis on the story. Storytelling is a difficult craft. It's not easy," stated Huggins.[2]

Although Dryer had been a successful football player during his thirteen-year career, he didn't want to transfer to acting on the back of his fame as an athlete. Acting lessons with Nina Foch provided essential training to attract casting agents looking for more than an "ex-jock." He auditioned for a new comedy show called *Cheers* (1982) and to his pleasant surprise found himself called back for the role of bartender Sam. He was up against Ted Danson and William Devane. Danson got the role and Dryer teamed up with Cannell on *The Rousters* (1983). The series failed but Dryer had caught the attention of Cannell, and *Hunter* followed. Huggins was also impressed with Dryer: "I think Fred is an actor who just happened to play football. People just love Fred Dryer."[3]

Stepfanie Kramer, a graduate of the American Academy of Dramatic Arts, made her television debut in 1977 on *Starsky and Hutch* (1975). Prior to being cast as Sgt. Dee Dee McCall on *Hunter*, she had a regular role on the sitcom *We Got It Made* (1983). She said,

"The original title of the show was *Hunter and McCall*. The reason it became a one-name title was that Stephen Cannell had another series named *Hardcastle and McCormick*. The network thought the H and M connection might confuse viewers. The characters were always well-defined and in the initial season the overriding tone was a great deal of action in keeping with the success of *Miami Vice*. We ultimately ended up replacing *Miami Vice* as the number one crime drama on NBC as a result of the restructuring following Roy Huggins' arrival.

Stephen told me he was bringing in a new executive producer during hiatus. Roy called and invited me to lunch. When I walked into the restaurant in my sun dress and sandals, Roy's face just dropped. His first words were, "Oh my God, you're just a kid."

I thought to myself, "What were you expecting?" I think he believed that I was very much like the character I portrayed, a tough detective. The character was written for a woman ten years older than me. In spite of that, Stephen Cannell always supported me for the role. For that I will always be grateful.

That first meeting with Roy set the tone for our relationship. I think he always looked upon me as a kid. There was more of a paternal energy in how he dealt with me in certain ways. That can also lead to not being taken seriously at a certain level but I proved myself to him in pretty short notice.

We always had strong character construction but it became more plot-driven and more of a West Side show as opposed to downtown Los Angeles. Roy emphasized the more lovely visuals that Los Angeles and Southern California offered as opposed to the horrible downtown locations. Fred Dryer felt strongly about this as well. That was a big shift in terms of the tone and energy of the show. He brought a lot of movement that helped to re-establish the show in such a way that it became a huge hit. He made a significant difference.

I only had one major area of conflict with Roy regarding a proposed rape storyline based on a book by former L.A. detective Dallas Barnes. Actor and director James Whitmore, Jr., who was always a dear friend, said, "Have you read the next script that's coming up? You need to read it."

"Is there something wrong with it?" I asked.

"You know what, honey, they want to rape you again on the show."

"What?"

I read the script and said, "We covered this scenario in season two and the story was written well and it was well-received. To rape the character again is purely for ratings, and it perpetuates the cycle of violently exploiting women on film. It's not necessary to repeat this, and I feel strongly that it should not be done."

I often wonder if Roy wasn't aware of that previous two-part episode "Rape and Revenge" (2:06–07). I have no idea. I think there had been a disconnect between the actors and the executive producers. I felt that they needed to talk to us about what they were doing in terms of storylines and character arcs. We need to communicate because we are working together on this show. The press got wind of this conflict and I ended up giving interviews to the press and on talk shows about it. Everybody got on board behind me and said, "The girl's right." Eventually Roy acquiesced and it was rewritten to reflect an "attempted" rape. After he changed the rape storyline, he came on the set afterwards and we hugged each other. I believe there's a level of acceptance and forgiveness in life and it serves no one to harbor bad feelings. I think that's important. In this conflict with Roy, it wasn't about control, for me it was just about doing the right thing.

After that event, it changed dramatically. Fred and I had input on all of the scripts and even decided who we would have and not have as directors. It changed a lot. There was more of a collaborative energy moving forward, not an old paternal pedagogy of "Here's what you do."

In the early seasons, one of the things I loved about my character was that I was often put "undercover." I don't think there was another role on television that offered that potential to an actress. I had the opportunity to portray other characters and colloquialisms. I was able to draw upon my theater training and that was a lot of fun for me. Initially one of the things they did a lot was to put me undercover as a prostitute. I was always walking around in skimpy outfits and that grew really old after awhile. I would stress that there were so many more interesting possibilities here, let's not go with the obvious. Roy agreed. I think that Roy was a product of his time. He was "old school."

I'm a writer and director as well as an actress. From a writing point of view you strive to create a fully developed character on the page. However, when you give that information on paper to somebody else and say "Breathe life into this person, manifest this person"—everyone has a different "perception" of who they think they're reading. They have their own personal projections and imprints onto that man or woman based on their own personal internal journeys. It's in our minds. When you give the part to an actor and say "Make this character real, embody this energy" ... hopefully you find the person who best embodies that individual you created. Ultimately it's the character brought to life by an actor, that people will resonate to. It really becomes a shared experience.

There were many times in my years on *Hunter* that I would sit in my trailer and rewrite our dialogue and scenes. Fred Dryer often did the same. Sometimes new writers would come in and write dialogue that McCall or Hunter would never say. Once you embody your character, you know them better than anybody. Luckily we had a talented group of writers who were always willing to work together. It became a natural progression of collaboration. I think Roy respected my position in this regard, and never took issue with it.

I left after the sixth season. I had achieved what I wanted and needed to do on the show. I had written and directed and had come to a place in my life as an artist and a woman where I needed to go to the next level of my life experience, both professionally and personally. It could not have done this, had I stayed on the show. I gave this a great deal of thought. It wasn't a haphazard decision. Some people judged my choice harshly, yet I find that sometimes people will judge "your" personal choice based on "their" personal needs. They had no idea what mine were. I made the right choice for me at the right time for the right reasons.

During an initial meeting with Roy where we were discussing what direction we wanted to take the show, he looked at me and said, "And I've figured out her name."

"I'm sorry?"

"Dee Dee. I've named her. Her name is Deidre Deandre."

"No it's not Roy. It's Deanna."

In my mind it was Deanna. I came from a theater background, so I always developed a character, which included at the very least her name. Roy didn't realize I had already done all this work and was so surprised. I don't think he quite knew what to make of me in the beginning, yet over time it proved to be a very beneficial and productive collaboration. He was a very talented man."[4]

Gary Winter worked as director and post-production executive on *Hunter*. He reminisced:

In 1983 *Hunter* was created in a co-partnership with Steve Cannell and Frank Lupo. Both Steven and Frank were paying way too much respect for each other when we got to the cutting sessions. They would also split the scripts. *Hunter* had all the potential in the world but it was floundering in the ratings. The show over-indulged in action above character. Cannell in his wisdom, probably in consultation with Jo Swerling, decided to bring Roy out of retirement. He made *Hunter* a partner show and as the weeks went on, Stepfanie Kramer was becoming more popular.

Before Roy joined *Hunter*, Cannell promised I could direct an episode. But when Roy came on board, Cannell said, "I don't know about your directing assignment, Gary. It's now up to Roy." I knew that was going to happen. Two days later, Roy called me down to his office. I was always joking with him about my being on the sixth floor and he was on the fourth floor. I would be a kind of Don Rickles to him. Roy enjoyed that.

"I just want you to know you get to keep your directing assignment."

I was really touched. "I have one piece of advice for you."

"Only one?" I laughed.

"This is a character-driven show. Not a gun- and car-driven show."

"I understand that."

I was given part one of the two-part episode "Rape and Revenge" (2:06) where Dee Dee McCall is raped by a South American diplomat who has diplomatic immunity. I was so fortunate that I got that script because it was really Stepfanie Kramer's defining moment. Being a new director, I went to Stepfanie and said, "This is really all about you. How about if I come up with the angle but you tell me what you want to do."

She had to repeatedly cry over and over. It was a drain on her emotions. We came up with a plan that when she was ready, she would call the roll of the camera. We took the bell off of the Negra and had minimal people on the set. Stepfanie would sit or stand and stare and when I could see her eyes were starting to fill up, everything was done in hand signals. No clapper. No marker. Nothing. Then she would go into the scene. We did that day after day. I really didn't direct that show. She didn't take my directing powers away but she was the one that made that episode. The second hour director had directed numerous *A-Team* episodes. It was written with more action and it was as if the two episodes didn't really belong together.

I'm on the set of my next episode "The Beautiful and the Dead" (2:20) and I get a call from Roy to see him in his office when I've completed shooting for the day. He loved to sit and talk and teach.

"Now, Gary. You see here where you're shooting behind Fred Dryer's car and he's on a surveillance and the car is down the street. In the real world, the bad guy would see Fred."

"But nowadays, Roy, we use lens compression."

"Gary, did you learn that from Glen? You must have learned that from Glen."

"No, actually I learned that from *The A-Team*."

"We don't do that any more on *Hunter*."

My moments with him were like father and son. He took great pleasure out of my jousting with him. There was an underlying thread of teaching that was going on.

He turned *Hunter* around. It would have been cancelled in the second year if not for Roy. He was the mentor who came in who had another view of what the show should be. And his view happened to be a much bigger success.

Stepfanie and Fred together were wonderful and that was all because of Roy. He started favoring Stepfanie in many of the episodes because she was the better actor and had more range and Roy could do more with her. When *Hunter* was at its highest with Stepfanie and Fred, they were a force to be reckoned with. Even Roy would have to play the politics of his leading stars. As time went on, Fred was becoming more difficult and was part of the reason Roy left the show after three seasons."[5]

Charlotte Clay (Huggins) joined Huggins for the second season. She said,

Prior to meeting Roy, I had a good career producing award-winning Super Bowl commercials. Then I became head of PR and marketing for Stephen Cannell Productions. They produced four of the top ten shows in the world, although before I worked for Stephen I had never heard of *The A-Team* [1983] which was the number one show in the world at the time. I didn't even own a television set The company had 1600 employees and filled a seven-story building in Hollywood with offices in Vancouver, so I had an important job.

One day I got a phone call from Stephen. "I want you to meet this guy, Roy Huggins."

I had no idea who Roy was when I was introduced to him. Stephen was so nervous around Roy he was stuttering. It was totally uncharacteristic of him and I could tell by the way Stephen was reacting, this guy was the real deal. I started asking around to find out who Roy was and I discovered Roy had given Stephen his first writing job.

I wrote a press release that Roy was coming out of retirement to take over on *Hunter*. In the course of writing it, I got to interview Roy. I really liked him and thought to myself, "This is a super smart guy." I spoke with the editor of *Variety* and we got a banner headline.

I decided I wanted to learn how to write a television show and what better person to learn from than Roy. So one morning I pretended my car had broken down and parked it on the side of the road. I phoned Roy to ask him if he could pick me up on his way to work from his home in Mandeville Canyon, Brentwood. I befriended him. He thought I lived in a building on Sunset when in fact I lived in Santa Monica. As we drove into work he would tell me story ideas. After a couple of days when we became friends, I started pitching him story ideas.

One day I marched into his office and said, "Roy, I want to be your writing assistant."

"No. I don't need a writing assistant." His response was definite.

So I launched a personal campaign to be Roy's writing assistant and every day I would chip away at it until I got him to agree to a "Well, maybe." He finally confessed something to me that was very important in my life. We were in a restaurant called Butterfields on Sunset Boulevard when he confided in me. "I've only had three writing assistants. All of them have gone on to become head of a studio or have started their own studio. I am too old and it's too late in my career for me to help you get there."

"Roy, you don't need to help me. If that's important to you, I will do that on my own. I really want you to hire me." At that lunch he hired me. I went to Mike Dubelko, the president of Cannell, who told me I would be making half the pay I was making in my current job. I didn't care because I became Roy's writing assistant. I went from a spectacular office with people working for me to this tiny little office next to Roy.

I would sit in his office and listen to him talking to writers. Roy would philosophize about writing. It wasn't just "Hunter does this and Hunter does that." He would explain to these writers why Hunter needs to do this. There are times in your life where great things are happening to you and you don't even know it. You're just working really hard and don't realize it. And there are times when you are conscious that what you're experiencing is really remarkable and special. That's what it was like with Roy. I would go to work every day and feel like I was getting paid just to sit with this amazing man who was not only successful and really good at his job but willing to teach. I would write to my parents in Louisville, Kentucky, and tell them I was in graduate school.

Roy was a completely humble individual. I learned as much about how to live life from Roy as I did about writing. Roy taught me so much. Like never give a character two first names. It's confusing to the audience. I'm constantly reminded of the things that Roy taught me and I constantly try to teach other people the things that Roy taught me.

Roy would tell me to elevate the story. People care about people who are doing important and interesting things that have a bigger impact than just on themselves. Roy's philosophy was, people don't care about stories about people who are down and out. Elevate the characters to a place where people connect and care about them.

Roy also said his stories didn't come from his head but his heart. Yes they come from his heart, his emotional center, but he's extremely intelligent about the way he approaches storytelling. And that's really what turned me on. He wasn't flippant. It wasn't haphazard to him. He was very thoughtful, articulate and extremely intelligent about his storytelling before he approached that emotional center. There was something about Roy that was rare. It's a balancing of emotion and intellect and personal and business. Roy had that balance. It was so important for me to meet a guy like that. In 1984 there weren't a lot of people in the industry with the kind of education and background that Roy had.

After working with Roy for about a year, one morning he told me, "I have this amazing son. He's handsome, smart, educated and well traveled."

"Roy, are you pitching me your son?"

"I think you two would really get along. By the way, I had an assistant named Frank Price and I introduced him to my daughter."

I said, "No thanks, I'm interested in learning to write but not interested in your son."

A month later I'm in my office and I see this tall handsome guy. It was Roy's son. I told Roy, "I've changed my mind. I want to meet your son."

"Oh, now you've seen him, you want to meet him."

He introduced me to Tom in 1986 and we wrote a *Hunter* script at the Huggins beach house in Malibu. When we told Roy we had written a script together, Roy said, "I can't read it because I can't be impartial." He sent it to Brandon Tartikoff, head of NBC, and removed our names. Brandon read it and said not only did he like it he thought it should be produced and put in the sweeps. There were two sweeps periods and our episode "Double Exposure" (3:15) aired on Valentine's Day 1987. Tom and I bought bicycles with the money. It won its time slot and we came on as story editors.

We rewrote many episodes we didn't obtain a credit for because we weren't on staff. At the time we didn't care, we were just writing partners in the Writers Guild making lots of money. It was a brilliant couple of years writing with Tom and Roy. Tom and I fell in love in the middle of those two years and were married April 9, 1990. During the Writers Guild strike, Tom decided to go back to UCLA and get his Ph.D. in Biology. I now have this husband whose name is Thomas Roy Huggins and who has the exact story sense Roy had. Tom can hear an idea and take that in real time and turn that into a story.

I knew that I was privileged to be with Roy. He had a confidence about his work that was fun to be around but he was also so humble. Stephen had an admiration not only for the style that Roy wrote, but also the intelligence and the speed. Writing television is like taking an entrance exam for a college. It's not just how much you know, it's how fast you know it. You can't just be good, you also have to be fast. You don't have time to gestate. Roy loved the speed of television. "You show up on Monday and you get the ratings. If you did really well, that's great. You move on. If you did really badly, that's a drag but you still move on because that Friday you're going to have another show." In my professional partnership with Tom, he was the ideas person and I could write them down. I'm fast and extremely focused. I stay on point and move on to the next thing whereas Tom would walk around with a cigar in his mouth and pace up and down. He'd tell me the idea and I would sit and write and re-write.

Tom is very much like Roy. Roy never threw ideas out. If he put an idea on the table, that was it. He didn't ruminate at all. A writer would pitch an idea and Roy would say, "What if?" He never put the person down or made them feel bad. He would re-write them in real time as he talked. He would take the idea and turn it left or right and go down that road. There was never an episode of *Hunter* that Roy didn't write the core story, idea. As the executive of the show he was involved in every story.

And then there was post-production. Roy could walk into an editing room and completely change the story. If he thought the dailies were bad, he would go home and go to bed and say, "I'm actually sick." He would become physically ill by watching bad footage on a television episode! Adele would nurse him for twelve hours and then he would return to work and say, "I know how to fix it." He would fix it in editing. You have to know the footage and have the intelligence to remember all that footage. Writing and shooting are just the first two steps. The editorial process is as challenging, if not maybe the most challenging in some regards. Roy would have up to four episodes in his head at any one time while he was writing upcoming episodes. I would sit and watch him in the editing room for hours. He would say, "Flip those two things around. Take that scene out. Put that line later rather than earlier and now let's see it." Many times I watched shows change from practically unusable to captivating.

Hunter made the change to digital editing and upset many film editors. But Roy loved new technology. He embraced it and anything that made the show better and faster; he was the first guy in line to use the digital editing at Cannell. A lot of film editors resisted and were upset when the Moviolas moved out. Cannell was one of the first production companies to make the switch to digital. We spent a lot of money training them. Working with Roy Huggins at Cannell during those transformative years in production was amazing. I guess I have pretty good karma.[6]

John Huggins also worked on *Hunter*:

When I got out of college, I was a cameraman on *Hunter* for four seasons and worked on about 100 episodes. I was lucky because I had a family connection called Roy Huggins. But I started out as a lowly film loader apprentice. I would see Roy very rarely on the set. I would give him a kiss when I greeted him. Roy was affectionate that way.

I spent 13,000 hours as a cameraman. We would get new directors but in many cases they would seen unnecessary because the episodes would shoot themselves. The director of photography would say, "Number five boys." That meant the walk from the police station to the morgue. We'd have the whole scene set up and the director would have nothing to do. The director was at times superfluous. In movies the director has time for an overriding vision. In episodic television the actors know their characters after a handful of episodes. They just shoot themselves.

I came in when Roy joined the show. Tom and I were just getting out of college. I kept my relationship to my father quiet. It wasn't until my second season on the show that the crew realized who I was. For me personally it didn't tickle my creative bone. But I look back on the camaraderie with the crew very fondly. They were hanging me out of helicopters and crashing cars and it was all very exciting. We were close to the actors and got up to lots of shenanigans. We talked freely with them. There wasn't a separation of any kind. It's always nice to be on a winning show. There's job security and a certain amount of pride.[7]

"*Hunter* was one of Roy's unheralded success stories," commented Frank Price. "Roy turned the series totally around and made a solid hit of it. He was no young guy when he did this."

Jo Swerling, Jr., then working for Stephen Cannell, was reunited with Huggins. "I didn't work with Roy on a day-to-day basis on *Hunter*. I was more on a studio management level. I would see him and talk with him every day. I had a great time with Steve Cannell but looked back on my years with Roy with a lot of fond memories. I basically had a very good time during those years of association with him."

Huggins expressed his respect for Swerling: "I love him. His talent knows no limits. When I needed someone to write in a hurry and I couldn't do it, I'd give it to Jo and he would do it and he would do it well. When we had problems with actors, Jo was always the most diplomatic human being in the world. Jo is a renaissance man."[8]

Frank Price stated, "Jo is a very nice guy and a knowledgeable professional. His father had a good reputation in the business. With Roy, Jo found his niche. He was never going to be the top dog on his own, but he performed the role of complementing Roy very well. Most of the mundane tasks of producing were carried out by Jo, an easygoing, affable but hardworking and conscientious guy, leaving Roy free to focus on creating good stories and turning them into scripts. Obviously Roy kept the film editing well under his own hand. Jo carried out Roy's judgments without disagreement."

In 1979, James Garner sued Universal for breach of contract and fraud for withholding his share of the profits on *The Rockford Files*. In December 1988 he received a check for $607,000. This was followed by an offer of $6 million a few months later. Garner resisted the offer and discovered Universal was syndicating *The Rockford Files*, with *Quincy* and billing *Quincy* at twice the rate of *The Rockford Files* thus cheating Garner out of profits. Universal offered Garner a settlement but once again he refused. Garner wanted to expose Universal's shady bookkeeping practices. But with the possibility of losing everything if it went to trial, Garner finally agreed on a multi-million dollar settlement on March 23, 1989.

No doubt encouraged by the outcome of Garner's lawsuit, Roy Huggins sued Universal in late July 1990. He claimed $5 million in compensatory damages and an unspecified amount for punitive damages based on a promised 25 percent of net profits from *The Rockford Files*. Huggins' attorney Donald Engel alleged that Universal sent Huggins false accounting statements to conceal the missing profits. The case never went to court and Huggins received an undisclosed settlement.

In 1991 Huggins was enticed out of retirement yet again to co-executive produce and co-write a crime drama pilot for CBS. *Perfect Crimes* featured two real-life murder stories linked by host-narrator Telly Savalas. In "Double Identity," Dr. Lori Forman (Lisa Hartman Black) arranges a murder to collect the insurance money and in "Murder in Triplicate" a man decides to murder his wife, girlfriend and blackmailer. The pilot failed to sell but Huggins refused to retreat into permanent retirement. In 1993 he accepted work as a consultant on a movie adaptation of *The Fugitive*. He still owned the movie rights and was able to license those rights to Warner Brothers for the film adaptation starring Harrison Ford as Dr. Richard Kimble. Now in his late seventies, Huggins played an active, creative role in bringing his creation to the big screen. A new generation was introduced to Kimble, and Sam Sheppard was once again called the inspiration for the character. As he did decades before, Huggins emphatically denied any connection but the fiction had more staying power than the truth.

During production of the movie, Huggins was diagnosed with mouth and throat cancer at the back of the tongue. The cancer was diagnosed in time and successfully treated. "Roy religiously smoked one cigar a day. He never smoked cigarettes. He enjoyed the cigar, which Adele would bring to him after dining. I think he thought it was relatively safe," stated Frank Price.

"The radiation destroyed his salivary glands. So thereafter he had to use constant water," commented Katherine Crawford. "It also took away all the fat in his cheeks and left him very gaunt. It was a dramatic change, but he handled it with his usual grace and lived happily. The radiation almost killed him, so he was grateful for whatever he had."[9]

The Fugitive was a major success. Howard Rosenberg of the *Los Angeles Times* (September 6, 1993) stated: "The movie and series necessarily differ in many ways, and it's Tommy Lee Jones who gives the former much of its intensity. Although equally obsessive, his charismatic, oft-ruthless, action-driven Gerard is stunningly unlike Barry Morse's bureaucratically bland, stuffy and methodical cop in the series, which is more or less a plug-along Javert automaton in a gray suit."

In 1993 while recovering from the radiation treatment, Huggins suffered another setback when he was diagnosed with colon cancer and underwent successful diverticulitis surgery. The following year saw another movie adaptation of a Huggins show: *Maverick* featured Mel Gibson in the lead role with James Garner playing Marshal Zane Cooper. "He did not control the rights to *Maverick*," declared Price. "Warners prepared the script, then sent it to Roy. He felt they had taken the wrong approach to it, so he quietly declined to participate. The movie didn't rise to a good level of more sophisticated humor and action. Too much was plain silly, which Roy wouldn't have permitted."[10]

Huggins received an executive producer credit but wasn't personally involved in the *Fugitive* spin-off *U.S. Marshals* in 1998. The finished product, which saw Tommy Lee Jones reprise his role as Chief Deputy Marshal Samuel Gerard, failed to impress the public or the film critics.

Huggins encountered more health problems in 1999 when he was diagnosed and received treatment and medication for prostate cancer. John Huggins stated, "I never heard Dad complain."[11]

In 2000, *The Fugitive* returned to the small screen with Tim Daly playing Dr. Richard Kimble and Mykelti Williamson as an African-American Lt. Philip Gerard. Production was based in Seattle with shows filmed in blocks of four to incorporate the various locales around

Washington state and beyond. Huggins was officially credited as executive producer but only served in a consultation capacity regarding scripts. Huggins expressed enthusiasm for the project in a *Los Angeles Times* interview with Susan King (August 29, 2000): "It's a continuation of the series in every way except it's in the 21st century. That means the Internet is everywhere, and that means his jeopardy is a little heavier than it was.... I am reading the scripts and meeting with John McNamara a little more than I expected. It's fun and John is very easy to work with. John has some ideas that make it a little different and, and I think his ideas are good."

Away from the public glare, Huggins was less enthusiastic about the show's prospects. The fact he wasn't personally involved in the casting added to his misgivings. Price said, "They did not contact Roy up front since they had negotiated those rights along with the movie rights. He generally gave them script notes, without the belief it would help much. He was not enthusiastic about the casting. Roy never would have agreed to cast Tim Daly. Tim was too weak for the role and no David Janssen." Huggins' misgivings proved justified as the updated series failed to attract a sizable audience and was cancelled after one season of twenty-three episodes.

Meanwhile Jo Swerling, Jr. had been informed that Universal was interested in doing a feature version of *Run for Your Life*:

> My lawyer called me to tell me I could get compensated for any future production. I disagreed and told him my contract at Universal gave them ownership of my material. My lawyer responded, "I don't think that's valid under Writers Guild rules." I told him I wrote the format under Roy's direction but I was under this slave labor contract to Universal at the time.
>
> "No. I think you're entitled to separation of rights as the writer of the story. You had the sole story credit." My lawyer made a claim at Universal and the Writers Guild supported our position. Roy gave an affadavit that I had written the story and Luther Davies signed an affadavit that I had presented him with the format and a story. The Writers Guild upheld my position and I received a big check from Universal which I gave Roy half of. They had a change of regime at Universal and that project fell by the wayside.

17

DENOUEMENT

From the end spring new beginnings.—Pliny the Elder (AD 23–79)

As Huggins approached the new century, the memory of the HUAC hearings still occupied his thoughts. The hearings had left a scar on the political landscape of America and on many of those who testified. Cooperative witnesses were labeled "snitches," "stoolies," and "informers." Huggins was particularly disappointed by journalists, writers and editors on the left, including Victor Navasky who interviewed Huggins in 1974 for his book *Naming Names*. "It became leftist dogma that a witness who 'informed' at a HUAC hearing had 'betrayed his friends and ruined their lives.' Victor Navasky, then editor of *The Nation*, unintentionally invalidated that claim by declaring that HUAC was 'in the business of ruining peoples' lives without profit to the nation." Huggins continued,

> In the mills of leftist propaganda, HUAC had become a neutral party; a synergistic relationship was being nurtured between HUAC and the Communist Party. The Committee subpoenaed ex–Communists, put them through the names ritual, thanked them for their cooperation, and the Party took it from there.... The Committee knew what was happening and played its part with joy, as a close perusal of the hearings makes clear. Without the left's help, HUAC's intention to punish former Communists would have come to nothing, but the Party could do what the HUAC could not, it could sell the proposition that cooperative witnesses were "rats".... The Party practice of ducking debate by aiming invective at adversaries had become an art, and nothing could render debate redundant as effectively as a good label. The Party found its label in the word "informer," a big improvement on Jean-Paul Sartre's lackluster slogan "anti–Communists are rats."[1]

Huggins addressed his internal thoughts through unpublished articles and looked to satisfy his curiosity about his past exploits. On March 21, 1995, he wrote to the FBI with a Freedom of Information Privacy Act request detailing dates of his history with the American Communist Party and to receive confirmation he had never joined a "Communist front" organization. "I was notified that the backlog of 'requesters' was so immense that I would have to wait in excess of two years for any information about me they might have."

Two years later in, on April 9, 1997, a frustrated Huggins contacted the FBI once again. "I will be 83 years old in ten weeks. I have recovered from two bouts with cancer (throat and colon) but my health is considerably short of robust. I am hoping that may make me eligible for some prescribed consideration. If not, perhaps you could let me know approximately how much longer I may have to wait...."

Huggins had to wait another six months before the FBI finally mailed his file in October 1997. He was disappointed: "Much of the 'information' was blacked out, making it a 99-page compendium of riddles, an impenetrable brew of ambiguous fact and random fiction." This initial reaction to the content of the FBI file would be replaced by a slow realization that some of the facts were so disturbing to Huggins that they sent him "into a shock from which, four years later (2001), I have not fully recovered."

Huggins' excerpt from the file has the names of FBI agents blacked out.

> ROY MARSHALL HUGGINS voluntarily appeared at the Los Angeles office by appointment on May 3, 1951, at which time he was interviewed by Special Agents XXXXX and XXXXX.
>
> *FRONT ACTIVITY:*
> HUGGINS states that he is not by nature "a joiner" and that he has never joined or sponsored organizations which have since been reported to have been dominated or controlled by the CP.
>
> In this connection it may be noted that previous investigation of HUGGINS tends to bear this out. Furthermore, it is reported that the Fourth Report of the (California) Senate Fact Finding committee on Un-American Activities in 1948, dealing specifically with Communist-front organizations, does not list Huggins' name.
>
> The Bureau will note from its file on ROY MARSHALL HUGGINS that his account of the circumstances surrounding his rejoining the CP in 1943 is substantially the same as was developed by prior investigation. It is noted further that investigation has failed to develop Communist activity on his part since approximately 1947, when HUGGINS' membership was last reported by XXXXX. HUGGINS gave the impression during the interview of sincerely trying to remember details of his career in the CP, and it is believed that possibly additional information of specific matter may be developed in the future.
>
> *Summary of information received:*
> This source has furnished the names of all individuals he knew as a Communist Party member in Hollywood between 1940 and 1947.
>
> *Value of information received:*
> This source is not interested in going back into the Communist Party as a confident informant, even if it could be arranged. His activity and interest in the Party when he was a member was not marked, and for this reason his information is limited.
>
> For the reason that the scope of his information is limited and has been previously obtained, HUGGINS is being cancelled by separate communication as an active confidential source.
>
> It is noted that HUGGINS is no longer a member of the Communist Party, from which he dissociated himself in 1947. His cooperation in furnishing such additional information as he may have, based on his experience of the Communist Party, is assured.
>
> It is recommended that the Security Index card with regard to ROY MARSHALL HUGGINS be cancelled."

Huggins had no recall of the meeting with the FBI in May 1951 where he told them "all I knew about the American Communist Party." Adele told her husband, "Have you forgotten I was there when you decided to do that? You asked for my advice and I said, 'Great. Go for it.'"

His total amnesia of the meeting puzzled and worried him. But it was a fact he had blocked it from his memory:

> As a television producer turning out hundreds of one-hour episodes each season, I had consistently refused to put a story based on amnesia into production, on the grounds that "amnesia is fictive shit," as I once observed in a memo to my executive assistant, Jo Swerling, Jr. I spent the next two weeks trying to the point of megrim to recall the meeting, but the amnesia was total, and remains so to this day. But I continued, at morbid length, to ponder the puzzle. Why would I react to a meeting with the FBI with a total and permanent onslaught of amnesia?

In 1950 the Internal Security Act, called "the concentration-camp bill" by opponents, was passed. It included an Emergency Detention Act, which allowed the president to declare a "state of emergency" under which "subversives" (citizens carried on the FBI's Security Index) could be rounded up and jailed. My awareness of the Detention Act no doubt focused my mind sharply on my being, however mistakenly, on the FBI Security Index.

One day [in 1998] I looked around and observed that Hollywood was in the midst of a rousing campaign of public meetings and motion pictures and television documentaries celebrating its newly minted cultural heroes, the Old Stalinists, the proud survivors and supporters of the bloodiest tyranny in our totalitarian 20th century. Their campaign revived and embellished the falsehoods of the '50s, supported by an enthusiastic post-modernist debasement of history itself. I could conceive of no rationale in which my amnesia could possibly be seen as anything but prejudicial to me, but I decided I was stuck with it.[2]

Almost two years after he read the FBI report, Huggins watched Elia Kazan and his wife walk onto the stage of the Dorothy Chandler Pavilion in Los Angeles. The date was March 21, 1999, and the event was the Academy Awards ceremony. On stage they were greeted by Martin Scorsese and Robert DeNiro, who presented Kazan with his award. Had Hollywood finally forgiven him for his cooperation with HUAC? His reception was a mixture of warm applause and unsmiling faces, hands placed at their side. Only half of Hollywood present that evening warmed to his presence.

Ten years earlier, in February 1989, Kazan had been rejected by the American Film Institute for its Life Achievement award. Board member Charlton Heston recalled, "When they opened the floor for debate, a young woman [Gail Hurd] 30 going on 17 and attending her first meeting, immediately stood up and vociferously denounced [Kazan] for his HUAC testimony. I was stunned. This was language out of the '40s and '50s. I asked to speak and excoriated her as fiercely as I could within the bounds of courtesy. I pointed out she had no idea of the historic realties of time.... No one defended her. But when the vote was taken, Kazan's name had disappeared from the list."

Writer-director Abe Polonsky, a reminder of the Stalinist left from Hollywood's past, spoke of HUAC witnesses who refused to take the Fifth Amendment with contempt: "I don't speak to them. I don't even acknowledge their existence." In Polonsky's view, Kazan was "a creep. I wouldn't want to be wrecked on an island with him because if he was hungry he'd eat me alive."

Huggins sought the opinion of other HUAC witnesses as a means to reflect on his own actions back in 1952:

> I spoke to dozens of Hollywood's ex–Communists and a few who were not, like Kazan, troubled by cooperation with HUAC, but all felt the choice they had made was the right one. The Committee had provided them with an otherwise unattainable public platform from which to denounce the Communist Party for its indifference to Soviet crimes and its disdain for the membership; and since I was one of them, they had no fathomable reason to lie to me. The word "puppet-like" was used by one of the defectors, who took a dictionary from her shelf and read to me the definition of "puppet": *A small figure of a person or an animal, having a cloth body and hollow head, designed to be fitted over and manipulated by hand.*
>
> Kazan had conceded that giving names to HUAC was "painful" and "distasteful" but not because it instituted informing. Giving authorities information for venal reasons that implicate others, which information the authorities need and do not have, is the definition of informing. Giving authorities information they admittedly have, and admittedly do not need, is not informing and never will be till the history and definition of "informer" are rewritten to conform to what the left wanted it to mean in the '50s and still wants it to mean today."[3]

In late 2001, Huggins was admitted to a hospital with internal bleeding. Two weeks later he was back home recuperating and looking forward to the New Year. He had been working on his memoirs until his illness, and hoped to complete them. But in early 2002 the internal bleeding re-commenced and he was once again admitted to St. John's Hospital in Santa Monica. Complications for the treatment of pulmonary fibrosis and additional complications resulting from the radiation therapy many years earlier for throat cancer contributed to his deteriorating health although the official cause of the internal bleeding was never discovered.

During Huggins lifetime he remained cynical about his mother's stories claiming her Crawford family line had a case for legal ownership of Trinity Church in New York. Frank Price's research into the family history uncovered the truth of her story. Belle Huggins (Crawford) was a descendant of Dutch clergyman Dominic Evaradus Bogardus, who made a new life in New Amsterdam, marrying widow Anneke Jans Borgardus. Her first husband had bought sixty-two acres of farmland in 1836 and died one year later. After ten years of marriage, Dominic died in a shipwreck. The land was sold, but a son who was out of the country at the time, returned to unsuccessfully challenge the sale of the farm. Trinity Church was eventually built on the land and the surrounding area became some of the most valuable land on earth in lower Manhattan. The descendants kept challenging the courts until a New York judge finally declared that no further cases concerning the Bogardus-Trinity Church land issue could ever come before the New York courts.

"I was able to tell Daddy before he died. He closed his eyes, and said 'Interesting....' I asked if he was glad to know his mother was right all along, and he nodded," commented Katherine Crawford.[4]

John Huggins recalled, "Father spent three months in hospital. Two days before his death he became unconscious. I was at his bedside along with mother, Tom, Jim and Kathy holding his hand as he slipped away. For a time Father was an agnostic but at the end of his life he wanted the last rites. I wonder if toward the end of his life, Mother had rubbed off on him or he decided perhaps there was a greater power out there. Someone as intelligent and educated as my father must have thought about the mysteries of creation."[5]

Katherine added, "I think privately, in himself, he had an unguarded allowance of God that he *liked*, perhaps even cherished, but could never outwardly admit. He was so mentally against being a follower in anything, that I think he felt a shame or embarrassment at admitting to it. Or it may simply have been too personal to admit. He always said he liked the 'tradition' of it, as though that covered it all. Whenever he said that, I just smiled inwardly and agreed."[6]

Roy Huggins passed away on April 3, 2002, a few months short of his 88th birthday. At his memorial service at St. Martin of Tours Catholic Church in Los Angeles, Frank Price delivered a moving personal eulogy:

> I can say today some of the things I'd like to have said to Roy. He would have cut me off with a witty or caustic comment. He was a skeptical guy and complimentary remarks would have triggered his suspicion that I was trying to con him.
>
> I met Roy when I was a young writer-producer under contract to Universal Television. Roy was a star producer, already famous as the creator of *Maverick, Cheyenne,* and *77 Sunset Strip.* He was brought in to save a troubled new series called *The Virginian.*
>
> From the beginning, Roy called me Francis. His Irish background told him that Frank was a fake name for me. In the schoolyard, a boy named Francis was barely a step up from A Boy Named Sue.

I worked for him for just a few months in that first season. Those few months turned out to be incredibly important to me because of what I learned from Roy. He was truly someone who marched to that sound of a different drummer. In show business, there is the truism "You'll never go broke underestimating the intelligence of the viewers." Much of the audience will accept whatever is put before them.

Roy made it clear to me that his goal was to please the top ten percent of the audience—the thinking, critical ten percent. He wasn't prepared to settle for "okay" or "good enough." He treated his audience as sophisticated, intelligent people. He pushed himself—and anyone working with him—to achieve a high standard. He worked and worked and worked on preparing the script. And he worked and worked and worked on editing the picture to perfection. He was a labor-intensive intellectual.

When I later ran Universal Television, I often maneuvered to have the most talented young writer-producer types work under Roy. I knew that once they learned what he could teach, they would be stars. Steve Cannell and Glen Larson were graduates of that school.

He had no real say in the matter but I also owe Roy thanks for producing such a remarkable daughter who made the amazing decision to marry me. It wasn't easy, but I can be a persuasive fellow. When I first met her, I was working for Roy on *The Virginian*, producing episodes that he executive produced. Katherine would sometimes see dailies and make helpful suggestions to Roy and me. There were times I could have throttled her. Unfortunately her criticisms were too often accurate, but a pain in the—neck to fix. A few years later when we married, she became not a bad secret weapon for a studio head.

Because of her, I also took a more personal interest in Roy's history. His grandfather was a lumberjack in Wisconsin. His father was a saw filer in the lumber business in Washington, and died when Roy was two. His mother ran a beauty shop to support four children in the Depression. From this family came a brother, Jack Huggins, an immensely popular university professor of Irish literature, and Roy Huggins, creator of novels, movies, and hit television shows. It must all be in the genes...

Roy had been sent to a military boarding school while his mother built her business. Military school was considered good for fatherless boys. I think it was that experience, the rigid, harsh discipline, the arbitrary authority, that played a seminal role in the way Roy saw the world. His creations were not generic cop, hospital or lawyer shows. He created unusual characters who were outsiders, drifters observing society. Alienated—but with a sense of humor. They were Mavericks... Fugitives... Running for their lives. I consider Roy to be the best producer of dramatic series in television history.

I was lucky to have been his co-worker, his friend, his son-in-law, his occasional brunch or dinner partner with his devoted wife—beautiful, enchanting Adele who as Roy pointed out to me more than once had that wry sense of humor that he appreciated so much. I—we all—will sure miss him.[7]

Jo Swerling, Jr. added his own words in remembrance at the service:

I learned so much from him, but I wasn't the only one who attended the Roy Huggins Academy of Public Arts. There is a large alumni association of writers, directors, actors and producers, who owe their success to him... I always thought that he'd be up here one day, saying a few kind words about me. Sadly, that isn't the way it turned out.

Those of us who were lucky to know him, to have the benefit of his leadership, his generosity, his wry sense of humor, and his kindness are truly blessed. We will all miss him terribly.

Roy ... wherever you are ... from the bottom of my heart, I love you ... thanks for everything you did for me and for the rest of us. We'll never forget you. And, if you need anything, just write it down on a yellow legal pad, and we'll take care of it.

Stephen J. Cannell, who also attended the memorial service, acknowledged the debt he owed Huggins and later commented, "I learned how to edit. I learned how to tell a story.

I learned how to deal with networks. I learned studio politics. He was my godfather. Roy had all these amazing ways of doing things, all of which I have ripped off and now call my own…. I loved Roy like a father."[8]

Before his passing, Roy Huggins told his son John, "I want to be cremated in the cheapest box possible." John commented, "He wasn't interested in us spending lots of money on an expensive coffin that was going to end up as ashes. My father was cremated in a humble cardboard box. When he died, Father had almost no personal possessions apart from his wedding ring, watch, St, Christopher's medal and a Celtic cross that he always wore. The cross connected him to his Irish roots."

Katherine added, "He had become an Irish citizen late in life. The law states that any American grandchild of an Irish-born citizen is eligible. And of course he was the grandchild of Irish-born Helen Hickey. He did it for the joy of being an official Irishman and for the advantages of having a European passport when traveling in Europe. Then there was always the fantasy of living in Ireland in old age. It was never a political statement."[9]

John Huggins concluded, "Before his death, Father ordered one urn and asked for his ashes to be co-mingled with our mother's ashes. When she passed away on May 7, 2010, our mother was also cremated in a cardboard box, their ashes combined and the urn sealed."

THE WORKS OF ROY HUGGINS

Television Movies—Pilots

Perfect Crimes (1991)
Air date: November 8, 1991; **Cast:** Bruce Greenwood (Faulkner); Lisa Hartman Black (Dr. Lori Forman), Dennis Farina (Armand Zero), Khrystyne Haje (Diane Lacoss), Michael Bowen (Jack O'Neill); **Credits:** Teleplay: Roy Huggins. R.J. Stewart; Music: Stanley Clarke; Executive Producers: Roy Huggins, Fred Silverman; Director: Armand Mastroianni; 90 minutes; Production Company: MGM Television Entertainment; Fred Silverman; Roy Huggins; Distribution Company: Columbia Broadcasting System (CBS); Color.

The Secret War of Jackie's Girls (1980)
Air date: November 29, 1980; **Cast:** Lee Purcell (Casey McCann), Dee Wallace (Maxine), Ben Murphy (Buck), Mariette Hartley (Jackie); **Credits:** Teleplay: D. Guthrie, Theodore Jonas; Story: Theodore Jonas; Music: Fred Karlin; Executive Producers: Florence Small, John Surgal, Roy Huggins (uncredited); Producer: Dorothy J. Bailey, Jo Swerling, Jr. (uncredited); Director: Gordon Hessler; 100 minutes; Production Company: Penthouse Productions, Public Art Films, Universal TV; Distribution: National Broadcasting Company (NBC); Color.

The Jordan Chance (1978)
Air date: December 12, 1978; **Cast:** Raymond Burr (Frank Jordan), Ted Schackelford (Brian Klosky), James Canning (Jimmy Foster), Jeannie Fitzsimmons (Karen Wagner), Stella Stevens (Virna Stewart); **Credits:** Teleplay: Stephen J. Cannell; Story: John Thomas James, Stephen J. Cannell; Music: Pete Rugolo; Executive Producer: Roy Huggins; Producer: Jo Swerling, Jr.; Director: Jules Irving; 120 minutes; R.B. Productions, Roy Huggins Productions, Universal TV; Distribution: Columbia Broadcasting System (CBS); Color.

The 3,000 Mile Chase (1977)
Air date: June 16, 1977; **Cast:** Cliff De Young (Matthew Considine/Marty Scanlon), Glenn Ford (Paul Dvorak/Leonard Staveck), Blair Brown (Rachel Kane), David Spielberg (Frank Oberon), Priscilla Pointer (Emma Dvorak); **Credits:** Teleplay: Philip DeGuere, Jr.; Story: Roy Huggins; Music: Elmer Bernstein; Executive Producer: Roy Huggins; Producer: Jo Swerling, Jr.; Director: Russ Mayberry; 120 minutes; Production Company: Universal TV–Public Arts; Distribution: National Broadcasting Company (NBC); Color.

Hazard's People (1976)
Air date: April 9, 1976; **Cast:** John Houseman (John Hazard), John Elerick (Michael Chowder), Jesse Welles (Trish Cornell), Roger Hill (Ernest Clay), Dr. Carl DeLacy (Michael Tolan), Hope Lange (Mrs. DeLacy); **Credits:** Story: Heywood Gould, Roy Huggins, Jo Swerling, Jr.; Music: John Cacavas; Executive Producer: Jo Swerling, Jr.; Producer: Roy Huggins; Director: Jeannot Szwarc; 60 minutes; Production Company: Universal TV–Public Arts; Distribution: Columbia Broadcasting System (CBS); Color.

The Invasion of Johnson County (1976)
Air date: July 31, 1976; **Cast:** Bill Bixby (Sam Lowell), Bo Hopkins (George Dunning), John Hillerman (Major Walcott), Billy Green Bush (Frank Canton), Stephen Elliott (Colonel Van Horn); **Credits:** Teleplay: Nicholas E. Baehr; Music: Mike Post, Pete Carpenter; Executive

Producer: Jo Swerling, Jr.; Producer: Roy Huggins; Director: Jerry Jameson; 120 minutes; Production Company: Universal TV–Public Arts; Distribution: National Broadcasting Company (NBC); Color.

Target Risk (1975)

Air date: January 6, 1975; **Cast:** Bo Svenson (Lee Driscoll), Meredith Baxter (Linda Flayly), Keenan Wynn (Simon Cusack), John P. Ryan (Ralph Sloan), Robert Coote (Julian Ulrich), Phil Bruns (Marty); **Credits:** Teleplay: Don Carlos Dunaway; Music: Eumir Deodato; Executive Producer: Jo Swerling, Jr.; Producer: Robert F. O'Neill; Director: Robert Scheerer; 90 minutes; Universal Television; Color.

This Was the West That Was (1974)

Air date: December 17, 1974; **Cast:** Ben Murphy (Wild Bill Hickok), Kim Darby (Calamity Jane), Jane Alexander (Sarah Shaw), Anthony Franciosa (J. W. McCanles), Stuart Margolin (Blind Pete); **Credits:** Teleplay: Sam H. Rolfe; Music: Richard DeBenedictis; Executive Producer: Roy Huggins; Producer: Jo Swerling, Jr.; Director: Fielder Cook; 90 minutes; Universal Television; Color.

The Story of Pretty Boy Floyd (1974)

Air date: May 7, 1974; **Cast:** Martin Sheen (Charles Arthur Floyd), Kim Darby (Ruby Hardgrave), Michael Parks (Bradley Floyd), Ellen Corby (Ma Floyd), Joseph Estevez (E. W. Floyd), Kitty Carl (Mary Floyd), Geoffrey Binney (Melvin Purvis), Bill Vint (Bill Miller); **Credits:** Teleplay: Clyde Ware; Music: Pete Rugolo; Executive Producer: Roy Huggins; Producer: Jo Swerling, Jr.; Director: Clyde Ware; 90 minutes; Universal Television; Color.

The Rockford Files (1974)

Air date: March 27, 1974; **Cast:** James Garner (Jim Rockford), Lindsay Wagner (Sara Butler), William Smith (Jerry Grimes), Nita Talbot (Mildred Elias), Joe Santos (Dennis Becker), Stuart Margolin (Angel); **Credits:** Teleplay: Stephen J. Cannell; Story: John Thomas James; Music: Pete Carpenter, Mike Post; Executive Producer: Jo Swerling, Jr.; Producer: Stephen J. Cannell; Director: Richard T. Heffron; 90 minutes; Universal Television; Color.

Drive Hard, Drive Fast (1973)

Air date: September 11, 1973; **Cast:** Brian Kelly (Mark Driscoll), Joan Collins (Carole Bradley), Henry Silva (Deek La Costa), Joseph Campanella (Eric Bradley), Karen Huston (Ellen Bradley), Todd Martin (Fielder), Charles H. Gray (Blond Man), Patrick White (Cartier); **Credits:** Teleplay: Matthew Howard; Music: Pete Rugolo; Executive Producer: Roy Huggins; Producer: Jo Swerling, Jr.; Director: Douglas Heyes; 120 minutes; Production Company: Universal TV–Public Arts; Distribution: National Broadcasting Company (NBC); Color.

Toma (1973)

Air date: March 21, 1973; **Cast:** Tony Musante (David Toma), Simon Oakland (Inspector Spooner), Susan Strasberg (Patty Toma), Michael Baseleon (Tully), Robert Yuro (Frank Barber), David Spielberg (Marlowe), Ron Soule (Harrison); **Credits:** Teleplay: Edward Hume, Gerald DiPegeo; Music: Pete Rugolo; Producer: Jo Swerling, Jr.; Director: Richard T. Heffron; 90 minutes; Universal Television; Color.

Set This Town on Fire a.k.a. The Profane Comedy (1973)

Air date: January 8, 1973; **Cast:** Chuck Connors (Buddy Bates), Carl Betz (Andy Wells), Lynda Day (Molly Thornburgh), Charles Robinson (Brad Wells), John Anderson (Henry Kealey), Jeff Corey (Walter Stafford), Nancy Malone (Shirley Hammond), James Westerfield (Carl Rickter); **Credits:** Teleplay: John Thomas James; Music: Pete Rugolo; Executive Producer: Roy Huggins; Producer-Director: David Lowell Rich; 120 minutes; Production Company: Universal TV–Public Arts; Distribution: National Broadcasting Company (NBC); Color.

How to Steal an Airplane a.k.a. Only One Day Left Before Tomorrow (1971)

Air date: November 10, 1971; **Cast:** Peter Deuel (Sam Rollins), Clinton Greyn (Evan Brice), Claudine Longet), Michelle Chivot), Sal Mineo (Luis Ortega), Julie Sommars (Dorothy); **Credits:** Teleplay: Robert Foster, Phillip DeGuere; Music: Pete Rugolo; Executive Producer: Roy Huggins; Producer: Jo Swerling, Jr.; Director: Leslie H. Martinson; 120 minutes; Production Company: Universal TV–Public Arts; Distribution: National Broadcasting Company (NBC); Color.

Sam Hill: Who Killed the Mysterious Mr. Foster? (1971)

Air date: February 1, 1971; **Cast:** Ernest Borgnine (Deputy Sam Hill), Stephen Hudis (Jethro), Judy Geeson (Jody Kenyon), Will Geer (Simon Anderson), J. D. Cannon (Mal Yeager), Bruce Dern (Doyle Pickett), Sam Jaffe (Toby); **Credits:** Teleplay: Richard Levinson, William Link; Music: Pete Rugolo; Executive Producer: Roy Huggins; Producer: Jo Swerling, Jr.; Director: Fielder Cook; 120 minutes; Universal Television; Color.

Do You Take This Stranger? (1971)

Air date: January 18, 1971; **Cast:** Gene Barry (Murray Jarvis), Lloyd Bridges (Steven Breck), Diane Baker (Rachel Jarvis), Joseph Cotten (Dr. Robert Carson), Sidney Blackmer (G.R. Jarvis), Susan Oliver (Mildred Crandall); **Credits:** Teleplay: Matthew Howard; Music: Pete Rugolo; Executive Producer: Roy Huggins; Producer: Jo Swerling, Jr.; Director: Richard T. Heffron; 120 minutes; Universal Television; Color.

The Young Country (1970)

Air date: March 17, 1970; **Cast:** Roger Davis (Stephen Foster Moody), Joan Hackett (Clementine Hale), Pete Duel (Honest John Smith), Wally Cox (Aaron Grimes/Ira Greebe), Walter Brennan (Sheriff Matt Fenley); **Credits:** Teleplay-Producer-Director: Roy Huggins; Music: Pete Rugolo; 90 minutes; Production Company: Universal TV–Public Arts; Distribution: American Broadcasting Company (ABC); Color.

The Challengers (1970)

Air date: February 20, 1970; **Cast:** Darren McGavin (Jim McCabe), Juliet Mills (Mary McCabe), Sal Mineo (Angel de Angelo), Anne Baxter (Stephanie York), Sean Garrison (Cody Scanlon), Nico Minardos (Paco), Susan Clark (Catherine Burroughs), Farley Granger (Nealy), Richard Conte (Ritchie); **Credits:** Teleplay: Dick Nelson; Story: Robert Hamner, John Thomas James; Music: Pete Rugolo; Producer: Roy Huggins; Director: Leslie H. Martinson; 120 minutes; Production Company: Universal TV–Public Arts; Distribution: Columbia Broadcasting System (CBS); Color.

The Lonely Profession (1969)

Air date: October 21, 1969; **Cast:** Harry Guardino (Lee Gordon), Fernando Lamas (Dominic Savarona), Dina Merrill (Beatrice Savarona), Joseph Cotten (Martin Bannister), Barbara McNair (Donna Travers), Troy Donahue (Julian Thatcher), Dean Jagger (Charles Van Cleave), Ina Balin (Karen Menardos); **Credits:** Teleplay-Director: Douglas Heyes; Music: Pete Rugolo; Executive Producer: Roy Huggins; Producer: Jo Swerling, Jr.; 120 minutes; Universal Television; Color.

Any Second Now (1969)

Air date: February 11, 1969; **Cast:** Stewart Granger (Paul Dennison), Lois Nettleton (Nancy Dennison), Joseph Campanella (Dr. Raul Valdez), Dana Wynter (Jane Peterson); **Credits:** Teleplay: Gene Levitt; Story: Gene Levitt, Harold Jack Bloom, Robert Mitchell; Music: Leonard Rosenman; Executive Producer: Roy Huggins; Producer-Director: Gene Levitt; 95 minutes; Production Company: Universal TV–Public Arts; Distribution: National Broadcasting Company (NBC); Color.

The Whole World Is Watching (1969)

Air date: March 11, 1969; **Cast:** Burl Ives (Walter Nichols), Joseph Campanella (Brian Darrell), James Farentino (Neil Darrell), Carrie Snodgrass (Megan Baker), Hal Holbrook (Chancellor Graham), Steve Ihnat (Officer Platt), Stephen McNally (The Governor); **Credits:** Teleplay: Richard Levinson, William Link; Music: Pete Rugolo; Executive Producer: Roy Huggins; Producer: Jo Swerling, Jr.; Director: Richard A. Colla; 120 minutes; Production Company: Universal TV–Public Arts; Distribution: National Broadcasting Company (NBC); Color.

The Sound of Anger (1968)

Air date: December 10, 1968; **Cast:** Burl Ives (Walter Nichols), Guy Stockwell (Brad Darrell), James Farentino (Neil Darrell), Lynda Day (Barbara Keeley), Dorothy Provine (Marge Carruthers), David Macklin (Barry Kochek); **Credits:** Teleplay: Dick Nelson; Music: Pete Rugolo; Producer: Roy Huggins; Director: Michael Ritchie; 120 minutes; Production Company: Universal TV–Public Arts; Distribution: National Broadcasting Company (NBC); Color.

The Outsider (1967)

Air date: November 21, 1967; **Cast:** Darren McGavin (David Ross), Nancy Malone (Honora Dundas), Edmond O'Brien (Marvin Bishop), Audrey Totter (Mrs. Bishop), Shirley Knight (Peggy Leyden), Anne Sothern (Mrs. Kozzek), Joseph Wiseman (Ernest Grimes), Ossie Davis (Lt. Wagner); **Credits:** Teleplay-Producer: Roy Huggins; Music: Pete Rugolo; Director: Michael Ritchie; 120 minutes; Production Company: Universal Television; Distribution: National Broadcasting Company (NBC); Color.

Television Mini-Series

The Last Convertible (1979)

Air dates: September 24–26, 1979; **Cast:** Perry King (Russ Currier), Deborah Raffin (Chris Farris), Bruce Boxleitner (George Virdon), Sharon Gless (Kay Haddon), Edward Albert (Ron Dalrymple), Kim Darby (Ann Rowan); **Credits:** Teleplay: Philip DeGuere, Stephen McPherson Clyde Ware; Based on the novel by Anton Myrer; Music: Pete Rugolo; Executive Producer: Roy Huggins; Producer: Robert F. O'Neill; Directors: Signey Haynes, Jo Swerling, Jr., Gus Trikonis; Universal Television; Color.

Arthur Hailey's Wheels (1978)

Air dates: May 7, 8, 9, 14, 15, 1978; **Cast:** Rock Hudson (Adam Trenton), Lee Remick (Erica Trenton), Blair Brown (Barbara Lipton), John Beck (Peter Flodenhale), Marj Dusay (Caroline Horton), Lisa Eilbacher (Jody Horton), Anthony Franciosa (Smokey Stevenson); **Credits:** Teleplay: Millard Campbell, Hank Searls, Robert Hamilton, Nancy Lynn Schwartz; Based on the novel by Arthur Hailey; Music: Morton Stevens; Executive Producer: Roy Huggins; Producer: Robert F. O'Neil; Director: Jerry London; 10 hours; Universal Television; Color.

Aspen a.k.a. *The Innocent and the Damned* (1977)

Air dates: November 5–7, 1977; **Cast:** Sam Elliott (Tom Keating), Perry King (Lee Bishop), Gene Barry (Carl Osborne), Martine Beswick (Joan Carolinian), Anthony Franciosa (Alex Budde), Joseph Cotten (Horton Paine), Roger Davis (Max Kendrick); **Credits:** Executive Producer: Michael G. Klein; Producers: Roy Huggins, Jo Swerling, Jr.; Teleplay: Douglas H. Heyes; Based on the novels *Aspen* by Bert Hirschfeld and *The Adversary* by Bart Spicer; Music: Tom Scott, Mike Melvoin; Producers: Roy Huggins, Jo Swerling, Jr.; Director: Douglas Heyes; 6 hours; Universal Television; Color.

Captains and the Kings (1976)

Air dates: September 30, October 7, 14, 28, November 4, 11, 1976; **Cast:** Richard Jordan (Joseph Armagh), Perry King (Rory Armagh), Patty Duke Astin (Armagh), Katherine Crawford (Moira Armagh), Jane Seymour (Marjorie Chisholm Armagh), Henry Fonda (Sen. Enfield Bassett), Celeste Holm (Sister Angela), Burl Ives ("Old Syrup"), Vic Morrow (Tom Hennessey), Joanna Pettet (Katherine Hennessey), Barbara Parkins (Martinique), Robert Vaughn (Charles Desmond), Pernell Roberts (Braithwaite); **Credits:** Teleplay: Douglas Heyes; Adaptation: Stephen Karpf, Elinor Karpf; Based on the novel by Taylor Caldwell; Music: Elmer Bernstein; Executive Producer: Roy Huggins; Producer: Jo Swerling, Jr.; Director: Douglas Heyes, Allen Reisner; 9 hours; Production Company: Universal Television-Public Arts; Color.

Television Series

The Fugitive (2000); Creator–Executive Producer (14 episodes × 60 minutes): Roy Huggins.

Hunter (1984); Executive Producer: (1985–1988); Writer: as John Thomas James (11 × 60 minutes); **"The Beautiful and the Dead"** (2:20–2:21) Air dates: April 1, 8, 1986; Writer: John Thomas James; Story: Jo Montgomery; Directors: Gary Winter, Tony Mordente; **"The Contract"** (3:09); Air date: December 13, 1986; Writers: Paul Ehrmann, John Thomas James; Director: Les Sheldon; **"The Cradle Will Rock"** (3:10); Air date: January 3, 1987; Writer: Rogers Turrentine; Story: E. Nick Alexander, John Thomas James; Director: Kim Manners; **"Down and Under"** (3:12); Air date: January 17, 1987; Writer: Howard Chesley; Story: Charlotte Clay, John Thomas James; Director: James Darren; **"Straight to the Heart"** (3:13); Air date: January 24, 1987; Writers: Michael Berlin, Eric Estrin, John Thomas James; Director: James Whitmore, Jr.; **"Any Second Now"** (3:17); Air date: February 28, 1987; Teleplay: Marianne Clarkson; Writers: Stephanie Garman, Hollace White; Story: Charlotte Clay, John Thomas James; Director: James Darren; **"Crossfire"** (3:19); Air date: April 11, 1987; Teleplay: Herman Groves, John Thomas

James, Terry Nelson; Director: Charlie Picerni; **"Night on Bald Mountain"** (4:05); Air date: October 31, 1987; Teleplay: Marianne Clarkson; Story: John Thomas James; Director: Dennis Dugan; **"Allegra"** (4:11); Air date: December 29, 1987; Writer: Joe Menosky; Story: John Thomas James; Director: James Whitmore, Jr.; **"Murder He Wrote"** (4:21); Air date: April 30, 1988; Writer: John Thomas James; Director: Jefferson Kibbee; Production Company: Stephen J. Cannell Productions; Distributor: National Broadcasting Company (NBC); Color.

Blue Thunder (1984); Executive Producer: (10 × 60 minutes); Production Company: Columbia Pictures Television; Distributor: American Broadcasting Company (ABC); Color.

Universal Television

City of Angels (1976); Producer: (13 × 60 minutes); Writer: (8 × 60 minutes); **"The November Plan"** (1:01–1:03); Air dates: February 3, 10, 17, 1976; Writer: Stephen J. Cannell; Story: Stephen J. Cannell, Roy Huggins; Director: Don Medford; **"The House on Orange Grove Avenue"** (1:06); Air date: March 16, 1976; Teleplay: Elinor and Stephen Karpf; Story: Roy Huggins; Director: Robert Douglas; **"Palm Springs Answer"** (1:07), Air date: March 23, 1976; Teleplay: Merwin Gerard; Story: Roy Huggins; Director: Allen Reisner; **"The Losers"** (1:08), Air date: April 6, 1976; Teleplay: John Thomas James, Gloryette Clark; Director: Barry Shear; **"A Sudden Silence"** (1:09), Air date: April 13, 1976; Teleplay: Douglas Heyes; Story: John Thomas James; Director: Douglas Heyes; **"Say Goodbye to Yesterday"** (1:11), Air date: May 4, 1976; Writers: Gloryette Clark, Roy Huggins; Director: Jerry London; Production Company: Roy Huggins–Public Arts Productions, Universal TV; Distributor: National Broadcasting Company (NBC); Color.

Baretta (1975); Writer as John Thomas James (7 × 60 minutes); **"Woman in the Harbor"** (1:03); Air date: January 31, 1975; Teleplay: Robert I. Holt, Don Balluck; Story: John Thomas James; Director: Bernard L. Kowalski; **"If You Can't Pay the Price"** (1:04); Air date: February 7, 1975; Teleplay: Tony Morgan, John Thomas James; Story: Tony Morgan; Director: Bernard L. Kowalski; **"The Half-Million Dollar Baby"** (1:05); Air date: February 14, 1975; Teleplay: Philip DeGuere; Story: John Thomas James; Director: Michael Schultz; **"Ragtime Billy Peaches"** (1:06); Air date: February 28, 1975; Teleplay: Don Carlos Dunaway; Story: John Thomas James; Director: Bernard L. Kowalski; **"The Coppelli Oath"** (1:07); Air date: Teleplay: Michael Butler; Story: John Thomas James. Michael Butler; Director: Don Medford; **"The Secret of Terry Lake"** (1:11); Air date: April 16, 1975; Teleplay: Philip DeGuere, Jr.; Story: John Thomas James; Director: Russ Mayberry; **"Sharper Than a Serpent's Tooth"** (2:13); Air date: December 17, 1975; Teleplay: Frank Dandridge; Story: John Thomas James, Robert Janes; Director: Charles R. Rondeau; Production Company: Roy Huggins–Public Arts Productions, Universal TV; Distributor: American Broadcasting Company (ABC); Color.

Switch (1975); (1 × 60 minutes); **"Death by Resurrection"** (1:11) Air date: December 2, 1975; Teleplay: Stephen J. Cannell; Story: John Thomas James; Director: Story: John Thomas James; Director: Alf Kjellin; Production Company: Glen Larson Productions, Universal TV; Distribution: Columbia Broadcasting System (CBS); Color.

The Rockford Files (1974–1980); Creators: Stephen J. Cannell, Roy Huggins; Writer—as John Thomas James (15 × 60 minutes); **"The Kirkoff Case"** (1:01); Air date: September 13, 1974; Teleplay: Stephen J. Cannell; Story: John Thomas James; Director: Lou Antonio; **"The Dark and Bloody Ground"** (1:02); Air date: September 20, 1974; Teleplay: Juanita Bartlett; Story: John Thomas James; Director: Michael Schultz; **"The Countess"** (1:03); Air date: September 27, 1974; Teleplay: Stephen J. Cannell; Story: John Thomas James; Director: Russ Mayberry; **"Exit Prentiss Car"** (1:04); Air date: October 4, 1974; Teleplay: Juanita Bartlett; Story: John Thomas James; Director: Alexander Grasshoff; **"Tall Woman in Red Wagon"** (1:05); Air date: October 11, 1974; Teleplay: Stephen J. Cannell; Story: John Thomas James; Director: Jerry London; **"This Case Is Closed"** (1:06); Air date: October 18, 1974; Teleplay: Stephen J. Cannell; Story: John Thomas James; Director: Bernard L. Kowalski; **"The Big Rip-off"** (1:07); Air date: October 25, 1974; Teleplay: Robert Hamner; Story: John Thomas James; Director: Vincent McEveety; **"Find Me If You Can"** (1:08); Air date: November 1, 1974; Teleplay: Juanita Bartlett; Story: John Thomas James; Director: Lawrence Doheny; **"In Pursuit of Carol

Thorne" (1:09); Air date: November 8, 1974; Teleplay: Stephen J. Cannell; Story: John Thomas James; Director: Charles S. Dubin; **"Caledonia—It's Worth a Fortune"** (1:11); Air date: December 6, 1974; Teleplay: Juanita Bartlett; Story: John Thomas James; Director: Stuart Margolin; **"Profit and Loss: Profit"** (1:12); Air date: December 20, 1974; Teleplay: Stephen J. Cannell; Story: John Thomas James; Director: Lawrence Doheny; **"Profit and Loss: Loss"** (1:13), Air date: December 27, 1974; Teleplay: Stephen J. Cannell; Story: John Thomas James; Director: Lawrence Doheny; **"Aura Lee, Farewell"** (1:14); Air date: January 3, 1975; Teleplay: Edward J. Lakso; Story: John Thomas James; Director: Jackie Cooper; **"Say Goodbye to Jennifer"** (1:18); Air date: February 7, 1975; Teleplay: Juanita Bartlett, Rudolph Borchert; Story: John Thomas James; Director: Jackie Cooper; **"Charlie Harris at Large"** (1:19); Air date: February 14, 1975; Teleplay: Zekial Marko; Story: John Thomas James; Director: Russ Mayberry; Production Company: Roy Huggins–Public Arts Productions, Cherokee Productions; Universal TV; Distributor: National Broadcasting Company (NBC); Color.

Toma (1973–1974); Executive Producer: John Thomas James; Writer—as John Thomas James (10 × 60 minutes); **"The Oberon Contract"** (1:01); Air date: October 4, 1973; Teleplay: Stephen J. Cannell; Story: Roy Huggins; Director: Jeannot Szwarc; **"Crime Without Victim"** (1:03); Air date: October 13, 1973; Teleplay: Stephen J. Cannell; Story: Roy Huggins; Director: Daniel Haller; **"Stakeout"** (1:04); Air date: October 25, 1973; Writer: Roy Huggins; Director: Nicholas Colasanto; **"The Cain Connection"** (1:05); Air date: November 1, 1973; Teleplay: Stephen J. Cannell; Story: Roy Huggins; Director: Gary Nelson; **"Blockhouse Breakdown"** (1:06); Air date: November 8, 1973; Teleplay: Lonne Elder III; Story: Roy Huggins; Director: Richard C. Bennett; **"The Bambara Bust"** (1:08); Air date: December 6, 1973; Teleplay: Judy Burns; Story: Roy Huggins; Director: Alexander Grasshoff; **"The Contract on Alex Cordeen"** (1:15); Air date: March 8, 1974; Teleplay: Stephen J. Cannell; Story: Roy Huggins; Director: Alexander Grasshoff; **"Joey the Weep"** (1:16); Air date: March 22, 1974; Teleplay: Don Carlos Dunaway; Story: Roy Huggins; Director: Charles S. Dubin; **"The Madam"** (1:18); Air date: April 12, 1974; Teleplay: Juanita Bartlett; Story: Roy Huggins; Director: Michael Schulz; **"Indictment"** (1:20); Air date: April 26, 1974; Teleplay: Juanita Bartlett; Story: Roy Huggins; Director: Gary Nelson; Production Company: Roy Huggins–Public Arts Productions, Universal TV; Distributor: American Broadcasting Company (ABC); Color.

Jigsaw (1973); Executive Producer: Roy Huggins (2 × 60 minutes); **"Kiss the Dream Goodbye"** (1:06); Air date: February 17, 1973; **"Girl on the Run"** (1:07); Air date: February 24, 1973; Production Company: Universal TV; Distributor: American Broadcasting Company (ABC); Color.

Cool Million (1972); Executive Producer: Roy Huggins (Pilot 120 minutes+ 4 × 90 minutes); **"Cool Million—Mask of Marcella"** (Pilot); Air date: October 16, 1972; Director: Gene Levitt; **"Hunt for a Lonely Girl"** (1:01), Air date: October 25, 1972; Director: Daryl Duke; **"Assault on Gavaloni"** (1:02); Air date: November 22, 1972; Director: John Badham; **"The Abduction of Bayard Barnes"** (1:03); Air date: December 6, 1972; Director: Barry Shear; **"The Million Dollar Misunderstanding"** (1:04); Air date: December 20, 1972; Director: Charles S. Dubin; Production Company: Public Arts Films, Universal TV; Distributor: National Broadcasting Company (NBC); Color.

Alias Smith and Jones (1971–1973); Writer as John Thomas James (43 × 60 minutes); **Season One: "The McCreedy Bust"** (1:01); Air date: January 21, 1971; Teleplay: Sy Salkowitz; Story: John Thomas James; Director: Gene Levitt; **"Exit from Wickenberg"** (1:02); Air date: January 28, 1971; Teleplay: Robert Hamner; Story: John Thomas James; Director: Jeannot Szwarc; **"The Great Shell Game"** (1:05); Air date: February 18, 1971; Teleplay: Glen A. Larson; Story: John Thomas James; Director: Richard Benedict; **"Return to Devil's Hole"** (1:06); Air date: February 25, 1971; Teleplay: Knut Swenson; Story: John Thomas James; Director: Bruce Kessler; **"A Fistful of Diamonds"** (1:07); Air date: March 4, 1971; Teleplay: Robert Hamner; Story: John Thomas James; Director: Jeffrey Hayden; **"Stagecoach Seven"** (1:08); Air date: March 11, 1971; Teleplay: Dick Nelson; Story: John Thomas James; Director: Richard Benedict; **"The Man Who Murdered Himself"** (1:09); Air date: March 18, 1971; Teleplay: Robert Hamner, John

Thomas James; Story: John Thomas James; Director: Jeffrey Hayden; "**The Fifth Victim**" (1:11); Air date: April 1, 1971; Teleplay: Glen A. Larson; Story: John Thomas James; Director: Fernando Lamas; "**Journey from San Juan**" (1:12); Air date: April 8, 1971; Teleplay: Dick Nelson; Story: John Thomas James; Director: Jeffrey Hayden; "**Never Trust An Honest Man**" (1:13); Air date: April 15, 1971; Teleplay: Phil DeGuere; Story: John Thomas James; Director: Douglas Heyes; **Season Two: "The Day They Hanged Kid Curry**" (2:01); Air date: September 16, 1971; Teleplay: Glen A. Larson; Story: John Thomas James; Director: Barry Shear; "**How to Rob a Bank in One Hard Lesson**" (2:02); Air date: September 23, 1971; Teleplay: David Moessinger; Story: John Thomas James; Director: Alexander Singer; "**Jailbreak at Junction City**" (2:03); Air date: September 30, 1971; Teleplay: John Thomas James; Director: Jeffrey Hayden; "**Smiler with a Gun**" (2:04); Air date: October 7, 1971; Teleplay: Max Hodge; Story: John Thomas James; Director: Fernando Lamas; "**The Posse That Wouldn't Quit**" (2:05); Air date: October 14, 1971; Teleplay: Pat Fielder; Story: John Thomas James; Director: Harry Falk; "**Something to Get Hung About**" (2:06); Air date: October 21, 1971; Teleplay: Nicholas E. Baehr, John Thomas James; Story: John Thomas James; Director: Jack Arnold; "**Six Strangers at Apache Springs**" (2:07); Air date: October 28, 1971; Teleplay: Arnold Somkin, John Thomas James; Story: John Thomas James; Director: Nicholas Colasanto; "**Night of the Red Dog**" (2:08); Air date: November 4, 1971; Teleplay: Dick Nelson, John Thomas James; Story: John Thomas James; Director: Russ Mayberry; "**The Reformation of Harry Briscoe**" (2:09); Air date: November 11, 1971; Teleplay: B.W. Sandefur, John Thomas James; Story: John Thomas James; Director: Barry Shear; "**Dreadful Sorry Clementine**" (2:10); Air date: November 18, 1971; Teleplay: Glen A. Larson; Story: John Thomas James; Director: Barry Shear; "**Shootout at Diablo Station**" (2:11); Air date: December 2, 1971; Teleplay: William D. Gordon; Story: John Thomas James; Director: Jeffrey Hayden; "**The Bounty Hunter**" (2:12); Air date: December 9, 1971; Teleplay: Nicholas E. Baehr; Story: John Thomas James; Director: Barry Shear; "**Everything Else You Can Steal**" (2:13); Air date: December 16, 1971; Teleplay: John Thomas James; Director: Alexander Singer; "**Miracle at Santa Marta**" (2:14); Air date: December 30, 1971; Teleplay: Dick Nelson, John Thomas James; Story: John Thomas James; Director: Vincent Sherman; "**21 Days to Tenstrike**" (2:15); Air date: January 6, 1972; Teleplay: Irving Pearlberg, John Thomas James; Story: John Thomas James; Director: Mel Ferber; "**The McCreedy Bust, Going, Going, Gone!**" (2:16); Air date: January 13, 1972; Teleplay: Nicholas E. Baehr; Story: John Thomas James; Director: Alexander Singer; "**The Men Who Broke the Bank at Red Gap**" (2:17); Air date: January 20, 1972; Teleplay: Ronson Howitzer, John Thomas James; Story: John Thomas James; Director: Richard Benedict; "**The Men That Corrupted Hadleyburg**" (2:18); Air date: January 27, 1972; Teleplay: Dick Nelson, John Thomas James; Story: John Thomas James; Director: Jeff Corey; "**The Biggest Game in the West**" (2:19); Air date: February 3, 1972; Story: John Thomas James; Director: Alexander Singer; "**Which Way to the OK Corral?**" (2:20); Air date: February 10, 1972; Teleplay: Glen A. Larson; Story: John Thomas James; Director: Jack Arnold; "**Don't Get Mad, Get Even**" (2:21); Air date: February 17, 1972; Teleplay: John Thomas James; Director: Bruce Bilson; "**What's in It for Mia?**" (2:22); Air date: February 24, 1972; Teleplay: William D. Gordon; Story: John Thomas James; Director: John Dumas; "**Bad Night at Big Butte**" (2:23); Air date: March 2, 1972; Teleplay: Glen A. Larson; Story: John Thomas James; Director: Richard Bare; **Season Three: "The Long Chase**" (3:01); Air date: September 16, 1972; Story: John Thomas James; Director: Alexander Singer; "**High Lonesome Country**" (3:02); Air date: September 23, 1972; Teleplay: Dick Nelson; Story: John Thomas James; Director: Alexander Singer; "**The McCreedy Feud**" (3:03); Air date: September 30, 1972; Teleplay: Juanita Bartlett; Story: John Thomas James; Director: Alexander Singer; "**The Clementine Ingredient**" (3:04); Air date: October 7, 1972; Teleplay: Gloryette Clark; Story: John Thomas James; Director: Jack Arnold; "**Bushwack!**" (3:05); Air date: October 23, 1972; Teleplay: David Moessinger, John Thomas James; Story: John Thomas James; Director: Jack Arnold; "**What Happened at the XST?**" (3:06); Air date: October 28, 1972; Teleplay: John Thomas James; Director: Jack Arnold; "**The Ten Days That Shook Kid Curry**" (3:07); Air date: November 4, 1972; Teleplay: Gloryette Clark; Story: John Thomas James; Director: Edward M.

Abrams; "The Day the Amnesty Came Through" (3:08); Air date: November 25, 1972; Teleplay: Dick Nelson, John Thomas James; Story: John Thomas James; Director: Jeff Corey; "The Strange Fate of Conrad Meyer Zulick" (3:09); Air date: December 2, 1972; Teleplay: Nicholas E. Baehr; Story: John Thomas James; Director: Richard Bennett; "McGuffin" (3:10); Air date: December 9, 1972; Teleplay: Nicholas E. Baehr; Story: John Thomas James; Director: Alexander Singer; "Witness to a Lynching" (3:11); Air date: December 16, 1972; Teleplay: Nicholas E. Baehr; Story: John Thomas James; Director: Richard Bennett; "Only Three to a Bed" (3:12); Air date: January 13, 1973; Teleplay: Richard Morris; Story: John Thomas James; Director: Jeffrey Hayden; Production Company: Roy Huggins–Public Arts Productions, Universal TV; Distributor: American Broadcasting Company (ABC); Color

The Bold Ones: The Lawyers (1969–1972); Creator-Executive Producer as John Thomas James (28 × 60 minutes); "A Game of Chance" (1:01); Air date: September 21, 1969; Writer: John Thomas James; Based on the novel by Whit Masterson; Director: Douglas Heyes; "The Crowd Pleaser" (1:03); Air date: November 2, 1969; Teleplay: Frank Fenton; Story: John Thomas James, David Giler; Director: Vincent Sherman; "A Shriek of Silence" (1:05), Air date: November 30, 1969; Teleplay: Robert Foster, John Thomas James; Story: John Thomas James; Director: Fernando Lamas; "Point of Honor" (1:07); Air date: January 25, 1970; Writer: John Thomas James; Director: Gene Levitt; "The Verdict" (2:01); Air date: September 27, 1970; Writer: John Thomas James; Director: Alexander Singer; "The Hyland Confession" (2:07); Air date: January 31, 1971; Teleplay: Frank Fenton; Story: John Thomas James; Director: Daniel Petrie; "The Strange Secret of Yermo Hill" (3:02); Air date: October 17, 1971; Teleplay: William D. Gordon; Story: John Thomas James; Director: Jeffrey Hayden; "In Defense of Ellen McKay" (3:04); Air date: November 14, 1971; Teleplay: David Chase; Story: John Thomas James; Director: Alexander Singer; "Lisa, I Hardly Knew You" (3:11); Air date: February 13, 1972; Teleplay: Elick Moll; Story: John Thomas James; Director: Alexander Singer; Production Company: Public Arts Productions, Universal TV; Distributor: National Broadcasting Company (NBC); Color.

The Outsider (1968–69); Creator; Roy Huggins; Production Company: Public Arts Productions, Universal TV; Distributor: National Broadcasting Company (NBC); Color.

Run for Your Life (1965–1968); Executive Producer: Roy Huggins (86 × 60 minutes); Writer— as John Thomas James (30 × 60 minutes); **Season One:** "The Cold, Cold War of Paul Bryan" (1:01), Air date: September 13, 1965; Teleplay: Frank Fenton, John Thomas James; Story: John Thomas James; Directors: Robert Butler, Leslie H. Martinson; "The Girl Next Door" (1:02); Air date: September 20, 1965; Teleplay: Luther Davis; Story: John Thomas James; Director: Leslie H. Martinson; "Never Pick Up a Stranger" (1:04); Air date: October 11, 1965; Writer: Howard Browne; Story: John Thomas James; Director: Leslie H. Martinson; "Our Man in Limbo" (1:06); Air date: October 22, 1965; Teleplay: Paul Tuckahoe; Story: John Thomas James; Director: Leslie H. Martinson; "Where Mystery Begins" (1:07); Air date: October 29, 1965; Writer: John Thomas James; Director: Leslie H. Martinson; (1:07); "The Savage Season" (1:08); Air date: November 8, 1965; Story: John Thomas James; Director: Richard Benedict; "The Time of the Sharks" (1:12); Air date: December 6, 1965; Teleplay: Frank Fenton; Story: John Thomas James; Director: Leslie H. Martinson; "Make the Angels Weep" (1:13); Air date: December 13, 1965; Teleplay: John T. Dugan; Story: John Thomas James; Director: Leslie H. Martinson; "The Carnival Ends at Midnight" (1:16); Air date: January 10, 1966; Teleplay: Boris Sobelman; Story: John Thomas James; Director: Richard Benedict; "The Rediscovery of Charlotte Hyde" (1:17); Air date: January 24, 1966; Writer: Harold Gast; Story: John Thomas James; Director: William Hale; "The Night of the Terror" (1:18); Air date: January 31, 1966; Teleplay: John Thomas James; Story: Gerald-Vaughn Hughes; Director: Alexander Singer; "In Search of April" (1:20); Air date: February 14, 1966; Teleplay: Alvin Sargent; Story: John Thomas James; Director: Stuart Rosenberg; "Who's Watching the Fleshpot?" (1:22); Air date: March 7, 1966; Writer: John Thomas James; Director: Leslie H. Martinson; "Night Train from Chicago" (1:27); Air date: April 11, 1966; Teleplay: Robert Bloch; Story: John Thomas James; Director: Richard Benedict; "The Last Safari" (1:28); Air date: April 25, 1966; Writers: John

W. Bloch, Mel Goldberg; Story: John Thomas James; Director: Abner Biberman; **Season Two:** "**The Borders of Barbarism**" (2:08); Air date: September 26, 1966; Teleplay: John Thomas James; Based on the novel by Eric Williams; Director: Richard Benedict; "**The Dark Beyond the Door**" (2:05); Air date: October 10, 1966; Writer: John W. Bloch; Story: John Thomas James; Director: Richard L. Bare; "**The Man Who Had No Enemies**" (2:10); Air date: November 21, 1966; Writer: John W. Bloch; Story: John Thomas James; Director: Michael Ritchie; "**A Rage for Justice**" (2:17); Air date: January 16, 1967; Writer: John W. Bloch; Story: John Thomas James; Director: Leo Penn; "**The List of Alice McKenna**" (2:18); Air date: January 23, 1967; Teleplay: Jerry Ludwig; Story: John Thomas James; Director: Michael Ritchie; "**East of the Equator**" (2:26); Air date: March 20, 1967; Teleplay: Henri Simon; Story: John Thomas James; Director: Fernando Lamas; **Season Three:** "**The Inhuman Predicament**" (3:02); Air date: September 20, 1967; Teleplay: Barry Pritchard; Story: John Thomas James; Director: Alexander Singer; "**Trip to the Far Side**" (3:05); Air date: October 11, 1967; Writer: Paul Tuckahoe; Story: John Thomas James; Director: Fernando Lamas; "**The Company of Scoundrels**" (3:06); Air date: October 18, 1967; Teleplay: Howard Browne; Story: John Thomas James; Director: Michael Ritchie; "**At the End of the Rainbow There's Another Rainbow**" (3:07); Air date: October 25, 1967; Teleplay: Henry Slesar, John Thomas James; Story: John Thomas James; Director: Nicholas Colasanto; "**The Mustafa Embrace**" (3:13); Air date: December 1, 1967; Teleplay: Robert Hamner; Story: John Thomas James; Director: Murray Golden; "**Fly by Night**" (3:15); Air date: December 22, 1967; Teleplay: Robert Foster, Philip DeGuere, Jr.; Story: John Thomas James; Director: Richard Benedict; "**One Bad Turn**" (3:17); Air date: January 10, 1968; Teleplay: Paul Mason; Story: John Thomas James; Director: Ben Gazzara; "**Sara-Jane, You Never Whispered Again**" (3:20); Air date: February 7, 1968; Teleplay: Adrian Joyce; Story: John Thomas James; Director: Alexander Singer; "**The Exchange**" (3:26); Air date: March 27, 1968; Teleplay: Howard Browne; Story: John Thomas James; Director: John Moxey; Production Company: Roncom Films, Roy Huggins Productions, Universal TV; Distributor: National Broadcasting Company (NBC); Color.

Bob Hope Presents the Chrysler Theatre (1967); Producer: (1 × 60 minutes); "**The War of Eric Kurtz**" (2:17); Air date: March 5, 1965; Writers: Howard Browne, Gene L. Coon; Director: Tom Gries; Writer: (1 × 60 minutes); "**Don't Wait for Tomorrow**" (4:23); Air date: April 15, 1967; Writers: Frank Fenton, Roy Huggins; Director: Harvey Hart; Production Company: Hovue Enterprises, Morpics, Universal TV; Distributor: National Broadcasting Company (NBC); Color.

Kraft Suspense Theatre (1963–1965); Writer: (3 × 60 minutes); "**Doesn't Anyone Know Who I Am?**" (1:17); Air date: February 27, 1964; Teleplay: Paul Tuckahoe; Story: Thomas Fitzroy; Director: William A. Graham; "**The Sweet Taste of Vengeance**" (1:24); Air date: April 30, 1964; Teleplay: Frank Fenton; Story: Thomas Fitzroy; Director: Roy Huggins; "**The Green Felt Jungle**" (2:20); Air date: April 1, 1965; Adaptation: Howard Browne; Story: Thomas Fitzroy; Director: Irving J. Moore; Production Company: Roncom Films; Distributor: National Broadcasting Company (NBC); Color.

QM–United Artists

The Fugitive (1963–1967); Creator: Roy Huggins; Executive Producer: Quinn Martin; Production Company: Quinn Martin Productions (QM), United Artists Television; Distributor: American Broadcasting Company (ABC); Color.

Revue Studios–Universal Television

The Virginian (1962–1971); Executive Producer: (17 × 75 minutes); Writer as Thomas Fitzroy and John Francis O'Mara (7 × 75 minutes); "**The Exiles**" (1:16); Air date: January 9, 1963; Teleplay: William P. McGivern, Howard Browne: Story: Thomas Fitzroy; Director: Bernard Girard; "**The Man Who Wouldn't Die**" (1:19); Air date: February 2, 1963; Teleplay: Harry Kleiner; Story: John Francis O'Mara; Director: David Friedkin; "**If You Have Tears**" (1:20); Air date: February 13, 1963; Teleplay: Frank Fenton, Frank Chase; Story: Thomas Fitzroy, Howard Browne; Director: Richard L. Bare; "**Vengeance Is the Spur**" (1:22); Air date: February 27, 1963; Teleplay: Harry Kleiner; Story: John Francis O'Mara; Director: Robert Ellis Miller; "**The Golden Door**" (1:24); Air date: March 13, 1963; Teleplay: Maxwell Shane; Story: Thomas Fitzroy, Maxwell

Shane; Director: John Brahm; **"A Distant Fury"** (1:25); Air date: March 20, 1963; Teleplay: Howard Browne; Story: Howard Browne, John Francis O'Mara; Director: John English; **"Strangers at Sundown"** (1:27); Air date: April 10, 1963; Teleplay; Morton Fine, David Friedkin; Story: Thomas Fitzroy; Director: David Friedkin; Production Company: Revue Studios, Universal TV; Distributor: National Broadcasting Company (NBC); Color.

20th Century–Fox Television

Kraft Mystery Theatre (1961), **"The House on Rue Riviera"** (1:12); Air date: August 3, 1961; Writer-Producer: Roy Huggins; 60 minutes; Production Company: 20th Century–Fox Television; Distributor: National Broadcasting Company (NBC); B&W.

Bus Stop (1961–1962); Executive Producer: (26 × 60 minutes); Writer: (2 × 60 minutes); **"Cry to Heaven"** (1:16); Air date: January 14, 1962; Teleplay: John Francis O'Mara; Original Screenplay: Nunnally Johnson; Based on the novel by Patrick Quentin; Director: Stuart Rosenberg; **"How Does Charlie Feel?"** (1:19); Air date: February 4, 1962; Writer: Roy Huggins: Director: Richard L. Bare; Production Company: Belmont Television Company, 20th Century–Fox Television; Distributor: American Broadcasting Company (ABC); B&W.

Follow the Sun (1961); Story: (1 × 60 minutes); **"The Highest Wall"** (1:03); Air date: October 1, 1961; Teleplay: Ellis Kadison; Story: Thomas Fitzroy; Director: Ted Post; Production Company: 20th Century–Fox Television; Distributor: American Broadcasting Company (ABC); B&W.

Warner Brothers

Adventures in Paradise (1961); Producer; Production Company: Warner Bros. Television; Distributor: American Broadcasting Company (ABC); B&W.

Hawaiian Eye (1960); **"Dead Ringer"** (1:31); Air date: May 11, 1960; Story: Roy Huggins; Director: Mark Sandrich, Jr.; Production Company: Warner Bros. Television; Distributor: American Broadcasting Company (ABC); B&W.

77 Sunset Strip (1960); (1 × 77 minutes; 2 × 60 minutes); **"Girl on the Run"** (1:01), Air date: May 20, 1960; Screenplay: Marion Hargrove; Story: Roy Huggins; Director: Richard L. Bare; **"Lovely Lady Pity Me"** (1:02); Air date: October 17, 1958; Teleplay: Douglas Heyes; Based on the novel by Roy Huggins; Director: Douglas Heyes; **"Perfect Setup"** (2;33); Air date: May 20, 1960; Story: Roy Huggins; Director: Montgomery Pittman; Production Company: Warner Bros. Television; Distributor: American Broadcasting Company (ABC); B&W.

Colt .45 (1957–1960); (2 × 30 minutes); **"The Peacemaker"** (1:01); Air date: October 18, 1957; Teleplay: Marion Hargrove; Story: Roy Huggins; Director: Douglas Heyes; **"Chain of Command"** (3:17); Air date: April 5, 1960; Teleplay: Howard Browne, Dean Riesner; Story: Roy Huggins; Director: Lew Landers; Production Company: Warner Bros. Television; Distributor: American Broadcasting Company (ABC); B&W.

Maverick (1957–1960); Writer: (8 × 60 minutes); **"Point Blank"** (1:02); Air date: September 29, 1957; Teleplay: Roy Huggins, Howard Browne; Director: Budd Boetticher; **"The Jeweled Gun"** (1:10); Air date: November 24, 1957; Writer: Roy Huggins; Director: Leslie H. Martinson; **"Rage for Vengeance"** (1:16); Air date: January 12, 1958; Teleplay: Marion Hargrove; Story: Roy Huggins; Director: Leslie H. Martinson; **"Diamond in the Rough"** (1:18); Air date: January 26, 1958; Teleplay: Marion Hargrove; Story: Roy Huggins; Director: Douglas Heyes; **"Shady Deal at Sunny Acres"** (2:10); Air date: November 23, 1958; Teleplay: Roy Huggins, Story: Douglas Heyes;; Director: Leslie H. Martinson; **"Passage to Fort Doom"** (2:23); Air date: March 8, 1959; Writer: Roy Huggins; Director: Paul Henreid; **"The Lass with the Poisonous Air"** (3:08); Air date: November 1, 1959; Teleplay: Catherine Turney; Story: Roy Huggins; Director: Richard L. Bare; **"Guatemala City"** (3:20); Air date: January 30, 1960; Story: Roy Huggins, Coles Trapnell; Writer: Leonard Praskins; Director: Arthur Lubin; Production Company: Warner Bros. Television; Distributor: American Broadcasting Company (ABC); B&W.

Conflict (1956–1957); Producer: (20 × 60 minutes); Story: (3 × 60 minutes); **"Silent Journey"** (2:08); Air date: December 25, 1956; Writer: Dean Riesner; Story: Roy Huggins; Director: Walter Doniger; **"Capital Punishment"** (2:13); Air date: March 5, 1957; Teleplay: Frederick Brady; Story: Roy Huggins; Director: Walter Doniger; **"Anything for Money"** (2:16); Air date: April 16, 1957; Teleplay: Frederick Brady; Story: Roy Huggins; Director: Walter Doniger; Production Company: Warner Bros. Television; Distributor: American Broadcasting Company (ABC); B&W.

Cheyenne (1956); Producer: (12 × 60 minutes); Writer: (5 × 60 minutes); **"Decision"** a.k.a. **"The Black Hawk War"** (1:07); Air date: January 24, 1956; Writer: Dean Riesner; Story: Roy Huggins; Director: Richard L. Bare; **"Quicksand"** (1:11); Air date: April 3, 1956; Writers: Dean Riesner, N. B. Stone; Story: Roy Huggins, N.B. Stone; Director: Leslie H. Martinson; **"Star in the Dust"** (1:13); Air date: May 1, 1956; Writer: Roy Huggins; Story: Douglas Heyes, Roy Huggins; Director: Richard L. Bare; **"Johnny Bravo"** (1:14); Air date: May 15, 1956; Writer: Dean Riesner; Story: Roy Huggins, Dean Riesner; Director: Richard L. Bare; **"The Dark Rider"** (2:01); Air date: September 11, 1956; Writers: Howard Browne, Roy Huggins; Director: Richard L. Bare; Production Company: Warner Bros. Television; Distributor: American Broadcasting Company (ABC); B&W.

Warner Brothers Presents (1956); **"The Deadly Riddle"** (1:36); Air date: May 22, 1956; Adaptation: Roy Huggins, based on "The Wife of Bath's Tale" by Geoffrey Chaucer; Director: Don Weis; Production Company: Warner Bros. Television; Distributor: American Broadcasting Company (ABC); 60 minutes; B&W.

Lux Video Theatre (1955); **"The Lady Gambles"** (6:08). Air date: October 27, 1955; Story: Lewis Meltzer, Oscar Saul; Based on the original screenplay by Halsted Welles and Roy Huggins; Director: Richard Goode; Production Company: J. Walter Thompson Agency; Distributor: National Broadcasting Company (NBC); 60 min; B&W.

Kings Row (1955); **"Ellie"** (1:03); Air date: October 25, 1955; Teleplay: Richard Morris; Story: Roy Huggins; Based on the novel by Henry Bellamann; Director: Paul Stewart; Production Company: Warner Bros. Television; Distributor: American Broadcasting Company (ABC); 60 minutes; B&W.

The Joe Palooka Story (1954); 26 × 30 minutes; Cast: Joe Kirkwood, Jr. (Joe Palooka), Cathy Downs (Ann Howe), Luis Van Rooten (Knobby Walsh), "Slapsie" Maxie Rosenbloom (Clyde); Based on the syndicated cartoon strip by Ham Fisher; Producers: Richard L. Bare, William Berke; Story Editor: Roy Huggins (uncredited); Production Company: Guild Films, New York; Distributor: Syndicated; B&W.

Theatrical Films

U.S. Marshals (1998)

Released: March 6, 1998; **Cast:** Tommy Lee Jones (Samuel Gerard), Wesley Snipes (Sheridan), Robert Downey, Jr. (Royce), Jo Pantoliano (Renfro), Kate Nelligan (Walsh); **Credits:** Executive Producer: Roy Huggins; Writer: John Pogue; Music: Jerry Goldsmith; Producers: Arnold Kopelson, Anne Kopelson; 138 minutes; Production and Distribution Company: Warner Bros.; Color.

The Fugitive (1993)

Released: August 6, 1993; **Cast:** Harrison Ford (Dr. Richard Kimble), Tommy Lee Jones (Samuel Gerard), Sela Ward (Helen Kimble), Julianne Moore (Dr. Anne Eastman), Jo Pantoliano (Renfro); **Credits:** Screenplay: Jeb Stuart, David Twohy, based on characters created by Roy Huggins; Music: James Newton Howard; Executive Producers: Keith Barish, Roy Huggins; Director: Andrew Davis; 130 minutes; Production and Distribution Company: Warner Bros.; Color.

A Fever in the Blood (1961)

Released: January 1961; **Cast:** Efrem Zimbalist, Jr. (Judge Hoffman), Angie Dickinson (Cathy Simon), Don Ameche (Senator A.S. Simon), Jack Kelly (Dan Callahan), Herbert Marshall (Governor Thornwall), Andra Martin (Laura Mayberry), Rhodes Reason (Walter Thornwall), Robert Colbert (Thomas Morely); **Credits:** Screenplay: Roy Huggins, Harry Kleiner; Based on the novel by William Pearson; Music: Ernest Gold; Producer: Roy Huggins; Director: Vincent Sherman; 117 minutes; Production and Distribution Company: Warner Bros. Pictures; B&W.

Girl on the Run (1958)

Released: October 10, 1958; **Cast:** Efrem Zimbalist, Jr. (Stuart Bailey), Edd Byrnes (Kenneth Smiley), Erin O'Brien (Kathy Allen/Karen Shay); **Credits:** Screenplay: Marion Hargrove, Roy Huggins; Executive Producer: William T. Orr; Producer: Roy Huggins; Director: Richard L. Bare; 77 minutes; Production and Distribution Company: Warner Bros. Pictures; B&W.

Three Hours to Kill (1954)

Released: September 3, 1954; **Cast:** Dana Andrews (Jim Guthrie), Donna Reed (Laurie Martin), Dianne Foster (Chris Plumber), Stephen Elliott (Sheriff Ben East), Richard Coogan (Niles

Hendricks), James Westerfield (Sam Minor); **Credits**: Screenplay: Richard Alan Simmons, Roy Huggins; Story: Alex Gottlieb; Music: Paul Sawtell; Producer: Harry Joe Brown; Director: Alfred Werker; 78 minutes; Production and Distribution Company: Columbia Pictures Corp.; Technicolor.

Pushover (1954)

Released: August 1954; **Cast**: Fred MacMurray (Paul Sheridan), Kim Novak (Lona McLane), Dorothy Malone (Ann Stewart), E.G. Marshall (Lt. Carl Eckstrom), Allan Nourse (Paddy Dolan); **Credits**: Screenplay: Roy Huggins, based on the novels *The Night Watch* by Thomas Walsh and *Rafferty* by William S. Ballinger; Producer: Jules Schermer; Director: Richard Quine; 88 minutes; Production and Distribution Company: Columbia Pictures Corp.; B&W.

Gun Fury (1953)

Released: November 1953; **Cast**: Rock Hudson (Ben Warren), Donna Reed (Jennifer Ballard), Phil Carey (Frank Slayton), Lee Marvin (Blinky), Neville Brand (Brazos), Roberta Haynes (Estella Morales), Leo Gordon (Jess Burgess); **Credits**: Screenplay: Irving Wallace, Roy Huggins; Based on the novel *Ten Against Caesar* by Kathleen B. Granger, George Granger, Robert A. Granger; Producer: Lewis J. Rachmil; Director: Raoul Walsh; 81 minutes; Production and Distribution Company: Columbia Pictures Corp.; Technicolor; 3-D.

Hangman's Knot (1952)

Released: November 1952; **Cast**: Randolph Scott (Maj. Matt Stewart), Donna Reed (Molly Hull), Claude Jarman, Jr. (Jamie Groves), Richard Denning (Lee Kemper), Lee Marvin (Rolph Bainter), Jeanette Nolan (Margaret Harris); **Credits**: Screenplay: Roy Huggins; Producer: Harry Joe Brown; Director: Roy Huggins; 80 minutes; Production Company: Producers-Actors Corp.; Distribution Company: Columbia Pictures Corp.; Technicolor.

The Las Vegas Story (1952)

Released: January 30, 1952; **Cast**: Jane Russell (Linda Rollins), Victor Mature (Lt. Dave Andrews), Vincent Price (Lloyd Rollins), Hoagy Carmichael (Happy); **Credits**: Screenplay: Earl Fenton, Harry Essex, Paul Jarrico (uncredited), Roy Huggins (uncredited); Executive Producer: Samuel Bischoff; Director: Robert Stevenson; 88 minutes; Production and Distribution Company: RKO Radio Pictures Inc.; B&W.

The Enforcer (1951)

Released: February 24, 1951; **Cast**: Humphrey Bogart (Martin Ferguson), Zero Mostel (Big Babe Lazick), Everett Sloane (Albert Mendoza), Ted de Corsia (Joseph Rico); **Credits**: Writers: Martin Rackin, Roy Huggins (uncredited); Producer: Milton Sperling; Directors: Bretaigne Windust, Raoul Walsh (uncredited); 87 minutes; Production Company: Warner Bros., United States Pictures; Distribution Company: Warner Bros.; B&W.

Sealed Cargo (1951)

Released: May 19, 1951; **Cast**: Dana Andrews (Pat Bannon), Claude Rains (Eric Skalder), Carla Balenda (Margaret McLean); **Credits**: Screenplay: Dale Van Every, Oliver H.P. Garrett, Roy Huggins; Based on the novel *The Gaunt Woman* by Edmund Gilligan; Music: Roy Webb; Executive Producer: Samuel Bischoff; Director: Alfred Werker; 90 minutes; Production and Distribution Company: RKO Radio Pictures Inc.; B&W.

The Good Humor Man (1950)

Released: June 1950; **Cast**: Jack Carson (Biff Jones), Lola Albright (Margie Bellew), Jean Wallace (Bonnie Conroy); **Credits**: Screenplay: Frank Tashlin, from the *Saturday Evening Post* Roy Huggins story "Appointment with Fear"; Producer: S. Sylvan Simon; Director: Lloyd Bacon; 80 minutes; Production and Distribution Company: Columbia Pictures Corp.; B&W.

His Kind of Woman (1950)

Released: August 25, 1950; **Cast**: Jane Russell (Lenore Brent/Liz Brody), Robert Mitchum (Dan Milner), Vincent Price (Mark Cardigan); **Credits**: Screenplay: Frank Fenton, Jack Leonard, Roy Huggins (uncredited); Story: Gerald Drayson Adams (uncredited); Producer: Robert Sparks; Directors: John Farrow, Richard Fleischer (uncredited); 120 minutes; Production and Distribution Company: RKO Radio Pictures Inc.; B&W.

The Great Manhunt a.k.a. *State Secret* (1950)

Released: September 11, 1950 (UK); **Cast**: Douglas Fairbanks, Jr. (Dr. John Marlowe), Glynis Johns (Lisa Robinson), Jack Hawkins (Colonel Gason), Herbert Lom (Karl Theodor); **Credits**: Producers: Sydney Gilliat, Frank Launder; Screenplay: Sydney Gilliat; Story: Roy Huggins; Director: Sydney Gilliat; 97 minutes; Production Company: London Films Productions; Distribution Company: Columbia Pictures Corp.; B&W.

Woman in Hiding (1949)

Released: December 27, 1949; **Cast:** Ida Lupino (Deborah Chandler Clark/Ann Carter), Stephen McNally (Seldon Carl), Howard Duff (Keith Ramsay), Peggy Dow (Patricia Monahan), John Litel (John Chandler); **Credits:** Screenplay: Oscar Saul; Adaptation: Roy Huggins, based on the *Saturday Evening Post* serial story "Fugitive from Terror" by James Webb; Producer: Michel Kraike; Director: Michael Gordon; 93 minutes; Production Company: Universal-International Pictures; Distribution Company: Universal Pictures; B&W.

Too Late for Tears (1949)

Released: June 8, 1949; **Cast:** Lizabeth Scott (Jane Palmer-Petrie), Dan Duryea (Danny Fuller), Arthur Kennedy (Alan Palmer), Don DeFore (Don Blake), Kristine Miller (Kathy Palmer), Barry Kelley (Lt. Breach); **Credits:** Screenplay: Roy Huggins, based on his novel *Too Late for Tears*; Music: Dale Butts; Producer: Hunt Stromberg; Director: Byron Haskin; 100 minutes; Production Company: Republic Pictures Corp., Streamline Pictures Inc.; Distribution Company: United Artists Corp.; B&W.

The Lady Gambles (1949)

Released: May 20, 1949; **Cast:** Barbara Stanwyck (Joan Phillips Boothe), Robert Preston (David Boothe), Stephen McNally (Horace Corrigan), Edith Barrett (Ruth Phillips), Elliott Sullivan (Barky), John Hoyt (Dr. Rojac), Philip Van Zandt (Chuck); **Credits:** Screenplay: Roy Huggins; Adaptation: Halsted Welles; Story: Lewis Meltzer, Oscar Saul; Music: Frank Skinner; Producer: Michel Kraike; Director: Michael Gordon; 99 minutes; Production Company: Universal-International Pictures; Distribution Company: Universal Pictures; B&W.

The Fuller Brush Man (1948)

Released: May 12, 1948; **Cast:** Red Skelton (Red Jones), Janet Blair (Ann Elliot), Don McGuire (Keenan Wallick), Hillary Brooke (Mrs. Trist), Adele Jergens (Miss Sharmley), Ross Ford (Freddie Trist), Trudy Marshall (Sara Franzen), Nicholas Joy (Commissioner Gordon Trist); **Cred**its: Screenplay: Frank Tashlin, Devery Freeman; Based on the *Saturday Evening Post* short story "Now You See It" by Roy Huggins; Music: Heinz Roemheld; Producer: Edward Small; Director: S. Sylvan Simon; 93 minutes; Production Company: Edward Small Productions Inc.; Distribution Company: Columbia Pictures Corp.; B&W.

I Love Trouble (1948)

Released: January 1948; **Cast:** Franchot Tone (Stuart Bailey), Janet Blair (Norma Shannon), Janis Carter (Mrs. Caprillo/Jane Breeger/Janie Joy), Adele Jergens (Boots Nestor), Glenda Farrell (Hazel Bixby); **Credits:** Screenplay: Roy Huggins, based on his novel *The Double Take*; Producer-Director: S. Sylvan Simon; 96 minutes; Production Company: Cornell Pictures Inc.; Distribution Company: Columbia Pictures Corp.; B&W.

Unsold Pilots Never Broadcast

The Jay Hawkers (1961)

Created by William Self and Roy Huggins—about two Kansans who wander the West. The unsold pilot starred Jack Betts and Jock Gaynor.

Rio (1961)

Unsold pilot starring James Best and Adam West.

During his long career Roy Huggins and his production company Public Arts Inc. were involved in many proposed television projects that never went into production.

Ambassador Yates (1975); TV drama; Story: A. James Panos
Big Wheels (1965); TV Western series
Chaplin: The Story of Charlie and Lita
Coffeyville, Counterforce (1977)
Day the Laughter Stopped (1979)
Destry (1964); TV Western
The Exile (1964); TV series; Story: Luther Davis
The Grape War (1974); "Movie of the Week"; Story: Clyde Ware
Hart, Hart and Nancy (1976); TV comedy series; Story: Bob Shayne
Hawaii's Vanishing Heritage; three-part TV special; Executive Producer: Roy Huggins; Writer: Richard L. Bare
Headhunters, Judas Gospel (1975); theatrical feature
Kentucky Run (1977)

Kill Me Once, Kill Me Twice (1967)
The Lonely Lady (1978); Screenplay: Edward Hume, based on the novel by Harold Robbins
Medi-Commandos (1970); "Movie of the Week"
Meet Me in Escrow (1979); romantic comedy
My Brother Rene (1970); TV Series
Nurse (1980)
Para Medical (1971)
Pursuit (1965)
Rescue (1975), "NBC Special"; Story: Clyde Ware, based on the book by Peter Maas
Rescuers (1978)
Silent Men (1964)
Sweet Savage Love (1977)
T.R.A.C. (1978); TV series
Twelfth of Never (1970); TV drama
Violent World of Jake Lingle (1968)

Novels

Lovely Lady, Pity Me, New York: Duell, Sloan and Pearce (1949).
Too Late for Tears, New York: William Morrow & Co. (1947).
The Double Take, New York: William Morrow & Co. (1946).

Short Stories and Serialized Novels

"Aunt Willie's Ghost," *Conflict—Stories of Suspense* (v 1 #1, Fall 1953).
"Death and the Skylark," *Esquire* (December 1952).
____, *Ellery Queen's Mystery Magazine* Vol. 43, #4 (April 1964).
"Appointment with Fear," *The Saturday Evening Post* (Vol. 219 #13, September 28, 1946).
"Too Late for Tears," (Part 1 of 6), *The Saturday Evening Post* (v 219 #42, April 19, 1947) (April 26, May 3, 10, 17, 24, 1947).
"Now You See It," *The Saturday Evening Post* (May 25, 1946).
"The Double Take," *Mammoth Mystery* (v 2 #2, March 1946).

Collections

The One That Got Away, New York: Detective Book Club-Walter J. Black (1946); Book Club edition comprised of *The One That Got Away* by Helen McCloy, *The Double Take* by Roy Huggins, *The Fifth Man* by Manning Coles.
Too Late for Tears, New York: Detective Book Club (1947); Book Club edition comprised of *Too Late for Tears* by Roy Huggins, *Murder on the Purple Water* by Frances Crane and Frank Gruber.
Coup Double, France: Hachette-Collection "L'Enigme" (1949): French edition of *The Double Take*.
77 Sunset Strip, Dell (1959)—"An original suspense novel" comprised of "Appointment with Fear," "Now You See It" and "Death and the Skylark."

Nonfiction

Poker According to Maverick. Dell (1959)

DVDs

Theatrical Features

The Fuller Brush Man. Sony Pictures Home Entertainment; Full Screen 1.33:1; NTSC1; B&W; 92 minutes; Release: April 16, 2012.
The Barbara Stanwyck Collection (Internes Can't Take Money / The Great Man's Lady / The Bride Wore Boots / The Lady Gambles / All I Desire / There's Always Tomorrow). Universal Studios; Full Screen 1.33:1; NTSC 1; Dolby Digital 2.0 Mono; 3 discs; B&W, 517 minutes; Release: April 27, 2010.
Too Late for Tears. Image Entertainment; Full Screen 1.33:1; NTSC 1; 99 minutes; B&W; Release: May 25, 2004.
Hangman's Knot. Sony Pictures Home Entertainment; Full Screen 1.33:1; NTSC1, Dolby Digital 1.0; Color; 81 minutes; Release: June 15, 2004.
Film Noir Classic Collection, Vol. 3 (Border Incident / His Kind of Woman / Lady in the Lake / On Dangerous Ground / The Racket). Warner Home Video; 1.33:1; NTSC 1; Dolby Digital 2.0 Mono; 6 discs; B&W; 557 minutes; Release: July 18, 2006.
Sealed Cargo. Odeon Entertainment Ltd.; PAL Region 2; B&W; 89 minutes; October 25, 2010; UK.
Gun Fury. Sony Pictures Home Entertainment; Full Screen 1.33:1; NTSC 1; Dolby Digital 2.0 Mono; Color, 83 minutes; Release: May 31, 2005.
Three Hours to Kill. Sony Pictures Home Enter-

tainment; Full Screen 1.33:1; NTSC1; Color; 76 minutes; Release: March 23, 2011.
Woman in Hiding. Universal Studios; Full Screen 1.33:1; NTSC 1; B&W, 93 minutes; Release: November 30, 2012.
Columbia Pictures Film Noir Classics II (Human Desire / The Brothers Rico / Nightfall / City of Fear / Pushover). Sony Pictures Home Entertainment; 1.33:1; NTSC1; Color-B&W; 5 discs; Release: July 6, 2010.
The Fugitive. Warner Home Video; Anamorphic, Widescreen 1.85:1; NTSC1; Dolby Digital 5.1; 130 minutes; Release: June 5, 2001.

Television Series

Cheyenne—The Complete First Season. Warner Home Video; Full Screen, NTSC1; Dolby Digital 1.0; 3 disc; 631 minutes; B&W; Release: June 6, 2006.
Maverick: The Complete First Season. Warner Home Video; Full Screen 1.33:1; Region: NTSC 1; 1350 minutes; 7 discs; B&W; Release: May 29, 2012.
Maverick: The Complete Second Season. Warner Home Video; Full Screen 1.33:1; Region: NTSC 1 1300 minutes; 6 discs; B&W; Release: April 23, 2013.
The Fugitive: Season One, Vol.1; Paramount Home Video; Full Screen 1.33:1; NTSC 1; Dolby Digital 2.0 Mono; 4 discs; B&W; 460 minutes; Release: August 14, 2007.
The Virginian: Complete First Season. Timeless Media; Full Screen 1.33:1; NTSC 1; 11 discs; Color, 2370 minutes; Release: May 25, 2010.
Alias Smith and Jones: The Complete Series. Timeless Media; Full Screen 1.33:1; NTSC 1; 10 discs; Color; 2989 min.; Release: October 19, 2010.
The Rockford Files Season One. Universal Studios; Full Screen 1.33:1; NTSC 1; Dolby Digital 2.0; 3 discs; Color, 874 minutes; Release: December 6, 2005.
Baretta Season One. Universal Studios; Full Screen 1.33:1; NTSC 1; Dolby Digital 2.0 Mono; Color, 612 minutes; Release: October 29, 2002.
Blue Thunder: The Complete Series. Sony Pictures Home Entertainment; Full Screen 1.33:1; NTSC1; Dolby Digital 1.0; 3 discs; Color, 529 min.; Release: August 22, 2006.
Hunter: The Complete Series. Mill Creek Entertainment; Full Screen 1.33:1; NTSC 1; 28 discs; Color, 7215 min.; Release: July 27, 2010.

Television Movies

Invasion of Johnson County/The Outlaw Trail. Timeless Media; Full Screen 1.33:1; NTSC 1; 2 discs; Color; 164 min.; Release: February 24, 2009.

Television Mini-Series

Captains and the Kings. Koch Vision; Full Screen 1.33:1; NTSC 1; 3 discs; Color, 540 min.; Release: January 13, 2009.
Aspen: The Complete Mini-Series. Shout! Factory / Timeless Media; Full Screen 1.33:1; NTSC 1; 2 discs; Color, 288 min.; Release: November 15, 2011.

Awards and Nominations

1959: *Maverick*: Prime-Time Emmy Award; Best Western Series.
1968: *Run for Your Life*: Prime-Time Emmy Award Nomination: Outstanding Dramatic Series.
1977: *Captains and the Kings*: Prime-Time Emmy Award Nomination (with Jo Swerling, Jr.): Outstanding Limited Series.
1991: Private Eye Writers of America: Lifetime Achievement Award.
1993: Producers Guild of America (PGA) Golden Laurel Awards: Lifetime Achievement Award in Television.
2002: Golden Boot Award.

Chapter Notes

Chapter 1

1. *British Civil Wars, Commonwealth and Protectorate 1638–1660*, "1649: The Siege of Drogheda," http://www.british-civil-wars.co.uk.
2. Thomas Carlyle, *Oliver Cromwell's Letters and Speeches: With Elucidations—Vol. 1 Pt. 1* (New York: Wiley & Putnam, 1845), 196–198.
3. *Library Ireland*, http://www.libraryireland.com/IrishPictures/III-Drogheda.php.
4. Peter Beresford Ellis, *Eyewitness to Irish History* (Hoboken, NJ: John Wiley, 2004), 121.
5. Hilary McD Beckles, "A 'riotous and unruly lot': Irish Indentured Servants and Freemen in the English West Indies, 1844–1713," *The William and Mary Quarterly* (October 1990): 503–522.
6. Frank Price, e-mail communication with author, 2007–2013. "I had an ancestor who came as an indentured servant at age 16 to Virginia in 1680. He became an overseer who married the widow of a plantation owner, which is how he and his descendants came to own big plantations."
7. *Fifty Years of Residence in the West Indies Vol. 2*, 209.
8. John Davy, *The West Indies, Before and Since Slave Emancipation* (London: W. & F.G. Cash, 1854), 478.
9. *The Family of Edward Huggins, Sr. and Jr. of Nevis*, http://www.tc.umn.edu/~terre011/edward.html.
10. *Ibid.*
11. Price.
12. Katherine Crawford, e-mail communication with author, March 1, 2013.

Chapter 2

1. "To Start New Town in County," *The Centralia Daily Chronicle*, November 15, 1912.
2. Steve Rogers, "Lewis County to Willapa Bay by Rail," *The Sou'wester* (Summer & Fall 2006): 12.
3. Roy Huggins e-mail to his daughter Katherine Crawford (January 17, 1996). He also stated: "About my father: I remember meeting a friend of his when I was not yet four years old. He took a look at me, turned to my mother and said, "He looks just like Ed." I don't remember him at all."
4. Doris B. Murphy, *Love and Labor* (New York: iUniverse, 2006), 26.
5. Roy Huggins e-mail to Katherine Crawford (January 17, 1996).
6. *Ibid.*
7. Roy Huggins e-mail to Katherine Crawford (January 20, 1996).
8. Katherine Crawford, e-mail communication with author, 2007–2013. All further quotes from Crawford in this chapter come from the same e-mail communication.
9. Roy Huggins e-mail to Katherine Crawford (January 20, 1996).
10. In his unpublished memoir "The Story of My Life" Roy Huggins states, "I'd spent ten years of my life in military schools, the first one run like a crazed boot camp, where I learned that Chickenshit had been invented by the army. I went AWOL from that school and my family shipped me off to another, and then to a third ... Hill [Military Academy] was awash in army lore and jargon, but it had a staff of good teachers and a long and noble tradition. I stayed, and learned what was meant by 'the old army game,' another reason I preferred to remain a civilian."
11. Frank Price, e-mail communication with author, 2007–2013.
12. Bonnie Porter, telephone interview with author, January 14, 2008. All further quotes from

Porter in this chapter come from the same telephone interview.

13. Murphy, 32.

14. Roy Huggins, "The Story of My Life," unpublished memoir, 2001. Unless otherwise stated all further quotes from Huggins in this chapter come from the same unpublished memoir.

15. Mark Morrall Dodge, *Pasadena City College* (Pasadena: Pasadena City College Foundation, 2002), 29–31.

16. Pasadena Junior College Yearbook, 1937, 130, 147.

Chapter 3

1. Roy Huggins, "The Story of My Life." Unless otherwise stated all further quotes from Huggins in this chapter come from the same unpublished memoir.

2. Bonnie Porter, telephone interview with author, January 14, 2008. All further quotes from Porter in this chapter come from the same telephone interview.

Chapter 4

1. Roy Huggins, "The Story of My Life." Unless otherwise stated all further quotes from Huggins in this chapter come from the same unpublished memoir.

2. Katherine Crawford, e-mail communication with author, 2007–2013. All further quotes from Crawford in this chapter come from the same e-mail communication. "We had no air conditioning back then, so it was best to write by the pool. The wall was built by Daddy. Cement 'boards' dropped into the post blocks with a lid was placed on top. We were surrounded by acres of wild flat undeveloped land with a train that ran through it twice a day. Bret and I always tried to go wave at the conductor as he passed. He always waved back. We'd RUN out into the field when we heard the whistle. It was great."

3. Bonnie Porter, telephone interview with author, January 14, 2008.

4. Katherine Crawford, e-mail communication with author, 2007–2013.

Chapter 5

1. Roy Huggins, "The Story of My Life." All further quotes from Huggins in this chapter come from the same unpublished memoir.

2. Larry Ceplair, *The Marxist and the Movies: A Biography of Paul Jarrico* (Lexington: University Press of Kentucky, 2007), 127.

Chapter 6

1. *Blacklist: A Different Look at the 1947 HUAC Hearings*, http://www.moderntimes.com/blacklist.

2. Roy Huggins, "The Story of My Life." Unless otherwise stated all further quotes from Huggins in this chapter come from the same unpublished memoir.

3. *Communist Infiltration of the Hollywood Motion-Picture Industry—Part 9* (Washington, D.C.: United States Government Printing Office, 1952), 4264–4282.

4. Victor S. Navasky. *Naming Names* (New York: Viking, 1980).

5. Roy Huggins, *Archive of American Television*, interviewed by Lee Goldberg, July 21, 1998. Visit http://www.emmytvlegends.org for more information. All *Archive of American Television* listings refer to this interview unless otherwise stated.

6. Doris B. Murphy. *Love and Labor* (New York: iUniverse, 2006), 292.

Chapter 7

1. Katherine Crawford, e-mail communication with author, 2007–2013. All further quotes from Crawford in this chapter come from the same e-mail communication..

2. John Huggins, telephone interview by author, November 2, 2012. All further quotes from John Huggins in this chapter come from the same telephone interview.

3. Roy Huggins, "The Story of My Life."

4. Roy Huggins, "Tears from a Glass Eye," unpublished memoir, 1998. Unless otherwise stated all further quotes from Roy Huggins in this chapter come from the same unpublished memoir.

5. Richard L. Bare, *Confessions of a Hollywood Director* (Lanham, MD: Scarecrow Press, 2001), 257.

Chapter 8

1. Roy Huggins, "Tears from a Glass Eye," unpublished memoir, 1998. Unless otherwise stated all further quotes from Roy Huggins in this chapter come from the same unpublished memoir.

2. Emily Belser, "Horse Opera Rules Broken by Cheyenne," INS Syndicated, February 27, 1956.

3. Mike Connelly, "Censor Bars TV Divorce," "Mr. Hollywood" Syndicated, May 31, 1957.
4. Raymond Strait, *James Garner: A Biography* (New York: St Martin's Press, 1985), 37–38.
5. Charles Mercer, "This Huggins Is a Maverick Producer," Associated Press, April 12, 1959.
6. Strait, 59.
7. *Archive of American Television*.
8. *Stars and Stripes*, November 14, 1958, 16.
9. Richard L. Bare, *Confessions of a Hollywood Director* (Lanham, MD: Scarecrow Press 2000), 276.
10. Sylvia Stoddard, *Television Chronicles*, January 1998, 76–80.
11. *Ibid.*
12. John Huggins, telephone interview by author, November 2, 2012, and April 6, 2013.

Chapter 9

1. Roy Huggins, "Tears from a Glass Eye." Unless otherwise stated all further quotes from Roy Huggins in this chapter come from the same unpublished memoir.
2. Jo Swerling, Jr., telephone interview by author, November 12 and 27, 2007. All further quotes from Swerling Jr. in this chapter come from the telephone interview.
3. Jerry Landauer, "Producer Defends Violence on TV," *Milwaukee Journal*, June 10, 1961.
4. "Fare on TV More Diverse," *Toledo Blade*, January 25, 1962.
5. Hal Humphrey, "Fabian the Sole Survivor," *Toledo Blade*, June 19, 1962.
6. Roy Huggins, "The Bloodshot Eye: A Comment on the Crisis in American Television," *Television Quarterly* (August 1962): 6–22.

Chapter 10

1. Jo Swerling, Jr., telephone interview by author, November 12 and 27, 2007. All further quotes from Swerling Jr. in this chapter come from the telephone interview.
2. Jane Galbraith, "The Fugitive, Kind of: Dr. Richard Kimble, Meet Dr. Sam Sheppard," *Los Angeles Times*, December 9, 1993.
3. Ed Robertson, *The Fugitive Recaptured* (Los Angeles: Pomegranate Press, 1993), 182–188.
4. "Fugitive Role Is Really a Running Part," *The Daily Intelligencer* (Pennsylvania), October 19, 1963, 11.

5. Chris Soldo, e-mail communication with author, December 28, 2012.
6. Samuel D. Goodis and William Goodis as Executors of the Estate of David Goodis, Deceased, Plaintiffs-Appellants, v. United Artists Television, Inc., and American Broadcasting Co., Inc., Defendants-Appellees., 425 F.2d 397 (2nd Cir. 1970).
7. Frank Price, e-mail communication with author, 2005–2013. All further quotes from Price in this chapter come from the same e-mail communication.
8. Roy Huggins, "Tears from a Glass Eye."
9. Bob Thomas, *Associated Press*, August 17, 1967.
10. *Archive of American Television*.
11. Paul Green, *A History of Television's* The Virginian, *1962–1971* (Jefferson, NC: McFarland, 2006), 19–20.
12. Richard L. Bare, *Confessions of a Hollywood Director* (Lanham, MD: Scarecrow Press, 2001), 16–19.

Chapter 11

1. Frank Price, e-mail communication with author, 2005–2013. All further quotes from Price in this chapter come from the same e-mail communication.
2. Cynthia Lowry, "Another Show with Message Due on Screen," *Idaho State Journal*, September 4, 1963, 12.
3. Jo Swerling, Jr., telephone interview by author, November 12 and 27, 2007. All further quotes from Swerling Jr. in this chapter come from the telephone interview.
4. Katherine Crawford, e-mail communication with author, 2008–2013. All further quotes from Crawford in this chapter come from the same e-mail communications.
5. Roy Huggins, speech to the Ministers' Symposium in Long Beach, California, November 14, 1966.
6. Roy Huggins. "What's Wrong with the Television Series?" *Action*: *Director's Guild of America* (September-October 1969).
7. "Cover Close-Up," *Independent Star News* (Pasadena), June 26, 1966, 64.
8. Roy Huggins. "Film and the Pornography of Cruelty," speech before congregation of Westminster Presbyterian Church, Morrison Hall (April 1967).
9. Huggins, speech to the Ministers' Symposium.

10. Ben Gazzara, *In the Moment: My Life as an Actor* (Boston: Da Capo, 2005), 134.
11. Ed Robertson, *Television Chronicles*, February 1988.
12. From an interview by Jon Burlingame, December 6, 1991.
13. From an interview by Jon Burlingame, May 8, 2000.
14. Huggins, "What's Wrong with the Television Series?"

Chapter 12

1. Roy Huggins, speech at the Ministers' Symposium, Long Beach, California, November 11, 1966.
2. Roy Huggins, "Tears from a Glass Eye." Unless otherwise stated all further quotes from Roy Huggins in this chapter come from the same unpublished memoir.
3. Roy Huggins, speech at the Jonathan Club, Los Angeles, October 23, 1958.
4. Roy Huggins, "Television: What's the Difference?" no date.
5. Frank Price, e-mail communication with author, 2008–2013. All further quotes from Price in this chapter come from the same e-mail communication.
6. Jo Swerling, Jr., telephone interview by author, November 12, 2007. All further quotes from Swerling Jr. in this chapter come from the same telephone interview.
7. From an interview by Jon Burlingame, May 8, 2000.
8. Paul Green, *Pete Duel: A Biography* (Jefferson, NC: McFarland, 2007), 116.
9. Sandra K. Sagala and JoAnne M. Bagwell, *Alias Smith & Jones: The Story of Two Pretty Good Bad Men* (Boalsburg, PA: BearManor Media, 2005), 373.
10. John Huggins, telephone interview by author, November 2, 2012. All further quotes from John Huggins in this chapter come from the same telephone interview.
11. "Round 2 for ABC's *Alias Smith and Jones*," *L.A. Herald Examiner*, August 7, 1971.
12. Cecil Smith, *Los Angeles Times*, December 9, 1971.
13. Christopher Anderson, "Cheyenne," Museum of Broadcast Communications, 1994.
14. Paul Green, *Pete Duel: A Biography* (Jefferson, NC: McFarland, 2007), 146.
15. Ed Robertson, personal interview with Roy Huggins, conducted at Huggins' home in Los Angeles, November 8, 1996.

Chapter 13

1. John Huggins, telephone interview by author, April 6, 2013.
2. Katherine Crawford, e-mail communication with author, April 14, 2013.
3. Jo Swerling, Jr., e-mail communication with author, April 4, 2013.
4. Jo Swerling, Jr., e-mail communication with author, April 10, 2013.
5. Jo Swerling, Jr., telephone interview by author, November 12, 2007. Unless otherwise stated all further quotes from Swerling Jr. in this chapter come from the same telephone interview.
6. Frank Price, e-mail communication with author, 2005–2013. All further quotes from Price in this chapter come from the same e-mail communication.
7. Jerry Buck, "New Shows Stress Enjoyment," Associated Press, August 5, 1972.
8. Marilyn Beck, "Hollywood Hotline," *Star-News* (Pasadena), February 21, 1973.
9. Don Freeman, "Winning Show Given Junk Pile," *The Montana Standard*, June 16, 1973.
10. Jo Swerling, Jr., e-mail communication with author, January 28, 2013.
11. Jo Swerling, Jr., interview by author, January 30, 2013.
12. Jo Swerling, Jr., interview by author, April 10–11, 2013.

Chapter 14

1. Frank Price, e-mail communication with author, 2008–2013. All further quotes from Price in this chapter come from the same e-mail communication.
2. Jo Swerling, Jr., telephone interview by author, November 12, 2007. All further quotes from Swerling Jr. in this chapter come from the same telephone interview.
3. Juanita Bartlett, telephone interview by author, February 8, 2013.
4. Susan Sackett, *Prime-Time Hits, Television's Most Popular Network Programs* (New York: Billboard, 1993), 238–239.
5. James Garner and Jon Winokur, *The Garner Files* (New York: Simon & Schuster, 2011), 123.
6. *Ibid.*

7. "Monday Movie Stars Svenson," *Danville Register*, January 24, 1977.
8. Barbara Wilkins, "TV's 'Manure' Says Wayne Rogers, Who Plays the Angles as Skillfully as *City of Angels*," *People*, March 8, 1976.
9. Jo Swerling, Jr., e-mail communication with author, January 31, 2013.
10. *Ibid.*

Chapter 15

1. Frank Price, e-mail communication with author, 2007–2013. Unless otherwise stated all further quotes from Price in this chapter come from the e-mail communications from this period.
2. Kay Gardella, "*Captain, Kings* Serialized; Reminder of Kennedy's?" *New York News*, April 1967.
3. Jo Swerling, Jr., telephone interview by author, November 12, 2007. Unless otherwise stated all further quotes from Swerling Jr. in this chapter come from the same telephone interview.
4. Jo Swerling, Jr., e-mail communication with author, January 29, 2013.
5. John Huggins, telephone interview by author, April 6, 2013.
6. *Archive of American Television*.

Chapter 16

1. Stephen Cannell, "Impressions of Roy Huggins," *The Journal of the Caucus* (Spring 1993).
2. Jerry Buck, "Philosophy of *Hunter* Producer Changed," *Wichita Eagle*, January 10, 1988.
3. Steve Weinstein, "Fred Dryer Scores with *Hunter*," *Los Angeles Times*, August 19, 1988.
4. Stepfanie Kramer, telephone interview by author, March 25, 2013.
5. Gary Winter, telephone interview by author, March 24, 2013.
6. Charlotte Huggins, telephone interview by author, October 30, 2012.
7. John Huggins, telephone interview by author, November 2, 2012.
8. Roy Huggins, *Archive of American Television* interview.
9. Katherine Crawford, e-mail communication with author, 2008–2013.
10. Frank Price, e-mail communication with author, October 19, 2005.
11. John Huggins, e-mail communication with author, April 22, 2013.

Chapter 17

1. Roy Huggins, "Forgiving Elia Kazan," unpublished article, November 2000.
2. Huggins, "The Story of My Life."
3. Huggins, "Forgiving Elia Kazan."
4. Katherine Crawford, e-mail communication with author, April 12, 2013.
5. John Huggins, telephone interview by author, April 6, 2013.
6. Crawford, April 15, 2013.
7. Frank Price, e-mail communication with author, October 9, 2005.
8. Stephen J. Cannell, *Archive of American Television*, interviewed by Stephen J. Abramson, June 25, 2004. Visit http://www.emmytvlegends.org for more information.
9. Katherine Crawford, e-mail communication with author, April 24, 2013.

BIBLIOGRAPHY

Books

Bare, Richard L. *Confessions of a Hollywood Director.* Lanham, MD: Scarecrow Press, 2000.

Carlyle, Thomas. *Oliver Cromwell's Letters and Speeches: With Elucidations—Vol. 1 Pt. 1.* New York: Wiley & Putnam, 1845.

Ceplair, Larry, and Steven Englund. *The Inquisition in Hollywood: Politics in the Film Community 1930–60.* Urbana: University of Illinois Press, 1979, 1980, 1983, 2003.

Chernow, Ron. *Alexander Hamilton.* New York: Penguin, 2004.

Dodge, Mark Morrall. *Pasadena City College.* Pasadena: Pasadena City College Foundation, 2002.

Ellis, Peter Beresford. *Eyewitness to Irish History.* Hoboken, NJ: John Wiley, 2004.

Everitt, David. *A Shadow of Red: Communism and the Blacklist in Radio and Television.* Chicago: Ivan R. Dee, 2007.

Garner, James, and Jon Winokur. *The Garner Files.* New York: Simon & Schuster, 2011.

Gazzara, Ben. *In the Moment: My Life as an Actor.* New York: Carroll & Graf, 2004.

Greenfield, Jeff. *Television the First Fifty Years.* New York: Crescent Books, 1981.

Longworth, James L., Jr. *TV Creators: Conversations with America's Top Producers of Television Drama Vol II.* New York: Syracuse University Press, 2002.

Marill, Alvin H. *Movies Made for Television: The Telefeature and the Mini-Series 1964–1979.* Westport, CT: Arlington House, 1980.

McGilligan, Patrick, and Paul Buhle. *Tender Comrades: A Backstory of the Hollywood Blacklist.* New York: St Martin's Press, 1997.

Murphy, Doris B. *Love and Labor.* New York: iUniverse, 2006.

Navasky, Victor S. *Naming Names.* New York: Viking, 1980.

O'Donnell, Edward T. *101 Things Everyone Should Know About Irish American History.* New York: Broadway Books, 2002.

Robertson, Ed. *The Fugitive Recaptured.* Los Angeles: Pomegranate Press, 1993.

_____. *Maverick: Legend of the West.* CreateSpace, 2012.

_____. *Thirty Years of The Rockford Files.* New York: ASJ Press, 2005.

Sackett, Susan. *Prime-Time Hits, Television's Most Popular Network Programs.* New York: Billboard, 1993.

Sagala, Sandra K., and JoAnne M. Bagwell. *Alias Smith & Jones: The Story of Two Pretty Good Bad Men.* Boalsburg, PA: BearManor Media, 2005.

Strait, Raymond. *James Garner: A Biography.* New York: St. Martin's Press, 1985.

Vaughn, Robert. *Only Victims: A Study of Show Business Blacklisting.* New York: Limelight Editions, 1996.

Wylie, Max. *Writing for Television.* New York: Cowles, 1970.

Zee, John Van Der. *Bound Over: Indentured Servitude & American Conscience.* New York: Simon & Schuster, 1985.

Articles

Huggins, Roy. "The Bloodshot Eye: A Comment on the Crisis in American Television." *Television Quarterly* (August 1962): 6–22.

Resources

Roy Huggins Papers, 353, Library Special Collections, University of California, Los Angeles.

Internet Sources

AFI Catalog of Feature Films. http://www.afi.com/members/catalog.

Ancestry.com. http://www.ancestry.com.

Archive of American Television. http://www.emmytvlegends.org.

British Civil Wars, Commonwealth and Protectorate 1638–1660. http://www.british-civil-wars.co.uk.

The Classic TV Archive. http://ctva.biz.

The Complete Rod Taylor Site. http://www.rodtaylorsite.com/hongkong.shtml.

The David Janssen Archive. http://www.davidjanssen.net.

Google News. http://news.google.com/newspapers.

IMDB. http://www.imdb.com.

The Irish Story. http://www.theirishstory.com.

Library Ireland. http://www.libraryireland.com.

Museum of Broadcast Communications. http://www.museumtv.

Mystery File. http://www.mysteryfile.com.

Spartacus Educational. http://www.spartacus.schoolnet.co.uk.

UCLA Film & Television Archive. http://www.cinema.library.ucla.edu.

INDEX

Page numbers in ***bold italics*** indicate pages with illustrations.

The A-Team 143
Abalone 55, 70, 72
Actors Laboratory 41
Adam-12 118–119, 160
Adams, Abigail "Tommye" 38
Adele, Maria 38, 41, 43, 52, ***57***, 60, 64–65, ***67***, ***71***, 115, ***138***, 145, 150, 153–154
Adventures in Paradise 77–79, 164
Alias Smith and Jones 107–114, 116, 126, 160–161; "The Day They Hanged Kid Curry" 111, 161; "Don't Get Mad, Get Even" 110, 161; "Dreadful Sorry Clementine" 110, 161; "Everything Else You Can Steal" 110, 161; "Exit from Wickenberg" 110, 160; "The Girl in Boxcar #3" 109; "Journey from San Juan" 110, 160; "The McCreedy Bust" 111, 160; Return to Devil's Hole" 109, 160; "Smiler with a Gun" 111, 161; "Stagecoach Seven" 110, 160; "Which Way to the OK Corral?" 110, 161
All in the Family 102, 113
Alpert, Herb 93
Altman, Robert 75, 88
American Broadcasting Company (ABC) 58, 59, 62–63, 66, 68, 75–80, 83, 104–105, 107, 109, 112–113, 118, 121–122, 125, 138–139, 157, 159–160, 162–165; ABC Continuity Acceptance department 76; ABC Department of Standards and Practices 118

American Communist Party 43, 149–150
American Legion 39, 42
American Theme 79
Amnesia 150–151
Anderson, Richard 75–76
Andrews, Dana 38, 53–54, 165–166
Anthology series format 60–61, 87–88, 90, 92, 105
Any Second Now 106, 157
Appointment with Fear 28, 166, 168
Arness, James 65
Arthur Hailey's Wheels 133, 158
Ash Wednesday 137
Audience Studies Institute (ASI) 101–10
Auerbach, Lt. Cdr. Harold M. 34
Aqualung 55
Armer, Alan A. 81
Aspen 133, 158
Astaire, Fred 26
Astin, Patty Duke 132–133, 158
Aston, Sir Arthur 7
Author's Guild 46

Bailey, Doris 15, 50
Bailey, Dorothy 110, 133–134
Bailey, F. Lee 79
Bailey, Stuart 18, 22, 72
Bailey, Stuart (Private Eye) 4, 21–22, 24, 26–27, 32, 68–69, 165, 167
Baldwin Hills, Los Angeles 19
Bare, Richard L. 53, 55, 59–60, 62, 68–69, 84, 161, 163–165
Baretta 3, 5, 121–123, 127–129, 159; "The Coppelli Oath" 129, 159; "The Half Million

Dollar Baby" 129, 159; "If You Can't Pay the Price" 128–129, 159; "The Secret of Terry Lake" 129, 159; "Woman in the Harbor" 128, 159
Barnathan, Julius 78
Barnes, Dallas 141
Bartlett, Juanita, 125–126, 159–161
Barzman, Ben 50
Bath Hotel, Nevis 8–9
Batman 96, 117
Bealey Military Academy ***13***, 18
Beecroft, Eric 17
Beekeeper 72, 115
Behind the Cameras at Warner Brothers 58
Ben Casey 92
Benedict, Richard ***95***, 97, 160–163
Benny, Jack 54, 66
Benson, Hugh 58, 64, 68
Benton, Douglas 88
Bergman, Ingrid 36
Best Sellers 132–136
Beverly Hills Hotel suite 78
Bewitched 69
The Big Sleep 4, 20–21
Bixby, Bill 131, 155
Blacklist 39, 41–42, 44, 50, 115
Blair, Janet 28, 167
Blake, Robert 3, 122–123, 127–129
Blau, Louis C. 105
Blees, Robert 88
Blue Thunder 138–139, 159
Bodie, Cheyenne 59–61
Bogardus, Anneke Jans 152
Bogart, Humphrey 34, 59, 80, 102, 166

The Bold Ones: The Lawyers 104, 120, 162; "The Rockford Riddle" 93
Borgnine, Ernest 116, 119, 157
Bowery Boys 59
Brando, Marlon 30
Brandt, Joe 26
"Brazil 65" 92–93
Brewster, Diane 61, 64
Browne, Howard 21–22, 36, 61, 63, 73, 162–165
Bryan, Paul 91–97, 162
Bumgarner, Jim 62
Burke, John, Jr. 9
"The Burning Sky" 42
Burr, Raymond 136, 155
Bus Stop 75–76, 100, 164; "A Lion Walks Among Us" 75–76; "Make My Bed in Hell" 77
Butch Cassidy and the Sundance Kid 107, 109
Byrnes, Edd 68–69, 165

Caldwell, Taylor 132, 158
California 4, 16–17, 34, 72, 93, 100, 116, 144
"Cameo Kirby" 62–63
Campanella, Joseph 103–104, 117, 157
Cancer 74, 147, 149, 152
Cannell, Stephen J. 25, 118–119, 122–126, 128, 130, 137, 140–146, 153, 155–156, 158–160
Captains and the Kings 132–134, 158
Casablanca 58, 61
Catholic 41, 43, 137
CBC Film Sales 26
Celtic cross 154
Censorship 61, 100, 118
Centennial 135
Century Plaza Hotel 104–105
Cesana, Renzo 36–37
The Challengers 106–107, 157
Chandler, Raymond 4, 20, 24, 32, 118, 124
The Charge at Feather River 59
Charlestown, Nevis 9
Chaucer, Geoffrey 61
Cheers 140
Cheyenne 3, 5, 55, 58–62, 74, 76, 112, 152, 165; "The Argonauts" 59; "The Dark Rider" 61, 165; "Decision" 60, 165; "Fury at Rio Hondo" 59; "Johnny Bravo" 60, 165; "Mountain Fortress" 59; "Quicksand" 60, 165; "Star in the Dust" 60, 165; "West of the River" 59
Chicerinos 91
Chinatown 130
Cinematographer 40–41
City of Angels 130, 159
Clarke, Gary 85
Clarke, Matt 119
Cockatoo 129
Cody, Buffalo Bill 119
Cohn, Harry 26–28, 32, 39, 42–55, 73
Colasanto, Nicholas 97, 160–161, 163
Cold War 4, 46, 95
Coleridge, Samuel Taylor 8
Colt .45 67–68, 74, 165; "Judgment Day" a.k.a. "The Peacemaker" 68, 164
Columbia Pictures 3–4, 25–26, *27*, 28, 31–33, 38–39, 52–55, 63, 73, 100, 135, 138–139, 159, 166–167
Communism 4, 17, 43, 49–50, 93
Communist Party 17–18, 39, 41–43, 45–50, 149–151
Conflict 61–62, 68, 74, 79, 87, 164; "Anything for Money" 68–69, 164; "The Deadly Riddle" 61, 165; "The Man from 1997" 62, 165; "The Money" 78, 165; "The Velvet Cage" 61–62, 165
Congress 42–43, *44*, 75
Cook, Fielder 119, 156–157
Cool Million 117–118, 160
Copyright 62, 80–81
Counterattack 42
Cousteau, Jacques 72
Crawford, Elizabeth Emeline Whittier 10
Crawford, Frank 12
Crawford, Joan 31, 33
Crawford, Katherine 13, 18–19, 29, 30, 51–52, 55, 88–89, 91, 93, *99*, 115, 120, 147, 152–154, 158; artist 30; Blind Man's Bluff 30; dancing 30; diving board 30; drive-in theater 29; pool parties 30
Crawford, Maybelle Therina 10; palm reader 13; permanent wave 12–13; spiritualist 13
Crawford, Sadie 12
Crawford, Samantha 61–64
Creator rights 63, 67–68, 79
Cremation 154
Cromwell, Oliver 7–8, 170
Crossing the proscenium 40, 136
Cugat, Xavier 52
Curtis, Tony 30
Cyborg 117

Daily Bruin 17–18
Daily Variety 58, 111, 127
Daly, Tim 147–148
Dann, Mike 104
Darby, Gentleman Jack 64–65
Darby, Kim 94, 96, 119, 129, 156
Dark Passage 80
Dateline: San Francisco 74
Daves, Delmer 26
Davies, Luther 91, 96, 148
Davis, Bette 84
Davis, Roger 107, *108*, 111–114, 119, 126, 157–158
Day, Doris 38, 90
Day, Lynda 106, 156–157
Day of Epiphany 52
Day of the Badman 85
Dearborn, Michigan 72, 115
Death and the Skylark 32, 168
DeGuere, Philip **95**, 155–156, 159–160, 163
Delgado, Angel and Eloisa 72
Democracy 45–50
Democratic Centralism 49
Detective Book Club 22, 168
Deuel, Pamela 112
The Dilettante 15
Diller, Barry 104–106, 113–114, 121
Director 1, 24, 26–27, 34, 36–37, **40**, 52–55, 62, 64, 68, 70–71, 81, 88–90, 92, 97, 99, 102, 106–107, 111, 114, 116, 119–120, 136, 139, 141–143, 146, 151, 153
Director's Guild of America (DGA) 102, 117, 136
Do You Take This Stranger? 116, 157
Dodd, Senator Thomas J. 75
"Don the Beachcomber," restaurant 38
Dorothy Chandler Pavilion 151
Double pneumonia 66
The Double Take 4, 20, 22, 24, 26–27, 129, 167–168
Douglas, Kirk 33, 85
Doyle, Bernadette 17
Doyle, Clyde 45, 48–50
Dozier, William 32
Drive Hard, Drive Fast 119–120, 156
Drogheda massacre 7–8
Dryer, Fred 3, 140–143

Index

Dubelko, Mike 144
Duel, Pete 3, 93, 107–109, 111–114, 116, 157
Duryea, Dan 33–34, 167

Eastman, Carol 94
Editing 1, 72, 83–84, 91, 102, 107, 111, 119, 124, 140, 145–146, 153
Eisenhower, President Dwight D. 106
Eisner, Michael 122
Electra Glide in Blue 122, 128
Elliott, Sam 133, 158
Emanuel, Jack 62–63
Emergency Detention Act 15
Emmy Awards 66, *67*, 94–95, 106, 128, 132–133, 135, 169
The Enforcer 34, 166
Engel, Charlie 134, 137
Engel, Donald 146
Erlick, Everett 78
Eyewitness to Murder 36

Fabian 75–77
Farentino, James 103–104, 117, 157
Farewell My Lovely 4, 20
Fascism 4, 17, 45, 49
"Fat Blonde Reporter" 120
Faust 92
Federal Bureau of Investigation (FBI) 39, 129, 149–151
Federal Communications Commission (FCC) 58, 76
Fenton, Frank 36, 162–163, 166
A Fever in the Blood 69, *70*, 71–72, 165
Fifth Amendment 5, 39, 43, 50, 151
Fisher, Ham 53
Fitzroy, Thomas 85, 163–164
Flip Wilson Show 111
Flynn, Errol 52, 54, 59
Foch, Nina 89, 109, 140
Follow the Sun 74–75, 79, 164
Ford, Harrison 147, 165
Ford, John 113
Forrest, Steve 108–109
Foster, Dianne 76, 166
Foster, Robert *95*, 156, 162–163
Frank, Charles 137
Fraser, Sir Robert 5
Freedom of Information Privacy Act 149
Freeman, Devery 27–28
Freeman, Luke 75–76
Freeman, Paul 95
Frye, William 2, 88

The Fugitive 3, 5, 73–74, 78–81, *82*, 83, 91, 97, 105, 147–148, 158, 163, 165; "Fear in a Desert City" 80
The Fuller Brush Man 27–28, 167

Gage, Ben 65
Garner, James 3–5, 60, 62–64, 66, 122–127, 137–138, 146–147, 156
The Gaunt Woman 38, 166
Gazzara, Ben 3, 91–93, *95*, 96–97, 163
Gerard, Lieutenant Philip 80, 147
Giant 70
Giesy, Don 15
Gilda 54
Girl on the Run 68–69, 160, 164–165
"Gladly, Said the Fly" 23–24, 28
Glasscock. C. B. 63
Glenn, Charles 49
Goldberg, Leonard 104–106
Golden Gate Award for Entertainment 93
Goldenson, Leonard 58, 77–78, 81
Goldwyn, Samuel 36
The Good-Humor Man 28, 166
Goodis, David 80
Gould, Heywood "Woody" 131
Gower Gulch, Los Angeles 26
Graham, Billy 92
Grant, Cary 66
Gray, Coleen 38
Green, Henry M. 10
Guild, Leo and Hazel 38
Gulager, Clu 85
Gun Fury 52–53, 166
Gunsmoke 65

Haglund, Oren 58
Hale, William 97, 162
Halsey, Brett 75
Hamer, Arthur 73
Hammett, Dashiell 20, 118
Hangman's Knot 39, *40*, 41, 52–53, 107, 166
Hard-boiled fiction 4, 20–23, 49, 117, 129
Hargrove, Marion 65–66, 68, 75, 164–165
Hayworth, Rita 26, 53–54
Hazard's People 130–131, 155
Heidegger, Martin 17
Heilpern, Steve *95*
Here We Go Again 114

Herman, Jerry 38
Hermanos, W. 66
Heston, Charlton 151
Heyes, Douglas 66, 102, 108, 120, 132–133, 156–160, 162, 164–165
Heyes, Hannibal 5, 107, 109–111
Hickey, Helen F. 10
Hickok, Wild Bill 119, 156
Hill, Joseph Wood 13
Hill Military Academy 13
His Kind of Woman 36–37, 166
Hitler, Adolf 4, 17
Hobson, Thayer 25
Hollywood 3–4, 19, 24–25, 27, 36, 38–39, 41–43, 46, 49, 59, 61, 65, 70, 77, 80, 88, 90, 96, 102, 105, 113, 124, 127, 139, 143, 150–151
The Hollywood group 46, 49
The Hollywood Reporter 42, 71–72, 107
"Hollywood Ten" 41
Hong Kong 74–75
Hook, Sidney 45
Hopper, Dennis 60
Hopper, Hedda 42
"The Horizontal Man" 20–21
"The House on Rue Riviera" 75, 164
House Un-American Activities Commission (HUAC) 3–4, 39, 41–43, *44*, 45–50, 52, 149–151
Houseman, John 130–131, 155
How to Steal an Airplane 93, 116, 156
Hoyle, E. Ross 18
Hudson, Rock 52, 117, 133, 158, 166
Huggins, Bret 18–19, *27*, 29–30, 51–52, 55, 171
Huggins, Charlotte Clay 143–145
Huggins, Edward Francis 10–11, *12*
Huggins, Edward, Jr. 9, 170
Huggins, Edward "Poor Man" 8
Huggins, Edward, Sr. 9, 170
Huggins, Eva 11–12, 14
Huggins, Jack Whittier 11–15, 29, 43, 138, 145
Huggins, James 72
Huggins, John 8–9
Huggins, John (son of Roy Huggins) 52, 72, 110–111, 115, 137, 145–147, 152, 154
Huggins, John Murdoch 9–10

INDEX

Huggins, Marvel 11–12, 14
Huggins, Maybelle Therina 11, *12*, 13–14, 93, 152
Huggins, Peter Thomas 9
Huggins, Thomas 72, 144–145
Hughes, Howard 34–41
Hugo, Victor 80
Hume, Edward 122
Hunter 140–146, 158; "The Beautiful and the Dead" 143, 158; "Double Exposure" 145; "Rape and Revenge" 141, 143
Hunter, Ross 90
"Hunter and McCall" 141
The Hunters 75
Hurd, Gale 151

I Love Trouble 27–28, 167
In Cold Blood 128
Indentured servant 8, 170
Informer 149, 151
Inge, William 75
The Invasion of Johnson County 131, 155
Irish Catholic 8, 132
Irish Confederate Wars 7–8
Ironside 135
It Takes a Thief 107, 135
Ives, Burl 103–104, 111, 157–158

James, John Thomas 5, 98, 111, 126, 128, 155–163
James, Monique 90, 132
Jane, Calamity 119, 156
Janssen, David 78–81, 83
Jarrico, Paul 38, 166
Javert, Inspector 80, 147
Jazz 97
Jessel, George 38
Jigsaw 118–119, 160
The Joe Palooka Story 53, 165
Johnson, Van 59
Johnson County War 86
Jonathan Club, Los Angeles 85
Jones, L. Q. 59
Jones, Tommy Lee 147, 165
Jordan, Richard 132–133, 158
The Jordan Chance 136, 155
Jungle Gents 59

Kadison, Ellis 75, 164
Kahane, Ben 52, 55
Kaiser Steel Company 63
Karloff, Boris 88
Kaufman, Dave 104–105, 127
Kazan, Elia 43–44, 151
Keith, Brian 85
Kelly, Jack 58, 64–66, 69, *70*, 137–138, 165

Kennedy, Senator Edward **103**
Kennedy, Senator Robert 103
Kenton, Stan 97
Kershner, Irvin 88–89
Keyes, Jefferson 117
Kimble, Richard 4, 78–81, 147, 165
King, Helen 22, 25
Kings Row 58–59, 61, 165
"Kookie" 68–69
Korean War 42, 49
Kraft Mystery Theatre 75, 164
Kraft Suspense Theatre 86–91, 163; "The Case Against Paul Ryker" 88; "A Cruel and Unusual Night" 90; "The End of the World Baby" 88–90; "The Rapture at 240" 91–92
Kramer, Stepfanie 3, 140–143
Kung Fu 113

The Lady Gambles 32–33, 165, 167
Landis, Perry 23
Landon, Michael 60
Lang, Jennings 91, 117
Larson, Glen A. 5, 107–109, 133, 135, 153, 159–161
Las Vegas 33, 39, 59, 95–96
Las Vegas Chamber of Commerce 95–96
The Las Vegas Story 38, 166
The Last Convertible 136
Lavery, Emmett 43
Lawton, Bud 40
Lear Jet 116
Lenthall, William 7
Leonard, Jack 36–37
Les Misérables 80
Levathes, Peter G. 73–74, 77
Levee, M.C. "Mike" 39
Levitt, Gene 102, 157, 160, 162
Lewine, Robert 62
Littell, Charles 11
Littell, Wash. 11
Little Orphan Annie 94, 111
Lockwood, Gary 75
The Lonely Profession 102, 157
Long, Richard 64–65
Longet, Claudine 92, 156
Lorre, Peter 88–89
Los Angeles 4, 16, 18–20, *23*, 26, 32, 34, 43, 52, 65, 80, 88, 102, 123, 130, 132, 140–141, 150–152
Lovely Lady, Pity Me 33, 68, 164, 168
Lowen, Barry 104–105
Lupino, Ida 34, 167

Lupo, Frank 140, 142

Macao 37
Malis, Mark 134
Maltz, Albert 46
Mammoth Detective 21
Mammoth Mystery 22, 168
Man Without a Star 85
Mandeville Canyon, Brentwood 72, 115, 144
Mansfield, Jayne 75
"The Mare's Nest" 21–22
Margie 75
Maria, Father Jose 137
Marlowe, Philip 20, 118
Martin, Quinn 79–81, 83, 130, 163
Martinson, Leslie 66, 107
Marvin, Lee 39, 88, 90, 166
Marxist 43–48
Maugham, Somerset 32, 132
Maverick 3–5, 61–66, **67**, 68–69, 74, 101, 107, 109–110, 113, 119, 123, 138, 147, 152, 164; "Escape to Tampico" 110; "Game of Chance" 110; "Gun-Shy" 65; "Hadley's Hunters" 68; "Point Blank" 63, 110, 164; "The Savage Hills" 110; "Shady Deal at Sunny Acres" 64, 110, 164; "The Spanish Dancer" 65, 101; "Two Tickets to Ten-Strike" 110
Maverick, Bart 63–65, 68, 137–138
Maverick, Bret 62–65, 107, 109–110, 123, 137–138
Maverick Solitaire 110
MCA 83, 90, 105, 123, 132
McCall Dee Dee 141–143
McClure, Doug 85
McGavin, Darren 102, 106
McNally, Stephen 33–34, 167
McNamara, John 148
McWilliams, Carey 18
"Meditation" 93
Melioration Act 9
Melnick, Daniel 78
Memorial service 152–153
The Men 118
Mendez, Sergio 92–93
Mephistopheles 92
Mexico 33, 51–52, 74, 128–129
Miami Vice 141
Michener, James 135
Ministers' Symposium 93–94
Les Misérables 80
Moab, Utah 113
Monroe, Marilyn 75

Index

Monsanto Chemical Company 59
"Moon over the South Seas" 32
Moore, Tom 78
Morrow, William 21–22, 24–25, 168
Morse, Barry 80, 147
Moulder, Morgan M. **44**, 45
Movie of the Week 104–105, 109, 116–117, 119, 121–122, 125, 167–168
Murder Incorporated 34
Murphy, Ben 108, 111, 113, 119, 155–156
Musante, Tony 121–123, 126, 156

The Name of the Game 104
National Broadcasting Company (NBC) 75, 83, 86–87, 92, 94–95, 97–98, 102–104, 111, 117, 119, 121–122, 124–125, 132–133, 135, 137, 140–141, 145, 155–160, 162–165
National Safety Council 94
Navasky, Victor 149
Nazi-Soviet Non-Aggression Pact 17–18, 48
NBC Mystery Movie 117, 121, 129
NBC World Premiere 101–102
Nelson, Lord 8
Nevis 8, 170
The New Maverick 137
Newman, Bobbie 34
Nichols 125
Nodella, Burt 78
Norris, Chuck 139
Northern Pacific Railway 11
Nothing but the Night 24–25
Novak, Kim 53–54, 166
The November Plan 130, 159
"Now You See It" 23–24, 27, 167–168

O'Connor, Carroll 70–71
Odets, Clifford 17
Office For Emergency Management (OEM) 18, 20, 23
Olsson, Harry R., Jr. 105
O'Mara, John Francis 85, 163–164
One-armed man 80–81
Only One Day Left Until Tomorrow 116
Oregon University 14–15
Orr, William T. 55, **56**, 58–59, 61–64, 69, 83
The Outsider 102, 158, 162
The Outsiders 39

Palm Springs 18, 28–31; Smoketree Ranch 29; The Tennis Club 30–31
Parliamentarian New Model Army 7–8
Pasadena Junior College 15–16, 171
Pearl Harbor 18, 136
Pearson, William 69
Penn, Leo 97, 163
Perfect Crimes 147, 155; "Double Identity" 147; "Murder in Triplicate" 147
Pettker, John 23
Phi Beta Kappa 17, 49, 120
Phi Rho Pi 16
Phoenix, Ariz. 32
Pioneer of the Year Award **138**
Pittman, Montgomery 74, 164
Plantation 8–9
Plymouth Colony 10
Point Doom 28, 33
Poland 17, 47
Political Affairs 46
Political Science 16–17, 77, 86
Political Theory 17, 77
Polonsky, Abe 151
Porter, Bonnie 14–19, 22, **23**, 25, 29–30, **31**, 37, **51**, 55; art class 14; artist 51–52; wax portraits 51–52
Portland, Ore. 12–13, 21, 28
Powell, William 51
Preston, Wayde 67–68
Price, Frank 81, 83–87, 90, 95, **99**, 102, 104, 107, 109, 113, 117–118, 120–125, 128, 132, 135, 138–139, 144, 146–148, 152–153
Promethean 92
Pseudonyms 39, 91
Public Arts Inc. 91, 104 106, 153, 155–160, 162, 167
Pulmonary fibrosis 152
Pulp fiction 33, 107
Pushover 53, 166

Quincy 109, 146

Rabelaisian 92
Rape 133, 141, 143
Reagan, Ronald 38, 58, 90
Red Channels 42, 50
Reed, Donna 39, 52, 54, 165–166
Reeve, Christopher 132
Remick, Lee 135, 158
Republic Pictures 33–34, 41, 167
Restless Gun 88

Reynolds, Paul 23–25, 34–35
Rich, David Lowell 106, 156
Rich Man, Poor Man 132, 135
Rickles, Don 96, 142
Riesner, Dean 60, 164–165
Ritchie, Michael 94, 97, 102, 158, 163
RKO Radio Pictures 3–4, 35–41, 100, 166
The Rockford Files 3–5, 119, 121–128, 146, 156, 159; "Caledonia—It's Worth a Fortune" 127; "A Dark and Bloody Ground" 126, 159; "Exit Prentiss Car" 127, 159; "Find Me If You Can" 127, 159, 159; "The Kirkoff Case" 126, 159; "Say Goodbye to Jennifer" 127, 160
Roddenberry, Gene 85
Rogers, Wayne 130
Rogosin, Joel 90, 133
"The Rondelet Room" 62
Roosevelt, President 18, 45, 48
Rosenberg, Meta 92, 124–126, 137
Rosenberg, Stuart 97, 162, 164
Rosenberg-Coryell Agency 92
The Rousters 140
Royal Academy of Dramatic Arts (RADA) 89
Rugolo, Pete 97, 106, 118, 155–158
Run for Your Life 3, 5, 91–98, 111, 148, 162; "Carol" 96; "The Committee for the 25th" 95–96; "Cry Hard, Cry Fast" 94; "Down with Willie Hatch" 96; "Flight from Tirana" 94; "Hang Your Head and Laugh" 94; "Hoodlums on Wheels" 93; "The Killing Scene" 96; "A Rage for Justice" 94, 163; "The Sadness of a Happy Time" 92–93; "The Saga of Onyx O'Neill" 62; "The Word Would Be Goodbye" 93
Russell, Jane 36, 37, 39, 166

St. John's Hospital, Santa Monica 152
St. Kitts 8–9
St. Martin of Tours Catholic Church, Los Angeles 152
St. Peter's Church, Drogheda 7
Sam Hill: Who Killed the Mysterious Mr. Foster? 116, 119, 157
San Francisco International Film Festival 92

Sartre, Jean-Paul 149
The Saturday Evening Post 23–25, 27–28, 31–32, 34–35, 68, 80–81, 166–168
Sawmill 11
Sayonara 62
The Scavengers 116
Schulberg, Budd 49
Scott, Lizabeth 33–34, 167
Scott, Randolph 39, *40*, 42, 68, 70, 166
Screen Gems 89
Screen Writers Guild 42
Screenplay 4, 24–25, 27, 31–34, 36, 39, 52–53, 91, 94, 124, 135
Screenwriter 3, 25–26, 32, *37*, 39, 42, 80, 84
Scuba diving *71*, 72
The Secret War of Jackie's Girls 136–137, 155
Sedona, Arizona 52–53
Sergeant Ryker 88
Set This Town on Fire 106, 156
77 Sunset Boulevard 68
77 Sunset Strip 3, 5, 68–69, 152, 164, 168
Shane 79
Sheen, Martin 129, 156
Sheinberg, Sid 104–105
Sheppard, Dr. Sam 79–80, 147
Shiloh Ranch 84–86
"Show Me a Hero" 34
Silverman, Fred 135, 155
Simms, Hank 75
Simon, Sylvan 24–25, 27–28, 31
Singer, Alexander 97, 161–163
Sipes, Don 134
Situation ethics 98
The Six Million Dollar Man 117
Skelton, Red 27–28, 52
Skouras, Spyros 77
Slaves 8–9, 132, 148
Small, Florence 136–137, 155
The Sound of Anger 103, 157
Soviet Union 17, 42, 47–49
Spade, Sam 118, 130
Sperling, Milton 34
Stalin, Josef 17, 45, 151
Stanwyck, Barbara 32–33, 167
Stark, Ray 24, 34–35
Stella 11
Stevens, Gary 58
Stevens, George 70–71
Stewart, Paul 55, 58–59, 165
Stockwell, Guy 103
Stone, N.B. 60
Storm Warning 38
The Story of Pretty Boy Floyd 129, 156

Strack, Celeste 17, 45–46
Streep, Meryl 132–133
Stromberg, Hunt 31, 34
Subpoena 4, 42–43, 149
Suicide 33, 37–38, 112–114, 127
Surgal, Alan 136–137, 155
Surgal, Jon 137
Swerling, Jo, Jr. *1*, 2, 73–75, 78–79, 90–92, 94, *95*, 96–97, 103–104, 109–110, 112–113, 119, 130–131, 146, 148, 150, 153, 155–158, 169

Target Risk 130, 136, 156
Tarkington, Booth 62
Tate, Larry 69
Tavenner, Frank S., Jr. 45, 47–49
Taylor, Rod 74
Television 2–5, 30, 32, 42, 53, 58–59, 61, 64–66, 68
Telford, Frank 88
Ten Against Caesar 52
Tent City 15
That Is the West That Was 119, 156
Thomas, J. Parnell 42
Thornburg, Roann Elizabeth 138
Thoroughbred horses 72
Three Hours to Kill 53–54, 165
The 3,000 Mile Chase 136, 155
Thriller 88
Tinker, Grant 104–105
Titus, Charles 17
To Have and Have Not 59
Toma 121–123, 126, 156, 160
Toma, David 123
Tone, Franchot 27–28, 37
Too Late for Tears 25, 31–35, 53, 60, 167–168
A Touch of Grace 114
"Training Within Industry" 23
The Treasure of the Sierra Madre 59
Treyz, Oliver 76–77
Trilling, Steve 69–71
Trinidad 9
Trinity Church, New York 152
Truman, President Harry S 42
Trumbo, Dalton 44
TV western 3–4, 63, 77, 83, 107, 167
20th Century–Fox 3, 38, 62, 73–78, 109, 133, 135, 164

United Artists Television 80, 163
Universal-International 3, 85
Universal-Revue Studios 83

Universal TV 32–33, 81, 83, 86, 88, 90–91, 97, *99*, 101, 104–105, 107–109, 112, 115, 118, 121–123, 125, 127, 132–133, 135–138, 140, 146, 148, 152–153, 155–160, 162–164, 167
University of Arizona 10, 138
University of California, Los Angeles (UCLA) 4, 16–18, 20–21, 24–25, 45, 77, 86, 138, 145; Associated Student's Peace Council 17–18; Royce Hall 17
United Nations (U.N.) 46, 49
The Untouchables 79, 130
U.S. Marshals 147, 165

Valjean, Jean 80
Van de Grift, Bob and Dorothy 30
Van Nuys, Calif. 29, 30, *31*
Violence on television 75–76, 100, 102, 11, 130
The Virginian 5, 77–78, 83–86 109, 135, 152–153, 163–164; "The Accomplice" 84; "Duel at Shiloh" 85; "The Exiles" 110, 163; "The Judgment" 85; "Run Away Home" 109; "Strangers at Sundown" 110, 163–164; "Vengeance Is the Spur" 110, 163
Vogue magazine 91

Wagon Train 74, 83, 88
Wainwright, James 118
Wald, Jerry 54
Walsh, Raoul 52–53, 166
Walker, Clint 59, 61, 112
Walker, Norman Eugene 59
"The War of the Copper Kings" 54, 63
Ware, Clyde 129, 156, 167–168
Warner, Jack L. 5, 58, 64, 68, 83
Warner Bros. Presents 58, 61, 104
Warren, Charles Marquis 83–84, 135
Wasserman, Lew 77, 81, 87, 105, 122–123
Weaver, Dennis 65, 117
Weld, Tuesday 89–90
Werner, Mort 97
West Indies 8, 68, 170
Whalen, Joe 20–21
"Wheel" format 104, 117–118
White, David 69
White, Jesse *70*

Index

Whitmore, James, Jr. 141
Whitmore, Stanford 80
Whittier, Bret 21
Whittier, John Greenleaf 10
The Whole World Is Watching 104, 157
The Wife of Bath's Tale 61
Wilder, John 135
Wilkerson, W. R. 42
Williamson, Mykelti 147
Willner, George 25, 39
Wilson, Stanley 97

Winchell, Walter 42
Winter, Gary 133–135, 142, 158
Woman in Hiding 34, 167
Wood, Honorable John S. 45
Wood, Natalie 61
Wright, Herb 118
Writer's Guild of America (WGA) 42–43, 66, 69, 145, 148
Wyoming 84, 86, 131
Wyoming Constitution 86

Yellow Quashy 9
You Were Never Lovelier 26
Young, Gig 88–89
The Young Country 107, **108**, 111, 157
Young Maverick 137–138

Zimbalist, Efrem, Jr. 64, 68–69, 165

www.ingramcontent.com/pod-product-compliance
Ingram Content Group UK Ltd.
Pitfield, Milton Keynes, MK11 3LW, UK
UKHW050523150426
5217IPUK00026B/1772